"This is the book that started it all—the book that, with great clarity and ardor, introduced Vipassana and mindfulness to the West. I still have and cherish my dog-eared, heavily underlined and annotated copy from way back when—with the price tag still on it: $3.00. Of course its content is timeless—and universal. All teachers of mindfulness-based programs would do well to carefully read and re-read this book and reflect upon the ways in which mindfulness is described in terms of both bare attention and clear comprehension."

—Jon Kabat-Zinn, author of *Mindfulness for Beginners* and *Full Catastrophe Living*

"*The Heart of Buddhist Meditation* is a work of unique importance in the literature about meditation. It is written with great depth, extraordinary knowledge, deep humanity, and in a style that is simple and direct. Although written from the Buddhist thinking, it is of equal value to the non-Buddhist reader. I highly recommend it to anyone who is seriously concerned with self-development."

Dr. Erich Fromm

"An appreciated contribution to the development of Buddhism in the West."

—*Karuna: A Journal of Buddhist Meditation*

"It's wonderful to see this new edition of an invaluable, classic meditation guide. Nyanaponika Thera's *The Heart of Buddhist Meditation* is sure to benefit many."

—Sharon Salzberg, Co-Founder of The Insight Meditation Society

THE HEART OF BUDDHIST MEDITATION

THE HEART OF BUDDHIST MEDITATION

THE BUDDHA'S WAY OF MINDFULNESS

NYANAPONIKA THERA

WEISERBOOKS
San Francisco, CA / Newburyport, MA

This edition published in 2014 by Weiser Books
Red Wheel/Weiser, LLC
With offices at:
665 Third Street, Suite 400
San Francisco, CA 94107
www.redwheelweiser.com

ISBN: 978-1-57863-558-0

Library of Congress Cataloging-in-Publication Data available upon request.

Cover design by Jim Warner.
Cover art: Drawing 8/7 Nymphaea capensis var. zanzibariensis (Cape Blue Water-Lily) 1907 (watercolour on paper), Church, Arthur Henry (1865-1937) / Natural History Museum, London, UK / The Bridgeman Art Library
Interior by Frame25 Productions
Typeset in Brill.

Printed in the United States of America.
EBM
10 9 8 7 6 5 4 3 2 1

Contents

Foreword

The Heart of Buddhist Meditation was the first serious, didactic Dharma book I read. It was the early nineteen-eighties. My teacher, Jack Kornfield, suggested it as the beginning of formal training to become a Mindfulness teacher. I have that original copy, and I am touched by how many underlined passages, how many exclamation points in margins, and how many addenda of my own written in tiny scrawl appear in its fading pages. I had been a serious practitioner for more than five years by that time, a participant at many retreats, and an ardent, inspired listener to Dharma talks. My own discoveries about suffering and the end of suffering as I experienced them had kept me committed. When, as a way of providing formal, authoritative, academic background for me as teacher, I began to read the works of the Venerable Nyanaponika Thera, I not only felt that I understood the whole process of what was happening to me in a fuller way, I felt as though I were adopting the Venerable Nyanaponika as my spiritual grandfather. I still feel that way.

Apart from the meticulous yet accessible writing style with which the Venerable Nyanaponika builds every point, I feel a warmth and friendliness in his tone that makes me feel as if he is talking to me. The fact that I feel him as family is multi-layered, I'm sure. My father, whom I greatly admired, was a wonderful high school mathematics teacher who taught me to swim and solve puzzles and ice skate. I always felt that he taught things he loved to people he loved. Like Nyanaponika Thera, my grandfather, with whom I was very close all of his ninety-eight year life, was a Jew born in German-speaking Europe. Although unschooled, he liked to talk to me philosophically. I felt, from my family teaching me and talking to me, that I was well cared for and respected. I feel the same reading *Heart of Buddhist Meditation.*

Look at this example, and see if you don't feel uplifted and cared for and inspired:

> In the actual, and not merely conceptual, confrontation with the fact of Impersonality, as afforded by Bare Attention, its full gravity will certainly make itself felt strongly, in consonance with the gravity of entire existence of which it is the most significant fact. But this will not be the only emotional experience issuing from the awareness of Anattā (Impersonality). **Testimonies of ancient and modern meditators speak of moods of lofty happiness covering a wide range from rapture and exultation to serene joy. They are expressive of the exhilaration and relief felt when the tight, vice-like grip of "I" and "Mine" loosens; when the tension it produces in the body and mind is relaxed; when we can lift, for a while, our heads above the fierce current and whirl in which the obsessions of "I" and "Mine" engulf us; when there is a growing awareness that the very fact of Impersonality holds open for us the door to Liberation** from the Ill which was sensed so poignantly in what we called the grave aspect of Impersonality.

(The bold-type addition to that text is mine.) In my thirty year old edition of this book, that paragraph is heavily underlined and exclamation pointed. I love it! I hear it as Dharma poetry.

The Heart of Buddhist Meditation sits on my book shelf next to *The Vision of Dhamma*, a later collection of essays from the Venerable Nyanaponika Thera. Amidst dozens of Dharma books, they are my most referenced and most consulted. When I read in *Vision* that he uses "tidying" to describe the effect that mindfulness has on the mind, I could hear the echo of his German, Victorian mother in his word choice, and perhaps that added yet another layer to my feeling that Nyanaponika Thera is familiar to me. I do believe, though, that it is the Venerable's expansive heart and ardent hope to spread these liberating teachings to all seekers that will make him feel familiar to you as well, whoever you are.

Sylvia Boorstein
July 24, 2013

Introduction

The Heart of Buddhist Meditation

The purpose of these pages is to draw attention to the far- and deep-reaching significance of the Buddha's 'Way of Mindfulness' (Satipaṭṭhana), and to give initial guidance to an understanding of these teachings and their practical application.

This book is issued in the deep conviction that the systematic cultivation of Right Mindfulness, as taught by the Buddha in his Discourse on Satipaṭṭhāna, still provides the most simple and direct, the most thorough and effective, method for training and developing the mind for its daily tasks and problems as well as for its highest aim: mind's own unshakable deliverance from Greed, Hatred and Delusion.

The teachings of the Buddha offer a great variety of methods of mental training and subjects of meditation, suited to the various individual needs, temperaments and capacities. Yet all these methods ultimately converge in the 'Way of Mindfulness' called by the Master himself 'the Only Way' (or: the Sole Way; *ekāyano maggo*). The Way of Mindfulness may therefore rightly be called 'the heart of Buddhist meditation' or even 'the heart of the entire doctrine' (*dhamma-hadaya*). This great Heart is in fact the centre of all the blood streams pulsating through the entire body of the doctrine (*dhamma-kāya*).

The Scope of the Satipaṭṭhāna Method

This ancient Way of Mindfulness is as practicable to-day as it was 2,500 years ago. It is as applicable in the lands of the West as in the East; in the midst of life's turmoil as well as in the peace of the monk's cell.

Right Mindfulness is, in fact, the indispensable basis of Right Living and Right Thinking—everywhere, at any time, for everyone. It has a vital message for all: not only for the confirmed follower of the Buddha and his Doctrine (Dhamma), but for all who endeavour to master the mind that is so hard to control, and who earnestly wish to develop its latent faculties of greater strength and greater happiness.

In the first words of the Discourse, stating its high purpose, it is said that this method makes 'for the overcoming of sorrow and misery for the destruction of pain and grief'. Is not that just what everyone wishes for? Suffering is the common human experience, and, therefore, a method for radically conquering it, is of common human concern. Though the final victory over Suffering may, in the individual case, still be far off, the road to it has been clearly indicated. And more than that: from the very first stages of that road, the method of Right Mindfulness will show immediate and visible results of its efficacy, by defeating Suffering in many a single battle. Such practical results, in terms of happiness, must be of vital importance to everyone, in addition to the efficient help given to mental development.

The true aim of Satipaṭṭhāna is nothing less than final Liberation from Suffering which is also the highest goal of the Buddha's teaching—Nibbāna. The straight and direct path towards it, as provided by Satipaṭṭhāna, and a continuous progress on that path, require, however, sustained meditative effort, applied to a few selected objects of Mindfulness. Brief initial instructions in that practice will be given in these pages.

But, for striving after that highest goal, a general application of Mindfulness, on the level of the normal life activities, is of no less importance. It will give invaluable support to the effort in specialized and intensified Mindfulness. It will further instil in minds still untrained, the general 'mood' and attitude of Mindfulness, and give familiarity with its 'mental climate'. Its beneficial results, in a narrower and 'worldly' field, will be an additional inducement to extend the range of application, and will be an encouragement to take up the systematic practice aiming at the highest goal. For these reasons, special attention has been given here to the general aspects of Mindfulness, i.e. its place in the fabric of human life in general.

In Satipaṭṭhāna lives the creative power as well as the timeless and universal appeal of a true doctrine of Enlightenment. It has the depth and the breadth, the simplicity and the profundity for providing the foundation and the framework of a living *Satipaṭṭhana dhamma for all*, or, at least, for that vast, and still growing, section of humanity that is no longer susceptible to religious or pseudoreligious sedatives, and yet feel, in their lives and minds, the urgency of fundamental problems of a non-material kind calling for solution that neither science nor the religions of faith can give. For the purpose of such a *Satipaṭṭhāna dhamma for all* it is essential to work out, in detail, the applications of this method to modern problems and conditions. Here, within the limits of these pages, only brief indications can be given in that respect (see, in particular, pp. 79f). Elaboration and additions must be left to another occasion or to other pens.

For the benefit of those, particularly in the West, who are not well acquainted with Buddhist literature, some information follows here, about the relevant texts on which the ancient tradition of Satipaṭṭhāna is based.

The Discourse, Its Title, and the Commentary

The Buddha's original 'Discourse on the Foundations of Mindfulness' (Satipaṭṭhāna Sutta) occurs twice in the Buddhist scriptures: (1) as the 10th Discourse of the 'Middle Collection of Discourses': (*Majjhima Nikāya*), (2) as the 22nd Discourse of the 'Long Collection' (*Digha Nikāya*) where it has the title *Mahā-Satipaṭṭhāna Sutta*, i.e. the Great Discourse, etc. The latter differs from the first version only by a detailed treatment of the Four Noble Truths, included in that section of the 'Contemplation of Mental Contents' which deals with them. In the present publication, the second and larger version has been reproduced (as Part Two), and, in the following, it will be briefly referred to as 'the Discourse.'

The title.—In the compound Pali term *'sati-paṭṭhāna,'* the first word, *sati* (Sanskrit: *smṛti*), had originally the meaning of 'memory', 'remembrance'. In Buddhist usage, however, and particularly in the Pali scriptures, it has only occasionally retained that meaning of remembering past events. It mostly refers there to the present, and as a general psychological term it carries the meaning of 'attention' or 'awareness'. But still more frequently, its use in the Pali scriptures is restricted to a kind of attentiveness that, in the sense of the Buddhist doctrine, is good, skilful or right (*kusala*). It should be noted that we have reserved the rendering 'mindfulness', for this latter use only. *'Sati,'* in this sense, is the seventh factor of the Noble Eightfold Path, under the name of *Sammā-sati,* i.e. Right Mindfulness, being expressly explained as the fourfold 'Foundations of Mindfulness' (Satipaṭṭhāna).

The second part of the compound, *paṭṭhāna,* stands for *upaṭṭhāna,* lit. 'placing near (one's mind)', i.e. keeping present, remaining aware, establishing. This expression, in various grammatical forms, is frequently used in connection with 'sati', e.g. in our Discourse, *satim upaṭṭhapetvā,* lit. 'having kept present his mindfulness'. Moreover, in the Sanskrit version which probably is very old, the title of the Discourse reads *Smṛti-upasthāna-sūtra.* According to that explanation, the complete word may be rendered by 'The Presence of Mindfulness'.

Among alternative ways of interpreting the title, the Commentary mentions that the four objects or contemplations (body, etc.), dealt with in the Discourse, are the 'principal place' (*padhānam ṭhānaṁ*) or the 'domain proper' (*gocara*) of Mindfulness; this suggests a rendering 'The Domain of Mindfulness' or 'The Foundations of Mindfulness', and this latter translation has been adopted here.

It is, however, desirable that the Pali word 'Satipaṭṭhāna' itself should become familiarized among Western readers of Buddhist literature, as in the case of such terms as Kamma (Karma), Dharma, etc.

The *Commentary* to the Discourse is included in the old exegetical works on the two aforementioned canonical collections in which our text occurs. These commentaries, at least in their substance, date, almost certainly, back to the very earliest time of the Doctrine. The complete original, however, of all the old commentaries to the Buddhist Pali Canon was no longer extant in the fourth century a.c. The version we possess now is a retranslation, and partly perhaps a recasting into the Pali language, from the early Sinhalese version that was found in Ceylon. This rendering into Pali was done by the great scholar and commentator of the fourth century a.c., Buddhaghosa, who, besides some illustrative stories, probably added not much more than a few comments of his own to those already in the Ceylon tradition.

Since there exists a faithful English translation of that Commentary, by the late Venerable Soma Mahathera of Ceylon (d. 1960),* it was considered unnecessary to duplicate here this material in full. It has, however, been utilized in the explanatory notes to the Discourse, and a few passages of general interest taken from that Commentary have been included in the Anthology which forms Part Three of this book.

To those, however, who wish to acquaint themselves with the full exegetical material concerning our Discourse, the study of the Commentary in the Venerable Soma's translation will be very rewarding. Apart from its direct relevance to our subject, the Commentary contains a wealth of information about various important Buddhist teachings, and, besides, a number of stirring stories showing the determined and heroic manner in which the Only Way was trodden by the monks of old, and giving instructive glimpses into details of their practice.

Satipaṭṭhāna in Eastern Tradition

No other Discourse of the Buddha, not even his first one, the famous 'Sermon of Benares', enjoys in those Buddhist countries of the East which adhere to the unadulterated tradition of the original teachings, such popularity and veneration as the Satipaṭṭhāna Sutta.

In Lankā for instance, the isle of Ceylon, when on full-moon days pious lay devotees observe eight of the ten principal precepts of novice monks, staying for the day and the night in a monastery, they frequently choose this Sutta to read, recite, listen to, and contemplate. Still, in many a home, the Satipaṭṭhāna book is reverently wrapped in a clean cloth, and from time to time, in the evening, it is read to the members of the family. Often this Discourse is recited at the bedside of a dying Buddhist, so that in the last hour of his life, his heart may be set on, consoled and gladdened by the Master's great message of liberation. Though ours is an age of print, it is still customary in Ceylon to have new palm-leaf manuscripts of the Sutta written by scribes, and to offer them to the library of a monastery. A collection of nearly two hundred such manuscripts of the Satipaṭṭhāna Sutta, some with costly covers, was seen by the writer in an old monastery of Ceylon.

Such great veneration paid to a single canonical text may partly be ascribed to the fact that the Satipaṭṭhāna Sutta is one of the very few Discourses which the Master himself marked out, by introducing and concluding them in a particularly emphatic and solemn way. But this alone would not be sufficient to explain the persistence, through thousands of years, of such singular veneration. It must be attributed also to the effects of a long and successful practice of the Way, throughout twenty-five centuries, which has enhaloed the Sutta, as it were, with an aura of power that inspires deep reverence.

May this Undying Speech of the Buddha continue to wield its beneficial power, even far from the place and time of its origin, in the Western hemisphere! May it be a bridge between the races, by pointing to the common roots of human nature and to a common future of an ennobled mind's mastery over human destiny!

The Anthology

Having now introduced to the reader the first two parts of this book—the essay and the Basic Text—it remains to add a few words about the Third Part in which additional Buddhist texts relevant to the Way of Mindfulness have been collected.

These texts will offer to the earnest student supplementary explanations of the Discourse and will present aspects and applications of Satipaṭṭhana which received only passing mention, or none, in the first two parts. This anthology is firstly intended as a source book on its subject; but beyond its informative purpose it is hoped that it will serve as a book of contemplation to which the reader will return again and again for fresh inspiration.

The major part of these texts has been taken from the Pali Canon of the Theravada school, in which the oldest and most faithful tradition of the Buddha's teachings has been preserved. From the Discourse Collection (Sutta Piṭaka) of that Canon, it was in particular the Samyutta-Nikāya (The Kindred, or Grouped, Sayings) that proved a rich source of texts on Satipaṭṭhāna: firstly in the Group named after the latter, the Satipaṭṭhāna-Saṁyutta; in the Anuruddha-Saṁyutta, named after that great Arahant who was an eminent practiser of Satipaṭṭhāna; and finally, in the Saḷāyatana-Saṁyutta, the Group of texts on the Six Sense-bases, which contains much valuable material on the development of insight (vipassanā) into the basic cognitive processes.

Though the emphasis of this selection is on the Theravāda literature, it would have been an omission if the beautiful echo evoked by Satipaṭṭhāna in the early Mahāyāna literature would not be heard here, along with the voices of the original Buddha Word. The early Mahāyāna Sūtras are represented here by extracts taken from Sāntideva's anthology, the *Śikṣa-samuccaya.* These extracts and also Śāntideva's own masterly work, the *Bodhicaryāvatāra*, show how deeply he appreciated the importance of Mindfulness in the framework of the Teaching. Some of Santideva's succinct and beautiful formulations may well be regarded as classic, and should be often remembered by those who walk the Way of Mindfulness.

If that high value placed on Mindfulness and Satipaṭṭhāna in the early Mahāyāna literature is not allowed to be a mere historical remnant, but becomes an active force in the life and thought of the followers, it may well fashion a strong and close link of common spiritual endeavour between Mahāyāna and Theravada, relegating to the background the differences between these two schools. To contribute to that end is one of the reasons for including here the section on Mahāyāna which, by one more familiar with that literature, can certainly be increased considerably.

Two facts, however, must be remembered in this connection. Firstly: as the Master himself says so emphatically in the Discourse, the attainment of final deliverance from suffering (Nibbāna) is the ultimate aim and inherent power of Satipaṭṭhāna. But an earnest follower of the Mahāyānic Bodhisattva Ideal who, with full awareness of the implications, vows to aspire after Buddha-hood, ceases thereby to strive after individual deliverance before he has achieved his lofty aspiration. Consequently, he will have to avoid the application of Satipaṭṭhāna to the methodical development of Insight (*vipassanā*) which may well lead him, in this very life, to a stage ('Stream-entry' or *Sotāpatti*) where final deliverance is irrevocably assured, at the latest after seven existences; and this would, of course, put an end to his Bodhisattva career. Such restraint imposed on the full practice of Satipaṭṭhāna creates a rather strange situation from the view point of Theravāda and in the light of the Buddha's own injunction. But be that as it may, there is no doubt that he who is determined to walk the arduous road to Buddhahood will require a very high degree of mindfulness and clear comprehension, of keen awareness and purposefulness, if he wishes to acquire, maintain and develop, the midst of life's vicissitudes, those high virtues, the Perfections or Pāramis, which are the requisite conditions of Buddhahood. And in that endeavour he will be, for a long stretch of the road, the companion of his Theravāda brother. In his final effort for Enlightenment and ultimate emancipation, he will of course, have to reach the summit of Insight (*vipassanā*) through the Only Way of fully developed Satipaṭṭhāna. This is the road that all Liberated Ones have gone and will go, be they Buddhas, Pacceka-Buddhas or Arahants (see the stanza in Part III, Text I).

Among the Mahāyāna schools of the Far East, it is chiefly the Chinese Ch'an and Japanese Zen that are closest to the spirit of Satipaṭṭhāna. Notwithstanding the differences in method, aim and basic philosophical conceptions, the connecting links with Satipaṭṭhāna are close and strong, and it is regrettable that they have hardly been stressed or noticed. In common are, for instance, the direct confrontation with actuality (including one's mind), the merging of every-day life with the meditative practice, the transcending of conceptual thought by direct observation and introspection, the emphasis on the Here and Now. The follower of Zen will, therefore, find much in Theravāda's presentation and practice of Satipaṭṭhāna that can be of direct help to him on his own path. Since the literature on Zen has grown considerably in the West, it would have been repetitive to include here illustrative texts often reproduced elsewhere.

For reasons of space, the author has refrained from adding to the anthology voices from the West, old and modern, which give independent testimony of the importance of Mindfulness for the basic structure and future evolution of the human mind.

Concluding Remarks

The first part of this book, *The Heart of Buddhist Meditation,* together with the shorter version of the Discourse, was published in Ceylon in two editions (Colombo 1954 & 1956, 'The Word of the Buddha Publishing Committee'). In the present edition, apart from several minor additions and changes, a new chapter on 'Mindfulness of Breathing' (Ch. 6) has been included. The shorter version of the Discourse was replaced by the longer one which, with its detailed explanation of the Four Noble Truths, embodies the essence of the Buddha's Teachings.

A shorter German version of the first part (without chapters 5 and 6) was also included in the author's *Satipaṭṭhāna, Der Heilsweg buddhistischer Geistesschulung,* issued in 1950 by Verlag Christiani, Konstanz. The same publishing house also issued a German version of the anthology, under the title *Der einzige Weg* (Konstanz 1956) from which the present English edition differs by a few added and a few omitted texts. The author's thanks are due to his German publisher, Dr. Paul Christiani, for his kind permission to use this copyright material in an English version. He also expresses his appreciation of the keen interest taken by Dr. Christiani in the promotion of Buddhist literature in Germany.

It is heartening to find that there is a growing interest in meditation in the East as well as in the West, and that it comes, at least partly, from a genuine inner need. It is hoped that the present book will be helpful to many, in many lands, who wish to develop the human mind's potential for greater calm and strength, for a more penetrative awareness of reality, and finally, for its unshakable deliverance from Greed, Hatred and Delusion.

The Forest Hermitage Kandy, Ceylon
NYANAPONIKA THERA

Notes

**The Way of Mindfulness*, translated by Bhikkhu Soma. Colombo 1949 (Lake House Bookshop).

Part One

THE HEART OF BUDDHIST MEDITATION

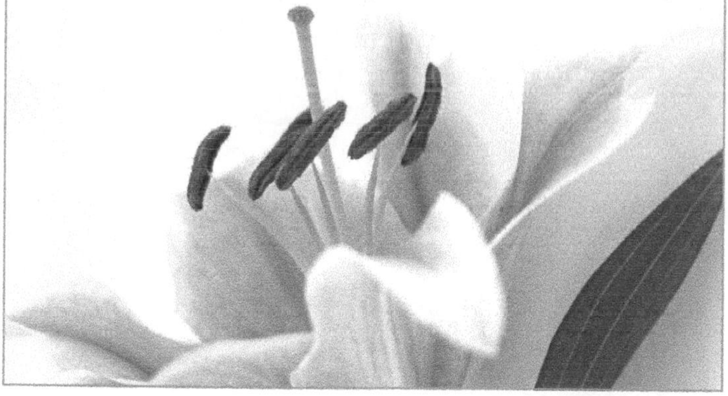

ONE

The Way of Mindfulness

Significance, Methods, and Aims

A Message of Help

In the present era after two world wars, history seems to repeat its lessons to humanity with a voice more audible than ever, because the turbulence and suffering that, alas, are generally equivalent with political history, affect increasingly larger sections of mankind, directly or indirectly. Yet it does not appear that these lessons have been learned any better than before. To a thoughtful mind, more gripping and heart-rending than all the numerous single facts of suffering produced by recent history, is the uncanny and tragic monotony of behaviour that prompts mankind to prepare again for a new bout of that raving madness called war. The same old mechanism is at work again: the interaction of greed and fear. Lust for power or desire to dominate are barely restrained by fear—the fear of man's own vastly improved instruments of destruction. Fear, however, is not a very reliable brake on man's impulses, and it constantly poisons the atmosphere by creating a feeling of frustration which again will fan the fires of hate. But men still bungle only with the symptoms of their malady, remaining blind to the source of the illness which is no other than the three strong Roots of Everything Evil (*akusala-mūla*) pointed out by the Buddha: greed, hatred and delusion.

To this sick and truly demented world of ours, there comes an ancient teaching of eternal wisdom and unfailing guidance, the Buddha-Dhamma, the Doctrine of the Enlightened One, with its message and power of healing. It comes with the earnest and compassionate, but quiet and unobtrusive question whether, this time, the peoples of the world will be prepared to grasp the helping hand that the Enlightened One has extended to suffering humanity through his timeless Teaching. Or will the world wait again till it has succeeded in conjuring up a new and still more gruesome ordeal that may well result in mankind's final decline, material and spiritual?

The nations of the world seem unthinkingly to assume that their reserves of strength are inexhaustible. Against such an unwarranted belief stands the universal Law of Impermanence, the fact of incessant Change, that has been emphasized so strongly by the Buddha. This Law of Impermanence includes the fact shown by history and by daily experience, that the external opportunities for material and spiritual regeneration, and the vital strength and inner readiness required for it, are never without limits, either for individuals or for nations. How many empires, mighty like those of our days, have not crumbled, and how many a man has not, in spite of his repentance and 'best intentions', been confronted with an implacable 'Too late!' We never know whether it is not this very moment or just this present situation that is opening to us the door of opportunity for the last time. We never know whether the strength that we still feel pulsating in our veins, however feebly, will not be the last capable of carrying us through our distressful plight. Hence it is this very moment that is most precious. 'Let it not escape from you!', warns the Buddha.

The Message of the Buddha comes to the world as an effective way of help in present-day afflictions and problems, and as the radical cure for ever-present ill. Some doubt may arise in the minds of Western men how they could be helped in their present problems by a doctrine of the far and foreign East. And others, even in the East, may ask how words spoken 2,500 years ago can have relevance to our 'modern world', except in a very general sense. Those who raise the objection of distance in space (meaning by it, properly, the difference of race), should ask themselves whether Benares is truly more foreign to a citizen of London than Nazareth from where a teaching has issued that to that very citizen has become a familiar and important part of his life and thought. They should further be willing to admit that mathematical laws, found out long ago in distant Greece, are of no less validity to-day, in Britain or elsewhere. But particularly these objectors should consider the numerous basic facts of life that are common to all humanity. It is about them that the Buddha preeminently speaks. Those who raise the objection of the distance in time, will certainly recall many golden words of long-dead sages and poets which strike such a deep and kindred chord in our own hearts that we very vividly feel a living and intimate contact with those great ones who have left this world long ago. Such experience contrasts with the 'very much present' silly chatter of society, newspapers or radio, which, when compared with those ancient voices of wisdom and beauty, will appear to emanate from the mental level of stone-age man tricked out in modern trappings. True wisdom is always young, and always near to the grasp of an open mind which has painfully reached its heights and has earned its chance to listen to it.

The Mind-Doctrine, the Heart of the Buddha's Message

Particularly does the culmination of human wisdom, the Teaching of the Buddha, deal not with something foreign, far, or antiquated but with that which is common to all humanity, which is ever young, and, nearer to us than hands and feet—the human mind.

In the Buddhist doctrine, mind is the starting point, the focal point, and also, as the liberated and purified mind of the Saint, the culminating point.

It is a significant fact and worth pondering upon, that the Bible commences with the words: 'In the beginning, God created the heaven and the earth . . .', while the Dhammapada, one of the most beautiful and popular books of the Buddhist scriptures, opens with the words 'Mind precedes things, dominates them, creates them' (translation by Bhikkhu Kassapa). These momentous words are the quiet and uncontending, but unshakable reply of the Buddha to that biblical belief. Here the roads of these two religions part: the one leads far away into an imaginary Beyond, the other leads straight home, into man's very heart.

Mind is the very nearest to us, because through mind alone are we aware of the so-called external world including our own body. 'If mind is comprehended, all things are comprehended', says a text of Mahāyāna Buddhism (*Ratnamegha Sūtra*).

Mind is the fount of all the good and evil that arises within and befalls us from without. This is declared precisely in the first two verses of the 'Dhammapada', and, among many other instances, in the following words of the Buddha: 'Whatsoever there is of evil, connected with evil, belonging to evil—all issues from mind.

'Whatsoever there is of good, connected with good, belonging to good—all issues from mind.'

—Anguttara Nikāya I.

Hence the resolute turning away from disastrous paths, the turning that might save the world in its present crisis, must necessarily be a turning inward, into the recesses of man's own mind. Only through a change within will there be a change without. Even if it is sometimes slow in following, it will never fail to arrive. If there is a strong and well-ordered inner centre in our mind, any confusion at the periphery will gradually be dissolved, and the peripheral forces will spontaneously group themselves around the focal point, sharing its clarity and strength. Order or confusion of society corresponds to, and follows, the order or confusion of individual minds. This does not mean that suffering humanity will have to wait till the dawn of a Golden Age 'when all men are good'. Experience and history show us that often just a very small number of truly noble men possessed of determination and insight, is required for forming 'focal points of the Good' around which will rally those who have not the courage to take the lead, but are willing to follow. However, as man's recent history shows, the same, and even greater, attraction may be exerted by the powers of Evil. But it is one of the few consolations in this not entirely disconsolate world, that not only Evil, but the Good also may have a strong infectious power that will show itself increasingly if only we have the courage to put it to the test.

'Thus it is our own mind that should be established in all the Roots of the Good; it is our own mind that should be soaked by the rain of truth; it is our own mind that should be purified from all obstructive qualities; it is our own mind that should be made vigorous by energy.'

—Gaṇḍavyūha Sūtra

Hence the message of the Buddha consists just in the help it gives to the mind. None, save he, the Exalted One, has given that help in such a perfect, thorough and effective way. This is maintained here with all due appreciation of the great curative and theoretical results achieved by modern analytical psychology which, in many of its representatives, particularly in the great personality of G. G. Jung, has taken a definite turn towards recognizing the importance of the religious element and towards appreciating Eastern wisdom. The modern science of the mind may well supplement, in many practical and theoretical details, the mind-doctrine of the Buddha; it may translate the latter into the conceptual language of the modern age; it may facilitate its curative and theoretical application to the particular individual and social problems of our time. But the decisive fundamentals of the Buddhist mind-doctrine have retained their full validity and potency; they are unimpaired by any change of time and of scientific theories. This is so because the main situations of human existence repeat themselves endlessly,[1] and the main facts of man's physical and mental make-up will remain essentially unaltered for a long time to come. These two relatively stable factors—the typical events in human life, and the typical physical and mental constitution of man—must always form the starting point for any science of the human mind and for any attempt to guide it. The Buddha's mind-doctrine is based on an exceptionally clear grasp of these two factors, and this bestows on it its 'timeless' character, i.e. its undiminished 'modernity' and validity.

The Buddha-Message, as a Doctrine of the Mind, teaches three things:

- to *know* the mind,—that is so near to us, and yet is so unknown;
- to *shape* the mind,—that is so unwieldy and obstinate, and yet may turn so pliant;
- to *free* the mind,—that is in bondage all over, and yet may win freedom here and now.

What may be called the theoretical aspect of the Buddha's mind-doctrine would come under the first of the above three headings, and will here be dealt with only as far as it is required for the pre-eminently practical purpose of these pages.

Right Mindfulness, the Heart of the Buddha's Mind-Doctrine

All the implications of the Buddha's healing message as well as the core of his mind-doctrine are included in the admonition 'Be mindful!' that pervades the Buddha's great sermon on the 'Foundations of Mindfulness' (Satipaṭṭhāna Sutta). This admonition requires, of course, the supplementary elucidation of the questions 'To be mindful of what?', and 'To be mindful, how?' The answer is given in the Discourse itself, in the ancient Commentary to it, and in the condensed interpretation that follows here.

If we have spoken above of the mind-doctrine being the starting, focal and culminating point of the Buddha-message, we may now add that Right Mindfulness holds the very same place within the Buddhist mind-doctrine.

Mindfulness, then, is the unfailing master key for *knowing* the mind, and is thus the starting point; the perfect tool for *shaping* the mind, and is thus the focal point; the lofty manifestation of the achieved *freedom* of the mind, and is thus the culminating point.

Therefore the 'Foundations of Mindfulness' (*Satipaṭṭhāna*) have rightly been declared by the Buddha as the 'Only Way' (*ekāyano maggo*).

What Is Mindfulness?

Mindfulness, though so highly praised and capable of such great achievements, is not at all a 'mystical' state, beyond the ken and reach of the average person. It is, on the contrary, something quite simple and common, and very familiar to us.

In its elementary manifestation, known under the term 'attention', it is one of the cardinal functions of consciousness without which there cannot be perception of any object at all. If a sense object exercises a stimulus that is sufficiently strong, attention is roused in its basic form as an initial 'taking notice' of the object, as the first 'turning towards' it.[2] Because of this, consciousness breaks through the dark stream of subconsciousness (—a function that, according to the Abhidhamma (Buddhist psychology), is performed innumerable times during each second of waking life). This function of germinal mindfulness, or initial attention, is still a rather primitive process, but it is of decisive importance, being the first emergence of consciousness from its unconscious subsoil.

From this first phase of the perceptual process naturally only a very general and indistinct picture of the object results. If there is any further interest in the object, or if its impact on the senses is sufficiently strong, closer attention will be directed towards details. The attention, then, will dwell not only on the various characteristics of the object, but also on its relationship to the observer. This will enable the mind to compare the present perception with similar ones recollected from the past, and, in that way, a coordination of experience will be possible. This stage marks a very important step in mental development, called in psychology 'associative thinking'. It also shows us the close and constant connection between the functions of memory and attention (or mindfulness), and will thereby explain why in Pali, the language of the Buddhist scriptures, both these mental functions are expressed by the one word *sati*.[3] Without memory, attention towards an object would furnish merely isolated facts, as it is the case with most of the perceptions of animals.

It is from associative thinking that the next important step in evolutionary development is derived: generalization of experience, i.e. the capacity of abstract thinking. For the purpose of this exposition we include it in the second stage of cognition as affected by the development of attention. We have found four characteristics of this second stage: increase of detail, reference to the observer (subjectivity), associative, and abstract, thinking.

By far the greatest part of the mental life of humanity to-day takes place on the plane of this second phase. It covers a very wide field: from any attentive observation of everyday facts, and attentive occupation with any work, up to the research work of the scientist and the subtle thoughts of the philosopher. Here, perception is certainly more detailed and comprehensive, but it is not necessarily more reliable. It is still more or less adulterated by wrong associations and other admixtures, by emotional and intellectual prejudices, wishful thinking, etc., and, primarily, by the main cause of all delusion: the conscious or unthinking assumption of a permanent substance in things, and of an Ego or soul in living beings. By all these factors the reliability of even the most common perceptions and judgements may be seriously impaired. On the level of this second stage, by far the greatest part of all those will remain who lack the guidance of the Buddha-Dhamma, as well as those who do not apply that instruction to the systematic training of their own minds.

With the next advance in the gradual development of Attention, we enter the very domain of Right Mindfulness or Right Attention (*sammā-sati*). It is called 'right' because it keeps the mind free from falsifying influences; because it is the basis as well as part and parcel of Right Understanding; because it teaches us to do the right thing in the right way, and because it serves the right purpose pointed out by the Buddha: the Extinction of Suffering.

The objects of perception and thought, as presented by Right Mindfulness, have gone through the sifting process of keen incorruptible analysis, and are therefore reliable material for all the other mental functions, as theoretical judgements, practical and ethical decisions, etc.; and notably these undistorted presentations of actuality will form a sound basis for the cardinal Buddhist meditation, i.e. for viewing all phenomena as impermanent, liable to suffering, and void of substance, soul or Ego.

To be sure, the high level of mental clarity represented by Right Mindfulness, will, to an unattuned mind, be anything but 'near' and 'familiar'. At best, an untrained mind will very occasionally touch its borderland. But in treading the way pointed out by the Satipaṭṭhāna method, Right Mindfulness may *grow* into something quite near and familiar, because, as we have shown before, it has its root in quite common and elementary functions of the mind.

Right Mindfulness performs the same functions as the two lower stages of development, though it does so on a higher level. These functions common to them are: producing an increasingly greater clarity and intensity of consciousness, and presenting a picture of actuality that is increasingly purged of any falsifications.

We have given here a brief outline of the evolution of mental processes as mirrored by the actual stages and qualitative differences of perception: from the unconscious to the conscious; from the first faint awareness of the object to a more distinct perception and a more detailed knowledge of it; from the perception of isolated facts to the discovery of their causal, and other, connections; from a still defective, inaccurate, or prejudiced cognition to the clear and undistorted presentation by Right Mindfulness. We have seen how in all these stages, it is *an increase in the intensity and quality of attention,* or mindfulness, that is mainly instrumental in enabling a transition to the next higher stage. If the human mind wants a cure for its present ills, and wishes to be set firmly on the road to further evolutionary progress, it will have to start again through the Royal Gate of Mindfulness.

The Road to the Development of Consciousness

The second stage of development—the more extensive, but still delusive knowledge of the world of objects—is already a secure possession of human consciousness. It allows now for growth only in the dimension of breadth, i.e. the addition of new facts and details and their use for material ends. Owing to the increase in the knowledge of details, over-specialization with all its attending beneficial and harmful effects, has gone very far in modern civilization. The biological consequences of one-sided development are well known: degeneration, and finally elimination of the species, as in the case of the prehistoric giant lizards, with their huge bodies and small brains. To-day's danger, however, is overdevelopment of one-sided brain-activity devoted solely to material ends, in the service of a thirst for sense pleasures and a lust for power. The concomitant danger is that mankind might, one day, be crushed by the very creations of its own hypertrophied brain—its body-killing inventions and its mind-killing 'distractions'. The fate of modern civilization might well be a repetition of the collapse of that technical marvel, the Babylonian Tower, all over again, with its builders not understanding, but fighting each other. The remedy that will prevent catastrophic developments is the Buddha's Middle Path. It is the eternal guardian that, if listened to, will protect humanity from shipwreck on the rocks of extremes, mental, spiritual and social.

To repeat: if humanity continues to move on the plane of the second evolution stage only, stagnation if not catastrophe awaits it. It is only by a new advance in mental clarity, i.e. in the quality of attention or mindfulness, that fresh movement and new progress will be introduced again into the structure of modern consciousness. This advance can be achieved by the Way of

Mindfulness taught here. The road, however, must be built on the safe foundation of 'human-heartedness' (Confucius), i.e. on a morality that is lofty as well as realistic. This, likewise, is to be found in the Buddha-Dhamma.

Right Mindfulness or Satipaṭṭhāna has been explicitly declared by the Buddha as the way to mind's liberation, and, thereby, to man's true greatness. It is a new type of man, the true 'superman', dreamed of by so many noble, but also misguided minds, an ideal aspired to by so many misdirected efforts. As evidence for our statement, the following remarkable conversation, which has been handed down to us in the Buddhist scriptures, may be included here:

Sāriputta, the Master's foremost disciple, addressed the Buddha: 'One speaks of "Great Men" (*mahā-purisa*), Lord! How far, Lord, is man great?' The Buddha replied: 'With liberated mind, Sāriputta, is one a Great Man; without a liberated mind one is not a Great Man. How then, Sāriputta, is mind liberated? Here a monk dwells contemplating the body . . . the feelings . . . consciousness . . . mind-objects, ardent, clearly comprehending and mindful . . . For him who dwells in that way, mind becomes detached from the defilements and liberated. Thus, Sāriputta, is mind liberated. With liberated mind, I declare, is one a Great Man; without liberated mind, I declare, one is not a Great Man' (*Saṃyutta Nikāya* 47, II).

It is this Right Mindfulness, of such a high objective and such a great potency, that will be treated in the following pages.

Right Mindfulness and Its Divisions

Right Mindfulness is the seventh factor of the Noble Eightfold Path leading to the Extinction of Suffering. In the canonical explanation of that Path, it is expressly defined as the four 'Foundations of Mindfulness' (Satipaṭṭhāna). Therefore, Right Mindfulness and 'Foundations of Mindfulness' or Satipaṭṭhāna, will be used here as interchangeable terms.

Right Mindfulness is fourfold with regard to its *objects*. It is directed (1) towards the body, (2) the feelings, (3) the state of mind, i.e. the general condition of consciousness at a given moment, (4) mental contents, i.e. the definite contents, or objects, of consciousness at that given moment.

These are the four 'Contemplations' (*anupassanā*), forming the main division of the Discourse. They are sometimes also called the four Satipaṭṭhānas, in the sense of being the basic objects of Mindfulness, or Sati.

In the Buddhist scriptures, the term 'mindfulness' (*sati*) is frequently linked with another term, translated here by 'clear comprehension' (*sampajañña*). These two concepts form, in the Pali language, the compound term *sati-sampajañña*, occurring very often in the Buddhist texts. In the context of that dual term, Mindfulness (*sati*) applies preeminently to the attitude and practice of Bare Attention in a purely receptive state of mind. Clear Comprehension (*sampajañña*) comes into operation when any kind of action is required, including active reflective thoughts of things observed.

These two terms may also serve as a general division of Right Mindfulness, or Satipaṭṭhāna, signifying two characteristic modes of its application. We shall deal with that twofold division first, while the fourfold one, according to the objects of Mindfulness, will be treated subsequently.

The Place of Mindfulness in the Framework of Buddhist Doctrine

The term 'mindfulness' occurs in the Buddhist scriptures in many contexts and is a member of several groups of doctrinal terms, of which only the most important ones shall be mentioned here.

'Right Mindfulness' (*sammā-sati*) is the seventh factor of the '*Noble Eightfold Path leading to the Extinction of Suffering*' that constitutes the fourth of the Four Noble Truths. In a threefold division of that eightfold path—into Virtue, Concentration and and Wisdom—Right Mindfulness belongs to the second group, Concentration (*samādhi*), together with Right Effort and Right Concentration.

Mindfulness is the first of the seven *Factors of Enlightenment* (*bojjhaṅga;* see p. 136). It is the first among them, not only in the order of enumeration, but because it is basic for the full development of the other six qualities, and in particular, it is indispensable for the second factor, the 'investigation of (physical and mental) phenomena' (*dhamma-vicaya-sambojjhaṅga*). Direct experimental insight into reality can be accomplished only with the help of the enlightenment factor Mindfulness (*sati-sambojjhaṅga*).

Mindfulness is one of the five Faculties (*indriya*); the other four are: confidence, energy, concentration and wisdom. Mindfulness, apart from being a basic faculty in its own right, has the important function of watching over the even development and balance of the other four, in particular of confidence (faith) in relation to wisdom (reason) and of energy in relation to concentration (or inner calm).

TWO

Mindfulness and Clear Comprehension

Among the two factors of that division, it is Mindfulness, in its specific aspect of Bare Attention, that provides the key to the distinctive method of Satipaṭṭhāna, and accompanies the systematic practice of it, from its very beginning to the achievement of its highest goal. It is, therefore, treated here first, and in greater detail.

I. Bare Attention

What Is Bare Attention?

Bare Attention is the clear and single-minded awareness of what actually happens *to* us and *in* us, at the successive moments of perception. It is called 'bare', because it attends just to the bare facts of a perception as presented either through the five physical senses or through the mind which, for Buddhist thought, constitutes the sixth sense. When attending to that sixfold sense impression, attention or mindfulness is kept to a bare registering of the facts observed, without reacting to them by deed, speech or by mental comment which may be one of self-reference (like, dislike, etc.), judgement or reflection. If during the time, short or long, given to the practice of Bare Attention, any such comments arise in one's mind, they themselves are made objects of Bare Attention, and are neither repudiated nor pursued, but are dismissed, after a brief mental note has been made of them.

This may suffice here for indicating the general principle underlying the practice of Bare Attention. Detailed information on the methodical practice will be given in Chapters Four and Five. In the following pages, we shall deal with the theoretical and practical significance of Bare Attention, and with the results to be expected from its application. It was thought advisable to dwell on these subjects in some greater detail, so that those who wish to take up a practice which, to some, will appear unusual, may start with some confidence in its efficacy, and an understanding of its purpose. It is, however, only by one's own personal experience gained in the course of persistent practice, that this initial confidence and understanding will find final and indubitable confirmation.

Thoroughness

Every effort of worth requires thoroughness if it is to achieve its purpose; particularly so if the work is as lofty and arduous as that mapped out by the Buddha in the Noble Eightfold Path, leading to the Extinction of Suffering. Among the eight factors of that Path, it is Right Mindfulness that represents that indispensable element of thoroughness, though Right Mindfulness has many other aspects in addition. In the Buddhist scriptures one of the qualities attributed to Right Mindfulness is called 'non-superficiality', and this is, of course, just a negative way of expressing our positive term 'thoroughness'.

It is obvious that the practice of Right Mindfulness itself will have to employ thoroughness of procedure, to the highest extent. The absence or neglect of it would be just the opposite of a quality deserving the name of Mindfulness, and would deprive the method of its chances of success. Just as detrimental consequences must result from an unstable and carelessly laid foundation, so the blessings of a solid and reliable one will extend far into the future.

Therefore, Right Mindfulness starts at the beginning. In employing the method of Bare Attention, it goes back to the seed state of things. Applied to the activity of mind this means: observation reverts to the very first phase of the process of perception when mind is in a purely receptive state, and when attention is restricted to a bare noticing of the object (see pp. 9 f). That phase is of a very short and hardly perceptible duration, and, as we have said, it furnishes a superficial, incomplete and often faulty picture of the object. It is the task of the next perceptual phase to correct and to supplement that first impression, but this is not always done. Often the first impression is taken for granted, and even new distortions, characteristic of the more complex mental functions of the second stage, are added.

Here starts the work of Bare Attention, being a deliberate cultivation and strengthening of that first receptive state of mind, giving it a longer chance to fulfil its important task in the process of cognition. Bare Attention proves the thoroughness of its procedure by cleansing and preparing the ground carefully for all subsequent mental processes. By that cleansing function, it serves the high purpose of the entire Method set forth in the Discourse: 'for the purification of beings . . . which, in the Commentary, is explained as the purification, or cleansing, of mind.

Obtaining the Bare Object

Bare attention consists in a bare and exact registering of the object. This is not as easy a task as it may appear, since it is not what we normally do, except when engaged in disinterested investigation. Normally man is not concerned with a disinterested knowledge of 'things as they truly are', but with 'handling' and judging them from the view point of his self-interest, which may be wide or narrow, noble or low. He tacks labels to the things which form his physical and mental universe, and these labels mostly show clearly the impress of his self-interest and his limited vision. It is such an assemblage of labels in which he generally lives and which determines his actions and reactions.

Hence the attitude of Bare Attention—bare of labels—will open to man a new world. He will first find out that, where he believed himself to be dealing with a unity, i.e. with a single object presented by a single act of perception, there is, in fact, multiplicity, i.e. a whole series of different physical and mental processes presented by corresponding acts of perception, following each other in quick succession. He will further notice with consternation how rarely he is aware of a bare or pure object without any alien admixture. For instance, the normal visual perception if it is of any interest to the observer will rarely present the visual object pure and simple, but the object will appear in the light of added subjective judgements, as: beautiful or ugly, pleasant or unpleasant, useful, useless or harmful. If it concerns a living being, there will also enter into it the preconceived notion: 'This is a personality, an Ego, just as "I" am, too'.

In that condition, i.e. closely intertwined with subjective additions, the perception will sink into the store house of memory. When recalled, by associative thinking, it will exert its distorting influence also on future perceptions of similar objects, as well as on the judgements, decisions, moods, etc., connected with them.

It is the task of Bare Attention to eliminate all those alien additions from the object proper that is then in the field of perception. These additions may be considered later singly if wanted, but the initial object of perception has to be kept free from them. This will demand persistent practice during which the attention, gradually growing in its keenness, will, as it were, use sieves of increasingly finer meshes by which first the grosser and then ever subtler admixtures will be separated until the *bare object* remains.

The necessity for such an exact definition and delimination of the object is emphasized in the Satipaṭṭhāna Sutta itself, by regularly mentioning twice the respective object of mindfulness, e.g. 'He dwells contemplating the body in the body', and not, e.g. his feelings or ideas concerned with it, as the Commentary expressly explains. Let us take the example of a person looking at a wound on his forearm. In that case, the visual object proper will consist exclusively of the respective part of the body and its damaged condition. Its different features, as flesh, blood, pus, etc., will be objects of the 'Contemplation of the Body', in particular of the exercise concerning 'the Parts of the Body'. Pain felt owing to the wound will form an object of the 'Contemplation of Feelings'. The more or less conscious notion that it is an Ego, a self that is wounded and suffers pain, will fall under the Contemplation of the State of Mind ('deluded mind') or under the 'Contemplation of Mental Contents': about the mental 'Fetters' that arise through bodily contact (see, in the Discourse, the section on the Sense Bases). The grudge one may feel (apparently at the same moment) against the person that caused the hurt, belongs to the Contemplation of the State of Mind ('mind with hate') or to the 'Contemplation of Mental Contents' (the Hindrance of Anger). This example will suffice to illustrate the sifting process undertaken by Bare Attention.

The far-reaching importance of getting at the *bare object* was stressed by the Buddha himself. When asked by a monk for a word of guidance in brief, the Master gave to him the following rule of practice:

"In what is seen there should be only the seen; in what is heard, only the heard; in what is sensed (as smell, taste or touch), only the sensed; in what is thought, only the thought."

(Udāna *I, 10*)

This concise but weighty saying of the Master may serve as a guide and companion for him who devotes himself to the practice of Bare Attention.

The Threefold Value of Bare Attention

Bare Attention has the same threefold value as attributed earlier to the Buddha's Mind-Doctrine and to Right Mindfulness, in general: it will prove a great and efficient helper in *knowing, shaping* and *liberating* the mind.

1. The Value of Bare Attention for Knowing the Mind

Mind is the very element in and through which we live, yet it is what is most elusive and mysterious. Bare Attention, however, by first attending patiently to the basic facts of the mental processes, is capable of shedding light on mind's mysterious darkness, and of obtaining a firm hold on its elusive flow. The systematic practice of Mindfulness, starting with Bare Attention, will furnish all that knowledge about the mind which is essential for practical purposes, i.e. for the mastery, the development and the final liberation of mind. But even beyond that intrinsically practical scope of the Satipaṭṭhāna method: when once clear awareness and comprehension have been firmly established in a limited but vital sector of the mind's expanse, the light will gradually and naturally spread, and will reach even distant and obscure corners of the mind's realm which hitherto had been inaccessible. This will mainly be due to the fact that the *instrument* of that search for knowledge will have undergone a radical change: the searching mind itself will have gained in lucidity and penetrative strength.

'Only things well examined by Mindfulness can be understood by Wisdom, but not confused ones' (Commentary, to Sutta Nipāta). A specimen of research that is to be examined with the help of a microscope has first to be carefully prepared, cleaned, freed from extraneous matter, and firmly kept under the lens. In a similar way, the 'bare object' to be examined by wisdom, is prepared by Bare Attention. It cleans the object of investigation from the impurities of prejudice and passion; it frees it from alien admixtures and from points of view not pertaining to it; it holds it firmly before the Eye of Wisdom, by slowing down the transition from the receptive to the active phase of the perceptual or cognitive process, thus giving a vastly improved chance for close and dispassionate investigation.

This preliminary work of Bare Attention is of importance not only for the analytic, i.e. the dissecting and discriminating function of mind by which the elements of the object's make-up are revealed. It is also of great assistance to the equally important synthesis, i.e. for finding out the object's connections with, and relations to other things, its interaction with them, its conditioned and conditioning nature. Many of these will escape notice if there is not a sufficiently long period of Bare Attention. As a maxim of great importance and of varied application, also to practical matters, it should always be kept in mind that the relations beween things can be reliably ascertained only if first the single members of that relationship have been carefully examined in their various aspects which are pointers to diverse connections. Insufficient analytic preparation is a frequent source of error in the synthetic part of philosophical systems and scientific theories. It is just this preparation that is carefully attended to and remedied, by the method of Bare Attention. Its consequences upon the spiritual practice that concerns us here have been mentioned before (pp. 19 f.) and will become still clearer in the following pages.

Bare Attention first allows things to speak for themselves, without interruption by final verdicts pronounced too hastily. Bare Attention gives them a chance to finish their speaking, and one will thus get to learn that, in fact, they have much to say about themselves, which formerly was mostly ignored by rashness or was drowned in the inner and outer noise in which ordinary man normally lives. Because Bare Attention sees things without the narrowing and levelling effect of habitual judgements, it sees them ever anew, as if for the first time; therefore it will happen with progressive frequency that things will have something new and worth while to reveal. Patient pausing in such an attitude of Bare Attention will open wide horizons to one's understanding, obtaining thus, in a seemingly effortless way, results which were denied to the strained efforts of an impatient intellect. Owing to a rash or habitual limiting, labelling, misjudging and mishandling of things, important sources of knowledge often remain closed. Western humanity, in particular, will have to learn from the East to keep the mind longer and more frequently in a receptive, but keenly observing, state—a mental attitude which is cultivated by the scientist and the research worker, but should increasingly become common property. This attitude of Bare Attention will, by persistent practice, prove to be a rich source of knowledge and inspiration.

What are now, in particular, the results, in terms of knowledge, obtainable through Bare Attention? We shall mention here only a few of them which are of primary importance. It must be left to one's own 'travel experience' on the Way of Mindfulness, to vindicate, elaborate and supplement what is said here in brief.

It has already been said, and is now repeated on account of its fundamental importance: in the light of Bare Attention, the seemingly uniform act of perception will, with increasing clarity, appear as a sequence of numerous and differentiated single phases, following each other in quick succession. This basic observation will gradually unfold its inherent wealth of single facts and their far-reaching implications. It will prove to be a truly scientific observation, in the literal meaning of the word, i.e. 'knowledge-yielding' (C. J. Ducasse). It will show, e.g., the basic differentiation of the perceptual process: the presentation of the comparatively bare sense data,[4] and the subsequent phase of interpreting and evaluating them. This is ancient psychological knowledge to the Buddhist, going back to the Discourses of the Master himself, and elaborated in later books and commentaries of the Abhidhamma. This distinction between the 'bare facts of the case' and the attitude to them, has, apart from its scientific ('knowledge-yielding') import, also a far-reaching practical significance: it locates the earliest, i.e. the most promising point where we can determine the further development of the given situation as far as it depends on our attitude towards it. The consideration of that aspect, however, belongs to the following chapter on Mind-shaping.

When practising Bare Attention, the first powerful impact on the observer's mind will probably be the direct confrontation with the ever-present fact of Change. In terms of the Dhamma, it is the first of the three Characteristics, or Signata, of Life: Impermanence (*anicca*). The incessant sequence of individual births and deaths of the events observed by Bare Attention, will become an experience of growing force and will have decisive consequences on the meditative progress. From that same experience of momentary change, the direct awareness of the two other Characteristics of Existence will emerge in due course, i.e. of ill (Suffering, Insufficiency; *dukkha*) and Impersonality (*anattā*).

Though the fact of Change is commonly admitted, at least to a certain extent, people in ordinary life will generally become conscious of it only when it challenges them fairly vehemently, in either a pleasant or, mostly, an unpleasant way. The practice of Bare Attention, however, will bring it forcibly home that Change is always with us; that even in a minute fraction of time the frequency of occurring changes is beyond our ken. Probably for the first time it will strike us—not only intellectually but touching our whole being—in what kind of a world we are actually living. (Joining face to face with Change, as experienced vividly in our own body and mind, we have now started 'to see things as they really are'. And this refers particularly to the 'things of the mind'. Mind cannot be understood without knowing it as a flux and remaining aware of that fact in all investigations devoted to the knowledge of mind. To show the fact as well as the nature of (Change in mental processes is, therefore, a fundamental contribution of the practice of Bare Attention to mind-knowledge. The *fact* of Change will contribute to it in a negative way, by excluding any static view of the mind, assuming permanent entities, fixed qualities, etc. The insight into the *nature* of Change will be a (contribution in a positive way, by supplying a wealth of detailed information on the dynamic nature of the mental processes.

In the light of Bare Attention focussed on sense perception, the distinctive character of material and mental processes, their interrelation and alternating occurrence as well as the basic 'objectifying' function of mind will gain in clarity.

In speaking here of 'objectifying' (i.e. having as object, taking as object), and of material and mental processes, we do so just for our practical purpose of analysis. These terms are not meant to express our advocating a dualism of subject/object and mind/matter. Nor do we side with any monism of Mind Only or Matter Only. The Buddha's Middle Teaching of Dependent Origination (*paṭicca-samuppāda*) transcends all these concepts of monism, pluralism and dualism. In a world of conditionality, relativity and flux, as directly experienced in the practice of Bare Attention, those rigid notions will soon appear as quite incongruous.

These latter casual remarks of ours point to another contribution to mind-knowledge of a more theoretical character concerning those aforementioned age-old philosophical attitude which arise from false factual premises, with vast theoretical superstructures framed to fit those premises. But we are not directly concerned with these problems here. In our context we need only point out that common experience as well as penetrative scrutiny show us differentiations in the process and the contents of cognition which are sufficiently strong to justify our pragmatic use of the traditional pairs of terms, subject/object, and mind/matter.

After the practice of Bare Attention has resulted in a certain width and depth of experience in its dealings with mental events, it will become an immediate certainty to the meditator that *mind is nothing beyond its cognizing function.* Nowhere, behind or within that function, can any individual agent or abiding entity be detected. By way of one's own direct experience, one will thus have arrived at the great truth of No-soul or Impersonality (*anattā;* Skr. *Anātma*), showing that all existence is void of an abiding personality (self, soul, over-self, etc.) or an abiding substance of any description. Also to modern psychology that unique and revolutionary teaching of Anattā may likewise become 'knowledge-yielding' in a high degree, through its strong impact on the root and various branches of the science of the mind. These implications will be evident to the student of that field of knowledge, and cannot be illustrated here. In calling the Anattā doctrine unique, we wanted to distinguish it from what is known in the West as a 'psychology without psyche' which is mostly of a materialistic hue, and which, with a deprecative undertone, is sometimes called 'soul-less'. Buddhist psychology, however, is not materialistic in either the philosophical or in the ethical sense of the word. The true philosophical and ethical significance of the No-self doctrine, and also its 'emotional tone', can be fully understood only in the context of the entire Buddhist doctrine, and not in isolation. We shall have occasion to return to that subject.

Bare Attention will, in addition, supply surprising as well as helpful information about the working of one's own mind: the mechanism of one's emotions and passions, the reliability of one's reasoning power, one's true and pretended motives, and many other aspects of mental life. Clear light will fall on one's weak and strong points as well, and of some of them one will become aware for the first time.

This method of Bare Attention, so helpful to mind-knowledge and, through it, to world-knowledge, tallies with the procedure and attitude of the true scientist and scholar: clear definition of subject-matter and terms; unprejudiced receptivity for the instruction that comes out of the things themselves; exclusion, or at least reduction, of the subjective factor in judgement; deferring of judgement until a careful examination of facts has been made. This genuine spirit of the research worker, manifested in the attitude of Bare Attention, will always unite the Buddha-Dhamma with true science, though not necessarily with all the theories of the day. But the *purpose* of the Buddha-Dhamma is not the same as that of secular science which is limited to the discovery and explanation of facts. The Buddha's mind-doctrine, however, is not restricted to a theoretical *knowledge* of the mind, but it aims at the *shaping* of mind, and, through it, of life. In that object, however, it meets with that branch of modern psychology which is devoted to the practical application of theoretical mind-knowledge.

2. The Value of Bare Attention for Shaping the Mind

The greater part of man-made suffering in the world comes not so much from deliberate wickedness as from ignorance, heedlessness, thoughtlessness, rashness and lack of self-control. Very often a single moment of mindfulness or wise reflection would have prevented a far-reaching sequence of misery or guilt. By *pausing* before action, in a habitual attitude of Bare Attention, one will be able to seize that decisive but brief moment when mind has not yet settled upon a definite course of action or a definite attitude, but is still open to receive skilful directions. The next moment may change the situation fully, giving final supremacy to tainted impulses and misjudgements from within, or harmful influences from without. Bare Attention slows down, or even stops, the transition from thought to action, allowing more time for coming to a mature decision. Such slowing down is of vital importance as long as unprofitable, harmful or evil words and deeds possess an all too strong spontaneity of occurrence, i.e. as long as they appear as immediate reactions to events or thoughts, without giving to the 'inner brakes' of wisdom, self-control and common sense a chance to operate. Acquiring the habit of 'slowing down' will prove an effective weapon against rashness in words and deeds. By learning, through Bare Attention, to pause, to slow down and to stop, the plasticity and receptivity of the mind will grow considerably, because reactions of an undesirable nature will no longer occur automatically, with the same frequency as before. When the supremacy of these habitual reactions, which are so often left unopposed and unquestioned, is regularly challenged, they will gradually lose their power.

Bare Attention will also allow us time for the reflection whether, in a given situation, activity by deed, word or mental application is necessary or advisable at all. There is often too great an inclination for unnecessary interference, and this becomes another avoidable cause of much suffering and superfluous entanglement. When acquainted with the peace of mind bestowed by the attitude of Bare Attention, one will be less tempted to rush into action or to interfere in other people's affairs. If, in that way, complications and conflicts of all kinds are lessened, the endeavour to *shape* the mind will meet with less resistance.

In regard to these two points mentioned last ('rashness' and 'interference'), the practical advice is in brief: to look well before leaping, to give the mind a chance to take a longer and larger view of things, to curb the urge for 'action at any cost'.

Bare Attention is concerned only with the *present.* It teaches what so many have forgotten: to live with full awareness in the Here and Now. It teaches us to *face* the present without trying to escape into thoughts about the past or the future. Past and future are, for average consciousness, not objects of observation, but of reflection. And, in ordinary life, the past and the future are taken but rarely as objects of truly *wise* reflection, but are mostly just objects of day-dreaming and vain imaginings which are the main foes of Right Mindfulness, Right Understanding and Right Action as well. Bare Attention, keeping faithfully to its post of observation, watches calmly and without attachment the unceasing march of time: it waits quietly for the things of the future to appear before its eyes, thus to turn into present objects and to vanish again into the past. How much energy has been wasted by useless thoughts of the past: by longing idly for bygone days, by vain regrets and repentance, and by the senseless and garrulous repetition, in word or thought, of all the banalities of the past! Of equal futility is much of the thought given to the future: vain hopes, fantastic plans and empty dreams, ungrounded fears and useless worries. All this is again a cause of avoidable sorrow and disappointment which can be eliminated by Bare Attention.

Right Mindfulness recovers for man the lost pearl of his freedom, snatching it from the jaws of the dragon Time. Right Mindfulness cuts man loose from the fetters of the past which he foolishly tries even to re-inforce by looking back to it too frequently, with eyes of longing, resentment or regret. Right Mindfulncss stops man from chaining himself even now, through the imaginations of his fears and hopes, to anticipated events of the luture. Thus Right Mindfulness restores to man a freedom that is to be found only in the present.

Thoughts of the past and the future are the main material of *day-dreaming* which by its tough and sticky substance of endlessly repetitive character crowds the narrow space of present consciousness, giving no chance for its shaping, and making it, in fact, still more shapeless and slack. These futile day-dreams are the chief obstacles to concentration. A sure way to exclude them is to turn the mind resolutely to the bare observation of any object close at hand, whenever there is no necessity or impulse for any particular purposive thought or action, and when, consequently, a mental vacuum is threatening that, otherwise, is quickly invaded by day-dreams. If they have entered already, one need only make these day-dreams themselves objects of close observation in order to deprive them of their mind-diluting power, and finally disperse them. This is an example of the effective method of 'transforming *disturbances* of meditation into *objects* of meditation' which will be treated later.

Bare Attention brings order into the untidy corners of the mind. It shows up the numerous vague and fragmentary pereptions, unfinished lines of thought, confused ideas, stifled emotions, etc., which are daily passing through the mind. Taken singly, these vain consumers of mental activity are weak and powerless, but by their accumulation they will gradually impair the efficiency of mental functions. Since these thought-fragments are mostly allowed to sink into the subconsciousness without being properly attended to, they will naturally affect the basic structure of character, dispositions and tendencies. They will gradually reduce the range and lucidity of consciousness in general, as well as its plasticity, i.e. its capacity of being shaped, transformed and developed.

The unflattering self-knowledge gathered through introspective Bare Attention, about the squalid and disreputable quarters of our own mind, will rouse an inner resistance to a state of affairs where clarity and order are turned into untidiness, and the precious metal of the mind into dross. By the pressure of that repugnance the earnest application to the practice of the Way of Mindfulness will increase, and the excessive squandering of mental energy will gradually come under control. It is the automatic 'tidying' function of Bare Attention that serves here for Shaping of Mind.

Bare Attention directed towards our own mind will supply that candid information about it which is indispensable for success in its shaping. By turning full attention to our thoughts as they arise, we shall get a better knowledge of our weak and our strong points, i.e. of our deficiencies and our capacities. Self-deception about the former and ignorance of the latter make self-education impossible.

By the skill attained through Bare Attention to call bad or harmful things at once by their true names, one will take the first step towards their elimination. If one is clearly aware, e.g. in the Contemplation of the State of Mind: 'There is a lustful thought', or, in the Contemplation of Mental Contents: 'In me is now the Hindrance of Agitation', this simple habit of making such express statements will produce an inner resistance to those qualities which will make itself felt increasingly. This dispassionate and brief form of mere 'registering' will often prove more effective than a mustering of will, emotion or reason, which frequently only provokes antagonistic forces of the mind to stiffer resistance.

Our positive qualities, too, will of course be focussed more clearly, and those which are either weak or not duly noticed will get their chance, and develop to full bloom and fruition. Untapped resources of energy and knowledge will come into the open, and capacities will be revealed which were hitherto unknown to oneself. All this will strengthen the self-confidence which is so important for inner progress.

In these and other ways the simple and non-coercive method of Bare Attention proves a most efficacious helper in *Shaping the Mind.*

3. The Value of Bare Attention for Liberating the Mind

The suggestion is proffered to the reader that he may try, at first for a few test days, to keep as well as he can to an attitude of Bare Attention towards people, inanimate environment and the various happenings of the day. By doing so he will soon feel how much more harmoniously such days are passing compared with those when he gave in to the slightest stimulus for interfering by deed, word, emotion or thought. As if protected by an invisible armour against the banalities and importunities of the outer world, one will walk through such days serenely and content, with an exhilarating feeling of ease and freedom. It is as if, from the unpleasant closeness of a hustling and noisy crowd, one has escaped to the silence and seclusion of a hill top, and, with a sigh of relief, is looking down on the noise and bustle below. It is the peace and happiness of detachment which will thus be experienced. By thus stepping back from things and men, one's attitude towards them will even become friendlier, because those tensions will be lacking which so often arise from interfering, desire, aversion, or other forms of self-reference. Life will become a good deal easier, and one's inner and outer world more spacious. In addition, we will notice that the world goes on quite well without our earlier amount of intervention, and that we ourselves are all the better for such a restraint. How many entanglements will not be avoided, and how many problems will not solve themselves without our contribution! Hereby Bare Attention shows visibly the benefit of abstaining from karmic action, be it good or evil, i.e. from a world-building, sorrow-creating activity. Bare Attention schools us in the art of letting go, weans us from busy-ness and from habitual interfering.

The inner distance from things, men and from ourselves, as obtained temporarily and partially by Bare Attention, shows us, by our own experience, the possibility of finally winning *perfect* detachment and the happiness resulting from it. It bestows upon us the confidence that such temporary stepping *aside* may well become one day a complete stepping *out* of this world of suffering. It gives a kind of foretaste, or at least an idea, of the highest liberty, the 'holiness during life-time' (*diṭṭhadhamma-nibbāna*) that has been alluded to by the words: '*In* the world, but not *of* the world'.

For achieving that highest, and final, liberation of mind, Bare Attention forges the principal tool—that highest penetration of truth which, in the Dhamma, is called *Insight* (*vipassanā*). This, and only this, is the ultimate purpose of the method described here, and it is the highest form of its mind-liberating function.

Insight is the direct and penetrative realization of the Three Characteristics of Existence, i.e. Impermanence, Suffering and Impersonality. It is not a mere intellectual appreciation or conceptual knowledge of these truths, but an indubitable and unshakable personal experience of them, obtained and matured through repeated meditative confrontation with the facts underlying those truths. *Insight* belongs to that type of life-transforming knowledge which the French thinker Guyeau had in mind when saying: 'If one knows but does not act accordingly, one knows imperfectly'. It is the intrinsic nature of *Insight* that it produces a growing detachment and an increasing freedom from craving, culminating in the final deliverance of the mind from all that causes its enslavement to the world of suffering.

That direct confrontation with actuality, which is to mature into Insight, is obtained by the practice of Bare Attention, and of Satipaṭṭhāna in general. Its methodical development will be described later on. But even its casual application in routine life will show its liberating influence on mind, and, if persistingly applied, it will create a mental background helpful to the strict and systematic practice.

It is the nature of Insight to be free from Desire, Aversion and Delusion, and to see clearly all things of the inner and outer world as 'bare phenomena' (*suddha-dhammā*), i.e. as impersonal processes. Just that is characteristic also of the attitude of Bare Attention, and therefore the practice of it will make for a gradual acclimatization to the high altitudes of perfect Insight and final Deliverance.

This high goal of perfect detachment and insight may still be very distant to the beginner on the Path, but owing to his own kindred experiences during the practice of Bare Attention it will not be completely foreign to him. To such a disciple the goal will have, even now, a certain intimate familiarity and thereby a positive power of attraction which it could not possess if it had remained to him a mere abstract notion without anything corresponding to it in his own inner experience. To him who has entered the Way of Mindfulness, the goal will appear like the contours of a high mountain range at the distant horizon; and these outlines will gradually assume a friendly familiarity for the wanderer who gazes at them while plodding his toilsome way that is still so far from these exalted summits. Though the chief attention of the pilgrim must needs be given to the often dull piece of road under his feet, to the various obstacles and confusing turns of his path, it will be of no small importance that, from time to time, his eyes turn to the summits of his goal as they appear on the horizon of his experience. They will keep before the eyes of his mind the true direction of his journey, helping him to retrace his steps when he has gone astray. They will give new vigour to his tired feet, new courage to his mind, and hope which often might fail him were the sight of the mountains always blocked, or if he had only heard or read about them. They will also remind him not to forget, with all the 'little joys on the way', the glory of those summits waiting for him on the horizon.

II. Clear Comprehension

The receptive and detached attitude of Bare Attention can and should certainly occupy far greater room in our mental life than it usually does, and therefore it has received here such a detailed treatment. But this should not make us forget the fact that Bare Attention can generally be maintained only during a limited time of ordinary life, apart from periods expressly given to its application. Every hour of the day demands some activity by deed, word or thought. First there are the numerous demands for bodily activity or movement, be it only that a change of posture becomes necessary. We have also again and again to abandon the protection and self-sufficiency of silence, and enter into relationship with others through speech. And the mind too cannot avoid defining its position, to itself and to the outer world, and issuing orders for action innumerable times during the day. Mind has to choose, to decide and to judge.

It is *Clear Comprehension* (*sampajañña*), the second aspect of Right Mindfulness, which is concerned with that greater part of our life, the active one. It is one of the aims of the practice of Satipaṭṭhāna that Clear Comprehension should gradually become the regulative force of all our activities, bodily, verbal and mental. Its task is to make them purposeful and efficient, accordant with actuality, with our ideals and with the highest level of our understanding. The term 'Clear Comprehension' should be understood to mean that to the *clarity* of bare mindfulness is added the full *comprehension* of purpose and of actuality, internal and external, or, in other words: Clear Comprehension is right knowledge (*ñāna*) or wisdom (*paññā*), based on right attentiveness (*sati*).

Though the Discourse itself speaks only of clearly comprehending action and speech, and consequently deals with

Clear Comprehension in the section on the Contemplation of the Body, it goes without saying that also thinking, the third 'door of action', has to be brought under the control of Clear Comprehension.

The Four Kinds of Clear Comprehension

Buddhist tradition as embodied in the commentaries to the Buddha's Discourses, distinguishes four kinds of Clear Comprehension: (1) the Clear Comprehension of Purpose (*sātthaka-sampajañña*), (2) the Clear Comprehension of Suitability (*sappāya-sampajañña*), (3) the Clear Comprehension of the Domain (of Meditation; *gocara-sampajañña*), (4) the Clear Comprehension of Reality (lit. of Non-delusion; *asammoha-sampajañña*).

1. Clear Comprehension of Purpose

This first kind of Clear Comprehension enjoins that, before acting, one should always question oneself whether the intended activity is really in accordance with one's purpose, aims or ideals, i.e. whether it is truly purposeful in the narrower practical sense as well as in view of the ideal. The timely pausing for putting that question—if this is not already customary with the practiser—will have to be learned through the training in Bare Attention.

Some may think that there is no need to make purposeful action a special subject of their study or training, because they believe that, as 'rational beings', they naturally act 'rationally', i.e. purposefully. But quite apart from the *ultimate* purpose of the Way of Mindfulness, it will certainly be admitted that man does not always behave rationally at all; not even when the purpose he has in mind is quite narrow and thoroughly selfish and materialistic. Man often forgets about his purposes, programmes and principles, neglecting even his most obvious advantage and all this not only through rashness or passion, but even on account of quite casual whims, childish curiosity or lazy indolence. For these, or other secondary reasons, people are often deflected into directions that are quite other than their proper aims in life and their true interests.

Under the impact of the innumerable impressions crowding upon man from the world of outer and inner multiplicity (*papañca*), an occasional deviation from the general direction of one's life is certainly understandable and, to a certain extent, even unavoidable, for the most of us. All the more does it become necessary to limit such deviations to the very minimum, and to strive for their complete elimination which however is realized only in the perfect Mindfulness of the Saint (*arahat*). But these deviations from the straight path of purposeful living cannot be excluded, or even considerably reduced, by an enforced subordination to the dictatorial commands of dry reasoning or moralizing. The emotional side in man for which such whimsical deviations or escapades are often an outlet or a kind of protest, would soon revolt and even retaliate by some demonstrative irrationality of behaviour. In order to achieve a 'peaceful penetration' of the irrational regions of mind, and to win them over for willing participation in the realization of clearly comprehended purpose, work has again to 'start at the beginning': on the broad foundation of Bare Attention. By the simple, non-coercive and harmonizing methods of that practice, the tension-creating forces within the mind which obstruct purposeful activity, will gradually be absorbed into the main current of one's aims and ideals. A purposeful co-ordination of the various tendencies and needs of the human mind, and of the numerous human activities, will be achieved only (through a systematic, but organic and natural extension of conscious control, or self-mastery. Only in such a way can an increasing balance of the emotions and a general harmony and stability of character result—to which finally all waywardness, all arbitrariness, down to the 'demonstrative irrationality' of behaviour and self-destructive tendencies, will become fundamentally alien. The safe basis of such a self-mastery, i.e. of sense-control and mind-control, is the non-coercive method of Bare Attention. By strengthening the habit 'to stop and think', it gives to Clear Comprehension of Purpose an increased chance of coming into operation; and by its presentation of undistorted facts it provides for Clear Comprehension the reliable material for making its decisions.

It may happen, and cause deep regrets afterwards, that a high ideal, or an important purpose that was forgotten or temporarily pushed aside for the sake of a passing whim or fancy, becomes, before being taken up again, completely unattainable owing to a changed *external* situation caused by oneself, through just these incidental excursions. The ideal, or purpose, may likewise become unattainable owing to an *inner* change in the individual himself, caused by the same behaviour. There will be less regrets for lost opportunities if one cultivates Clear Comprehension of Purpose until it becomes deeply engrained in one's nature.

If, on the other hand, one habitually yields to all whims, or allows oneself too easily to be deflected from one's purpose, then such qualities as energy, endurance, concentration, loyalty, etc., will gradually be undermined and weakened to such an extent that they become insufficient for achieving that original purpose, or even for truly appreciating it any longer. In that way, it often happens that, unheeded by the person concerned, his ideals, religious convictions, and even his ordinary purposes and ambitions, are turned into empty shells which he still carries along with him, solely through habit.

These remarks may suffice to show the urgent necessity for a strengthening of purpose in action, and for extending its orbit. This is done by the constant presence of Clear Comprehension of Purpose. It has the *negative* function of counteracting the desultoriness, aimlessness and wastefulness of an inordinately great part of human activity, in deeds, words and thoughts. Its *positive* function is to concentrate the dispersed energy of man, to render it a fit tool for the task of winning mastery over life. In this way, Clear Comprehension of Purpose makes for the formation of a strong inner centre in one's character, powerful enough to coordinate gradually all one's activities. Again, Clear Comprehension of Purpose strengthens *mind's leadership* by giving to it skilful and determined *initiative* in cases where mind used to yield passively or react automatically to pressure from within and without. It also takes care of wise *selection* and *limitation* in man's activity, which is necessitated by the confusing multitude of impressions, interests, demands, etc., with which we are faced in life. Strong purposefulness will not easily be diverted by them.

The proper aim of that *initiative,* and the truly befitting governing principle of that *selection,* is *growth in the Dhamma* (*dhammato vuddhi*), i.e. increase in the understanding, and progress in the practice, of the liberating doctrine of the Buddha. This is, according to the Teachers of old, the true purpose meant in that first kind of Clear Comprehension. If once the Truth of Suffering has been understood in its full gravity, progress on the Path leading to the Extinction of that Suffering will actually become the most pressing need, the only true and worthy purpose of man's life.

2. Clear Comprehension of Suitability

The Clear Comprehension of the Suitability of an action under given circumstances gives due consideration to the fact that it is not always in our power to choose that course of action which is the most purposeful and the most desirable one, but that our selection (spoken of before) is often restricted by circumstances or by the limitations of our own capacities. This second kind of Clear Comprehension teaches the Art of the Practicable, the adaptation to the conditions of time, place and individual character. It restrains the blind impetuosity and wilfulness of man's wishes or desires, aims or ideals. It will save many unnecessary failures which man, in his disappointment or discouragement, often blames on the purpose or the ideal itself, instead of attributing it to his own wrong procedure. Clear Comprehension of Suitability teaches the 'Skilfulness in the choice of the right means' (*upāya-kosalla*), a quality which the Buddha possessed in the highest degree and which he so admirably applied to the instruction and guidance of men.

3. Clear Comprehension of the Domain of Meditation

The first two divisions of Clear Comprehension apply also to the purely practical purposes of ordinary life, though conformity to the religious ideal (*dhamma*) is insisted upon with regard to that practical application too. Now we enter the proper domain of the Dhamma as a life-transforming force. By the third kind of Clear Comprehension the characteristic *methods* of mind-development used in the Dhamma are incorporated in everyday life itself; and by the fourth kind ('Reality') the same is done with the fundamental *tenet* of the Dhamma, i.e. the teaching of impersonality, or absolute fluidity of the 'individual'.

The Clear Comprehension of the Domain of Meditation is explained by the old commentators as 'Not abandoning the subject of meditation' during one's daily routine. This has to be understood in a twofold way.

1. If a particular, i.e. single, subject of meditation is practised, one should try to blend it with the work or thought directly required by the day's occupations; or, expressed conversely—the work at hand should be given a place in the framework of the meditation, as an illustration of its subject. For instance, the function of eating may easily be related to contemplations on the impermanence of the body, the four elements, conditionality, etc. Thus

the two domains of meditation and ordinary life will merge—to the benefit of both. If, as it may be in many cases, no link can be established between one's present work and one's particular meditation, or if such connection would seem too vague or artificial to be of real value, then the subject of meditation should be deliberately 'put down like goods carried in the hand', but one should not forget to take it up again as soon as the work in question has been attended to. That procedure will also count as 'not abandoning the subject of meditation'.

2. But if one's meditative practice is all-round Mindfulness, as advocated here, there will be no need ever to lay aside the subject of meditation which, in fact, will include everything. Step by step the practice of Right Mindfulness should absorb all activities of body, speech and mind, so that ultimately the subject of meditation will never be abandoned. How far one succeeds in that, will depend on the presence of mind available at the single occasions, and on the habit-forming and growing strength of diligent practice. The aim to be aspired to by the disciple of this method is that *life* becomes one with the spiritual *practice,* and that the *practice* becomes full-blooded *life.*

The 'domain' (*gocara*) of the practice of Right Mindfulness has no rigid boundaries. It is a kingdom that constantly grows by absorbing ever new territories of life. It was in reference to this all-comprehensive domain of the Satipaṭṭhāna method, that once the Master spoke as follows: 'Which, O monks, is the monk's domain (*gocara*)[5] his very own paternal place? It is just these four Foundations of Mindfulness'.

Therefore the disciple of this method should always ask himself, in the words of Santideva:

'How can the practice of Mindfulness be
performed under these very circumstances?'

One who does not forget thus to question himself and also to act accordingly, may be said to possess 'Clear Comprehension of the Domain' of Right Mindfulness.

To attain to it is certainly no easy task, but the difficulties will be less if the first two kinds of Clear Comprehension have prepared the ground. By Clear Comprehension of Purpose, the mind will have acquired a certain degree of firmness and 'moulding power', needed for the absorption of ordinary life into the 'domain of practice'. On the other hand, Clear Comprehension of Suitability will have developed the complementary qualities of mental plasticity and adaptability. If in that way an approximation to the level of the meditative mind has been achieved, the entrance into (the 'domain of practice' and its gradual extension will be easier.

4. Clear Comprehension of Reality

The Clear Comprehension of Reality (lit.: of Non-delusion) removes, through the clear light of an unclouded comprehension of actuality, the deepest and most obstinate delusion in man: his belief in a self, a soul, or an eternal substance of any description. This delusion, with its offspring of craving and hatred, is the true motive power of that revolving Wheel of Life and Suffering to which, like to an instrument of torture, beings are bound, and on which they are broken again and again.

'Clear Comprehension of Reality' is the clarity and presence of knowledge that in, or behind, the functions performed by the first three modes of Clear Comprehension, there is no abiding personality, self, Ego, soul, or any such substance. Here the meditator will be confronted with the strongest inner opposition, because against this greatest achievement of human thought, the Anattā doctrine of the Buddha, an obstinate resistance will be offered by the world-old habit of thinking and acting in terms of 'I', and 'Mine', as well as by the instinctive and powerful 'Will to live', manifesting itself as self-affirmation. The main difficulty will be not so much the theoretical grasp and approval of the Anattā doctrine, as the patient, repeated and constant application of it to particular instances of thought and action. To help in that difficulty is the special task of the fourth, the 'undeluded', kind of Clear Comprehension; and in that task it receives the vital help of the three other modes. Only by training oneself again and again in viewing the presently arisen thoughts and feelings as mere impersonal processes, can the power of deep-rooted, ego-centric thought-habits and egotistic instincts be broken up, reduced and finally eliminated.

Here, as a brief excursion, a few words on the 'emotional tone' of the truth of Impersonality will be appropriate, since it is misjudged so often. The discernment of the fact of Impersonality, by reflection or as the result of the methodical practice of Bare Attention, is, in itself, certainly as unemotional and sober as the attitude of the scientist. But, except in the saint (Arahant) of perfect equipoise, emotional repercussions may well arise, as they also may arise in connection with irrefutable results of scientific research. These emotional repercussions of the insight into Impersonality are, however, not restricted to a single note, and certainly not to the disconsolate and plaintive one implied in the deprecating word 'soulless' (see p. 27). The 'emotional tone' will vary according to the angle of observation and the stage of the observer's inner development; it will reach its *finale* in the undisturbed rhythm of the saint's serenity. In the actual, and not merely conceptual, confrontation with the fact of Impersonality as afforded by Bare Attention, its full gravity will certainly make itself felt strongly, in consonance with the gravity of entire existence of which it is the most significant fact. But this will not be the only emotional experience issuing from the awareness of Anattā (Impersonality). Testimonies of ancient and modern: meditators speak of moods of lofty happiness covering a wide range, from rapture and exultation to serene joy. They are expressive of the exhilaration and relief felt when the tight, vice-like grip of 'I' and 'Mine' loosens; when the tension it produces in body and mind is relaxed; when we can lift, for a while, our head above the fierce current and whirl in which the obsessions of 'I' and 'Mine' engulf us; when there is a growing awareness that the very fact of Impersonality holds open for us the door to Liberation from the Ill which was sensed so poignantly in, what we call the grave aspect of Impersonality.

The fourth kind of Clear Comprehension has yet another function to perform that is of great consequence to steady progress on the Path to Ill's extinction.

In taking up the practice of the first three modes of Clear Comprehension, the disciple has left behind the relative security and detachment of Bare Attention, and has returned to the perilous world of purposive action—action that provokes reaction from that which is acted upon. But leaving aside the reactions, the disciple will first of all be faced by the fact that nearly every action of his drags him further into the labyrinths of the world's diffuseness (*papañca*) to which this action itself is adding its share. Action has the inherent tendency to multiply and to reproduce, to intensify and to expand itself. The disciple will experience, even in his endeavour to practise the first three modes of Clear Comprehension, that his actions will tend to entangle him in new interests, plans, duties, aims, complications, etc. That means, he will always be exposed to the danger of losing what he has achieved in his earlier practice, or of losing *sight* of it, unless he is extremely watchful. Here, the Realistic, or Undeluded, Clear Comprehension, i.e. the vivid awareness of Impersonality, will come to his assistance. '*Within* there is no self that acts, and *outside* there is no self affected by the action!' If this is kept before the mind, not only in great undertakings, but also in those no less important minor activities of ordinary life, then a beneficent feeling of inner distance from one's so-called 'own' actions will develop, and a growing detachment as to any success or failure, praise or blame, resulting from such action. The action, after its purpose and suitability have been clearly established, is now performed for its own sake and in its own right. For that very reason, the apparent indifference with which the action is done will not cause any loss of energy in its performance. On the contrary, when sidelong glances at oneself, at others, or at the results, are absent, this exclusive devotion to the work itself will enhance its chances of success.

If one no longer clings to an action with one's whole heart and being, if there is no more hankering after personal success or fame, then there will be less danger of being carried away by the self-created current of one's action to ever new reaches of the samsāric ocean. It will also be easier to keep a certain control over the steps resulting from the first action, or when advisable, to 'break up action' and to withdraw into 'non-action', i.e. the peace and protection of the attitude of Bare Attention.

Action in pursuit of worldly ends, as performed by an unliberated mind, is mostly mere creation of additional bondage. To preserve, within this world of 'bondage by action' (*kamma*), the highest possible '*freedom of action*' is one of the particular tasks and achievements of the Clear Comprehension of Reality, in cooperation with the other three modes. The complementary 'freedom in non-action' or the 'freedom in letting go' is taught by Bare Attention (see p. 28). We have quoted previously (p. 14) a word of the Master to the effect that the liberated mind of a truly great, i.e. holy man is the result of the consummate practice of Satipaṭṭhāna. Now after having learned of the two kinds of freedom bestowed by Mindfulness and Clear Comprehension, we shall be in a better position to understand that saying of the liberating effect of the Satipaṭṭhāna practice.

In conclusion, another significant feature of the fourth mode of Clear Comprehension deserves mentioning. Through the Clear Comprehension of Reality the active part of life, too, will be permeated by the truly revolutionary thought of Impersonality (anattā), which is the central teaching of the Buddha and the most decisive one for the actual deliverance from suffering. Its influence should therefore not be restricted to the few hours of reflection or meditation granted to men with worldly duties. Our life is short. We cannot afford to regard the greatest part of it, devoted to the practical routine tasks, as mere dead ballast, or to treat it like a pariah caste of necessary, but despised slave labourers who are kept at a low cultural level, either intentionally or out of negligence. We cannot afford to leave that great sector of our life unused and uncontrolled, allowing most of our thoughts, emotions and activities to roam at will, so often to our greatest harm.

Quite apart from the cardinal principle of the Satipaṭṭhāna method, the merging of life and spiritual practice, the brief span of our life alone makes it imperative that every moment of it, according to the opportunities it offers, and *any, even the most ordinary activity in its own way, should be utilized for the work of Liberation.* This penetration of life with liberating knowledge is undertaken by the Clear Comprehension of Reality, with special regard to the immediate experience of Impersonality.

Tibetan wisdom says:

> *'A system of meditation, which will produce the power of concentrating the mind upon anything whatsoever, is indispensable. An art of living, which will enable one to utilize each activity in an aid on the Path is indispensable.'*
>
> (From *Tibetan Yoga,* by Evans-Wentz)

Such a 'system of meditation' and such an 'art of living' is Satipaṭṭhāna.

Concluding Remarks on the Two Modes of Practice

Now, at the end of our treatment of Clear Comprehension, we have come to a feature of it, closely corresponding to that which we mentioned when concluding our exposition of Bare Attention. It is an encouraging fact that even the initial stage of earnest practice shows kinship and correspondence with the highest goal of complete detachment and freedom.

At the stage of Bare Attention, disclosing the 'freedom in non-action', we saw that the temporary stepping *aside* to a vantage point of observation corresponds to the Saint's final stepping *out* from this world of suffering. At the stage of Clear Comprehension, particularly its fourth kind, the growing detachment with regard to any action, corresponds to the 'perfect act' of the Saint, which, though purposeful in itself, is completely selfless and free from any clinging. Though the world perceives it as a 'good act', it has no karmic result for the Saint, it does not lead him to any renewed existence.[6] An act done with Clear Comprehension is, in the degree of its detachment and in its function of reducing karmic entanglement, an approximation to the 'perfect act' of the Saint.

The two modes of practice, Mindfulness (Bare Attention) and Clear Comprehension, help and supplement each other. The high degree of alertness and self-control achieved in the school of Bare Attention, will make it considerably easier to guide one's deeds and words by Clear Comprehension, instead of being taken unawares by situations, carried away by passions or misled by deceptive appearances. On the other hand, Clear Comprehension makes more room, and creates a more suitable atmosphere, for Bare Attention, by the control and the quietening influence it exercises upon the world of end-seeking action and restless thought.

Bare Attention presents those carefully and dispassionately sifted facts upon which clearly comprehending action may safely base its decisions, and clearly comprehending thought its conclusions. Bare Attention eliminates the wrong concepts and false values which have been blindly tacked to the bare facts. Clear Comprehension replaces these by critically examined concepts and true values as furnished by the Dhamma.

Bare Attention heightens the susceptibility and refines the sensitivity of the human mind; Clear Comprehension guides as well as strengthens the actively shaping and creative energies. Bare Attention makes for the growth, preservation and refinement of intuition—that indispensable source of inspiration and regeneration for the world of action and rational thought. Clear Comprehension, on the other hand, as an active and activating force works for making the mind a perfect instrument for its hard task of harmonious development and final liberation. It trains one, at the same time, for selfless work in the service of suffering humanity by bestowing the keen eye of wisdom and the sure hand of skilfulness which are as necessary for that service as a warm heart. Clear Comprehension is capable of giving this training because it provides an excellent schooling in purposeful, circumspect and selfless action.

Hence Satipaṭṭhāna, in the entirety of both its aspects, produces in the human mind a perfect harmony of *receptivity* and *activity*. This is one of the ways in which the Middle Path of the Buddha appears in this method of Right Mindfulness.

THREE

The Four Objects of Mindfulness

1. Body, 2. Feeling, 3. State of Mind, 4. Mental Contents

The objects of Right Mindfulness comprise the entire man and his whole field of experience. They extend from the body and its functions to the feelings as well as to the processes and contents of perception and thought. Right Mindfulness includes in its range the most primitive as well as the most lofty aspects of that complex being called 'man': from the functions he has in common with animals, e.g. nutrition and excretion, up to the exalted heights of the Factors of Enlightenment. We meet here again this method's fundamental principle of thoroughness, together with its character as a Middle Path, which, avoiding onesidedness or exclusiveness, aspires to completeness and harmony. The work of spiritual practice receives here a broad and secure foundation, being based upon the entire personality. Without such a foundation it may happen that from what is overlooked, underrated, neglected or ignored, strong antagonistic forces may grow, which may seriously damage, or even destroy, the results of long spiritual effort. Thoroughness of procedure will make the road of inner progress as safe as one may reasonably expect in a venture that aspires to such heights. There are further to be considered those various inner conflicts which consume so much energy and are the cause of so many defeats in the spiritual struggle: e.g. the conflict between 'the mind that is willing and the flesh that is weak', between emotion and reason, etc. These conflicts, too, will be greatly reduced or mitigated by the equal attention and the wise understanding which in this method of harmonious development, is givcn to each side of the conflict. What is to be mastered, transformed or transcended, has first to be known and understood.

Therefore it is necessary that the disciple of this method should cultivate all four Contemplations, or Objects, of Mindfulness mentioned in the Discourse, whenever they come into the range of his daily experience. The systematic meditative practice, however, centres (as will be shown later) on a very few selected subjects taken from the 'Contemplation of the Body', but the other objects of mindfulness will likewise have ample opportunity to come into the range of observation and should then receive full attention.

'The Instructions for Practice'

The thoroughness and completeness of the method applies to other fields too, as exemplified in what we may call 'the Instructions for Practice', which are repeated in the Discourse after every single exercise.[7] They begin as follows: 'Thus he dwells contemplating the body internally (in himself) . . . externally (in others) . . . both internally and externally . . .'

According to that first part of the 'Instructions', each single exercise has to be applied first to oneself, then to others (in general or to a definite person just observed) and finally to both. This threefold rhythm of each aspect of the practice was obviously regarded as very important. It occurs, in different connections and applications, in various Discourses of the Buddha and also in later Pali literature. By following the instruction, incomplete statements and misjudgements, resulting from an insufficient range of mindfulness, and one-sided attitudes, will be eliminated.

As to the latter, there are, for instance, those basic types of character as formulated by C. G. Jung: introverts and extraverts, i.e. people turned predominantly inward or outward, respectively. The former type will naturally prefer the contemplation of things internal; the latter, of those external. The deficiencies resulting from each partial contemplation will be compensated by faithfully following the instructions given above. The natural outcome of that threefold application of practice will be that each characterological type will remedy its shortcomings until an ideal balance is achieved. This method of Right Mindfulness, as an embodiment of the Middle Path, does in fact provide what each extreme type is lacking, and it does so in a form acceptable and intelligible to each. But in this brief exposition it is not possible to enter into these details.

Many things permit of better understanding when observed in others, or in external objects, than in oneself. A closer scrutiny, and one more impartial, may thus be possible, and defects, virtues and their consequences may appear in a clearer light. On the other hand, by an exclusive attention to persons or things external, one may conveniently forget the all-important application of mindfulness to oneself. This may happen quite unconsciously even in contemplating Impermanence, etc. If such contemplations proceed only in a very general way, without direct reference to one's own case, they will have only a very limited effect.

The third phase in this threefold rhythm of practice is that of viewing internal and external things in immediate succession.

In comparing them, the observed similarities as well as the differences will be highly instructive. In addition, attention will be drawn to the interconnections existing between internal and external components of the same group of things, e.g. the matter composing this body of ours, and external nature; to the causal, and other relations among the various internal and external phenomena, in brief: to the fact of conditionality or relativity. This scrutiny of relations and conditions is as important for a comprehensive understanding of actuality as are the results of analysis. Finally, this third, combined, phase of the practice serves to show the *general* validity of the knowledge and experience gathered, and the impersonal character of any object under view. This will gradually lead to the result that both internal and external things, i.e. those pertaining to oneself or to others, are instantly viewed as impersonal processes.

It should be noted, however, that in the systematic meditative development of Insight only *internal* objects are taken up and brought into the focus of Bare Attention. This is so because only one's own bodily and mental processes are accessible to direct experience. And it is a knowledge by direct experience (*paccakkha-ñāna*), in the strictest sense, which is aimed at, and which is the distinguishing mark of the Buddhist meditation of Insight (*vipassanā-bhāvanā*). Inference, reflection, etc., are entirely excluded at the beginning of the practice, and only at a later stage may they receive a limited place in it, as a kind of interlude, when inference is made from the meditative observation of the facts present, to past and future events of the same type. Mindfulness on *external* objects, however, may, and should, be cultivated outside the strict meditative practice. Those external objects, i.e. bodily and mental activities of others, will present themselves to us either„ by direct sense-perception or by inference. The contemplation of them will assume a different character according to the specific details of each exercise (as given in the Discourse), and will claim varying degrees of importance-a subject which here can only be intimated, but not treated in detail.

The *second* way of application of the single exercises proceeds likewise in a threefold rhythm: it is the attention to (1) the origination, (2) the dissolution, (3) both the origination and dissolution of the respective objects. As pointed out earlier, this direct experience of the fact and the nature of Change is a key-point of the practice, and of decisive consequences for its success. The Commentary to the Discourse should be consulted at each repetitive occurrence of that passage. The Commentary, however, does not deal with the actual meditative observation of the facts and the nature of Change, for this does not so much require comment as diligent practice. It deals rather with the utilization of those meditative observations for analytic reflection, and with a penetrative understanding of them in the wider context of the Dhamma. Here we shall mention, in addition, only the fact. By way of reflection, this contemplation on origination and dissolution may be used with advantage for the avoidance as well as the refutation of certain speculative theories. According to the Buddha, the belief in annihilation (philosophical nihilism, materialism, etc.) is countered by the fact of origination; the belief in eternalism (theism, pantheism, naive realism, etc.), by the fact of dissolution.

The remaining part of this textual passage indicates the *result* of the aforementioned twofold practice, i.e. concerning things internal, etc. and origination, etc. 'The body exists', feeling exists, etc., but no separate self, no abiding personality or soul. These words of the text indicate the results in terms of insight, i.e. ' the realistic view of things as they actually are. We read further in the text: 'He lives independent and clings to naught'. This indicates the resulting attitude of detachment. This concluding part of the repetitive passage shows, as the result of the practice, the liberation from the two principal 'dependencies', or attachments, of man, as formulated in the Commentary: false views (*diṭṭhi*) and craving (*taṇhā*), i.e. liberation from intellectual and irrational, theoretical and practical bondage.

The whole passage that we have now considered is a striking instance of the distinctive qualities apparent in statements coming from the source of Perfect Enlightenment (*sammā-sambodhi*). They have a quality of unique completeness and finality as to their meaning and their way of expression, carrying deep conviction for those able to appreciate this quality at least partly. It is very nature of these enunciations to combine profundity with simplicity, and, consequently, they are felt to be satisfying on any level of understanding. Their action on the mind is both tranquillizing and stimulating: tranquillizing, by stilling doubts and conflicts, and by imparting that feeling of deep satisfaction we have spoken of; stimulating, by their depth, or, as we may also express it, by their 'expanding horizon'.

Here we have been able to give only a bare indication of the far- and deep-reaching significance of these seemingly simple -words of the Master. He who practises accordingly, and reflects wisely, will discover more about them.

We now proceed to the consideration of the single Contemplations and exercises, given in the Discourse.

I. The Contemplation of the Body (*Kāyānupassanā*)

1. Mindfulness of Breathing

The section on Contemplation of the Body starts with 'Mindfulness on breathing in and breathing out' (*ānāpāna-sati*). It is an exercise in *mindfulness,* and not a '*breathing* exercise' like the *prāṇayāma* of Hinduistic Yoga. In the case of the Buddhist practice there is no 'retention' of breath or any other interference with it. There is just a quiet 'bare observation' of its natural flow, with a firm and steady, but easy and 'buoyant' attention, i.e. without strain or rigidity. The length or shortness of breathing is noticed, but not deliberately regulated. By regular practice, however, a calming, equalizing and deepening of the breath will result quite naturally; and the tranquillization and deepening of the breath-rhythm will lead to a tranquillization and deepening of the entire life-rhythm. In this way, Mindfulness of Breathing is an important factor of physical and mental health, though that is only incidental to the practice.

Breath is always with us. Therefore we can, and we should, turn our attention to it in any free or 'empty' minute during our daily occupations, even though we may not be able to do so with that highest attention demanded by the exercise proper. Even such a brief and casual application of the mind to the 'breath-body' lays the foundation for a very noticeable feeling of well-being, self-sufficient happiness and invulnerable quietude. Such happy conditions of mind, as well as the keenness and naturalness of attention, will grow with repeated practice.

To put in a few conscious, deep and calm respirations before starting any continuous work, will likewise be found most beneficial to oneself and to the work as well. To cultivate the habit of doing so before taking important decisions, making responsible utterances, talking to an excited person, etc., will prevent many rash acts and words, and will preserve the balance and efficiency of mind. By simply observing our breath, we can easily and unnoticed by others withdraw into ourselves if we wish to shut ourselves off from disturbing impressions, empty talk in a large company, or from any other annoyance. These are only a few examples of how even a casual Mindfulness of Breathing, as applicable in the midst of ordinary life, may have beneficial results.

These instances will show that Mindfulness of Breathing is very effective in *quietening* bodily and mental unrest or irritation, for ordinary as well as for higher purposes. It is further a simple way to the initial stages of *concentration* and meditation, used either as a prelude to other exercises, or as a practice in its own right. For attaining, however, to a more advanced degree of concentration, or even for achieving complete mental one-pointedness in the meditative 'Absorptions' (*jhāna*), Mindfulness of Breathing is not at all a simple method but, for all that, most worthy of adoption. Progress on that higher level of the practice can lead to the four stages of meditative Absorption, and even to still higher attainments. About this developed stage of the practice, Buddhist tradition says: 'Mindfulness of Breathing takes the first place among the various subjects of meditation (*kammaṭṭhāna*). To all Buddhas, Pacceka-Buddhas, and holy disciples it has been the basis of their attainment of the Goal, and of their well-being here and now'.

Breath stands on the threshold between the voluntary and the involuntary bodily functions, and thus offers a good opening to extend the scope of conscious control over the body. In this way, Mindfulness of Breathing is able to contribute to that partial task of Satipaṭṭhāna which may be formulated in the words of Novalis: 'Man should become a perfect self-instrument!'

Though, according to tradition, Mindfulness of Breathing is regarded primarily as a subject for Tranquillity-meditation (*samatha-bhāvanā*), i.e. for inducing the meditative Absorptions (*jhāna*), it can, however, be used also for the development of Insight (*vipassanā-bhāvana*); because in respiration, used as an object of Bare Attention, the heaving of the Ocean of Impermanence, its continuous rise and fall, can be well observed.[8]

Mindfulness of Breathing will also contribute to a general understanding of the body's true nature. Just as, in ancient mystical thought, breath was identified with the life force itself, so does Buddhist tradition regard breathing as representative of the bodily functions (*kāya-sankhāra*). In the obvious evanescence of breath we perceive the *impermanence* of the body; in heavy, short or strained breath, or in the ailments of the respiratory organs, we become aware of the *suffering*, associated with the body; in breath as a manifestation of the vibrant, or Wind Element (*vāyo-dhātu*) the nature of the body as activated by impersonal processes becomes evident, i.e. the *absence of any substance* in the body; the dependence of breath on the efficient functioning of certain organs, and, on the other hand, the dependence of the living body on breathing, show the *conditioned* nature of the body. Thus does Mindfulness of Breathing help towards a true understanding of the body and to detachment from it resulting from such understanding.

2. *Mindfulness of the Bodily Postures*

In the general application of this exercise, during one's routine life, its first purpose is to increase the awareness of one's momentary bodily behaviour when going, standing, sitting or reclining. It frequently happens that the preoccupation with thoughts about the *aim* of going, completely blots out the full consciousness of the *act* of going; and that, through giving sole attention to the activity performed while standing or sitting, there may be no conscious awareness of those two postures themselves. Though, in ordinary life, it will neither be possible nor even desirable to be always fully conscious of the postures, nevertheless a practice of this awareness of postures will be wholesome for many practical reasons too. By directing one's attention to the posture, any nervous haste in going will be restrained; unnecessary and harmful distortions of the body, in the case of the other postures, will be avoided, or corrected, and thereby those postural defects with which medical science has to deal in the case of children, and adults too, will be prevented. Unnecessary fatigue of the body and, consequently, of mind, will be avoided, and reduction of the range of conscious control over the body is prevented. Controlled movement of the body is necessarily an expression of a self-possessed mind.

As to the ultimate purpose of Satipaṭṭhāna, Mindfulness on Postures will bring an initial awareness of the impersonal nature of the body, and will be conducive towards an inner alienation trom it. In the course of the practice, one will come to view (the postures just as unconcernedly as one views the automatic movements of a life-sized puppet. The play of the puppet's limbs will evoke a feeling of complete estrangement, and even a slight amusement like that felt by an onlooker at a marionette show. By looking at the postures with such a detached objectivity, the habitual identification with the body will begin to dissolve.

In strict meditative training, the awareness of the bodily postures forms the starting point of the whole day of practice and the meditator's attention has to return to it whenever he is not engaged in attending to the other objects of mindfulness (see Chapter 5). Particularly through the sharpened awareness developed in strict practice, the postures, too, will afford an opportunity to observe the momentary rise and fall of phenomena and to make those other observations on the nature of the body to which we have referred earlier.

3. *Clear Comprehension*

Clear Comprehension extends to all functions of the body to the four postures again, to the acts of looking, bending, stretching, dressing, eating, drinking, excreting, speaking, keeping silent, being awake and falling asleep, etc. The general principles of that practice, its purpose and value, have been described earlier. To summarize briefly: the practice of Clear Comprehension teaches circumspect and purposeful action, (1) for practical ends; (2) for the purpose of progress in the Dhamma; (3) for a gradual merging of ordinary life and spiritual practice; (4) for a deepening of insight into the impersonality of bodily processes, by visualizing it in daily experience; (5) for the resulting detachment from the body.

In the previous exercise, Mindfulness accompanies the postures while they are assumed, simply registering their occurrence. In distinction to it, the first and the second kind of Clear Comprehension ('Purpose' and 'Suitability') exercise a *directing* influence upon the various bodily activities. The previous exercise consisted of a full, but only general, awareness of the postures and their impersonal character. The fourth kind of Clear Comprehension ('Reality') may also include a more detailed analysis of the processes involved, leading thereby to a deeper penetration of their impersonal nature.

4. The Parts of the Body

This contemplation opens, as it were with a scalpel, the skin of this body of ours, and exposes to view what is hidden under it. This mental dissection dissolves the vaguely held notion of the oneness of the body, by pointing to its various parts; it removes the delusion of the body's beauty, by revealing its impurity. When visualizing the body as a walking skeleton loosely covered by flesh and skin, or seeing it as a conglomeration of its various strangely-shaped parts, one will feel little inclination to identify oneself with one's so-called 'own' body, or to desire that of another being.

If, in the visualization of the Parts of the Body, one can obtain a fairly good concentration of mind, without being diverted into an emotional repulsion or attraction, one will be able to achieve, in the course of that practice, a growing detachment from the body and an effortless disenchantment from sensuality. Though this will be of a temporary and imperfect nature until the second and third stage on the Path to Accomplishment (*arahatta*) is reached,[9] diligent practice of this contemplation, within the framework of general mindfulness, will be a helpful approximation to that high goal. Skill attained in swiftly and easily resorting to it will stand one in good stead, if, in practical life, one wishes to counter a strong and upsetting attachment to one's own body (for instance, in serious illness or danger) or wishes to resist sensual temptations.

This contemplation, however, is not directed to a repression of feelings of bodily attraction through producing the emotional counter-pressure of revulsion, but it aims at and results in an effortless alienation from attachment and in a growing realization of the body's true nature. Though this contemplation of the Parts of the Body is sometimes called 'the meditation on loathsomeness', the 'mood' produced by its correct practice is not one of violent revulsion or of gloom, but of unruffled calm or even of exhilaration resulting from sober, analytical observation.

Benefits can be derived from this contemplation also by those who do not envisage giving up what is called 'the pleasures of the flesh', but wish to gain a greater measure of control over their emotional and sense responses. The modern city dweller is now constantly subjected to a veritable barrage of sense titillation, particularly directed to the sex instinct. The channels by which it reaches him are manifold: stage and screen, radio and television, art and literature, pseudo-art and pseudo-literature, advertisements and garish magazine covers. The average cultured citizen may shrug it off, may not take it very seriously. He will believe himself superior to all that, even if he partakes of that dubious fare as far as it pleases or amuses him. But, in its daily repetition, the subtle impact on his conscious and subconscious mind will be stronger than it may be apparent to him, and may effect deep-reaching gradual changes in his whole mental make-up, emotionally, ethically, intellectually—unless there is a determined self-protection against these insidious influences. Here the Contemplation of the Parts of the Body may prove helpful by building up a conscious and subconscious defence against infection.

5. The Four Elements

This practice continues the dissection of the body into components of a more and more impersonal nature, by reducing it to those four primary manifestations of matter which it has in common with inanimate nature. The result will likewise be disenchantment, alienation and detachment, as well as an intensified awareness of the egolessness of the body.

As an exercise in its own right, the Analysis of the Body into the Four Elements (*dhātu-vavatthāna*) has always enjoyed a very high esteem in Buddhist tradition because it serves as a very effective breaking-up of the seeming compactness and substantiality of the body.[10] Though in the methodical practice of Satipaṭṭhāna as described in Chapter 5, this meditation does not figure as a separate exercise, yet an intimate knowledge will result, in particular of the Element of Vibration (or Air; *vāyo-dhātu*) which is the one chiefly concerned in the two alternative primary subjects recommended: the abdominal movement and breathing. To the meditator it will become evident that the characteristic features and functions of the Air- or Vibratory Element within the body, as formulated in the later commentarial literature of Pali Buddhism,[11] are not a matter of mere deduction, abstraction or speculation but are based on actual meditative experience. Also the nature of the other three material elements will gradually gain in distinctness, during diligent practice.

6. The Cemetery Contemplations

One either obtains the actual objects of these contemplations for direct observation, or, if that is not possible, the objects are viewed by vivid visualization. They show the dead body in various stages of decay. They are meant to arouse, in a passionately sensual nature, disgust towards the object of his desire (though, in some cases, other methods may prove more suitable). They are further an object lesson of impermanence, by showing the dissolution of this composite body, which, in other exemplars but particularly in that of one's own, one sees moving about full of life: 'Thus he applies it to himself. "Verily, this body of mine, too, is of the same nature as that body, it will become like that, and will not escape it" '.

These contemplations will also point to the self-deception in regarding and cherishing as 'Mine' this body which tomorrow may 'belong' to the elements or, as prey, to the birds and worms. These contemplations will also make one more familiar with the fact of death.

Here, too, the sequence of development will proceed as before: from disgust through disenchantment and alienation, to a detachment with regard to the body which comes from a vivid awareness of its impersonal nature.

In ancient India, the objects of these contemplations could be seen easily on the charnel grounds where the dead bodies of the poor, and of executed criminals, were exposed to the elements and to the beasts of sky and earth. Nowadays opportunity for seeing these actual objects is rare, but it might still be available in the morgues, mortuaries or dissecting rooms of our cities, and, alas, the greed, hatred and stupidity of man still sees to it that battlefields, too, offer such sights.

Concluding Remarks on Body Contemplation

The exercises in the section now concluded, on 'Contemplation of the Body', cover both types of the practice: they belong partly to Bare Attention and partly to Clear Comprehension.

As a feature common to all these exercises we have found that they lead to a *detachment* with regard to the body, grown from the observation of its nature and from a true understanding of it. Detachment gives, with regard to its objects, mastery as well as freedom. This holds true in the case of the body, too. No mortification of the body is here required to assert mind's mastery over it. Above the extremes of mortification and sensuality leads the Middle Path, the simple, realistic and non-coercive Way of Mindfulness and Clear Comprehension, bringing mastery and freedom. In following that 'Only Way to the destruction of pain and grief', the body will become light and pliant to the wanderer on the path; and even if the body succumbs to sickness and pain, the serenity of his mind will not be affected.

II. The Contemplation of Feeling (*Vedanānupassanā*)

The Pali term *vedanā*, rendered here by 'feeling', signifies, in Buddhist psychology, just pleasant, unpleasant or indifferent sensation of physical or mental origin. It is not used, as in the English language, in the sense of 'emotion', which is a mental factor of a much more complex nature.

Feeling, in the sense spoken of, is the first reaction to any sense impression, and, therefore, deserves the particular attention of those who aspire to mastery over the mind. In the formula of 'Dependent Origination' (*paṭicca-samuppāda*) by which the Buddha shows the conditioned 'arising of this whole mass of suffering', Sense Impression is said to be the principal condition of Feeling (*phassa-paccayā vedanā*), while Feeling, on its part, is the potential condition of Craving, and, subsequently, of, more intense, clinging (*vedanā-paccayā taṇhā, taṇhā-paccayā upādānaṁ*).

This, therefore, is a crucial point in the conditioned Origin of Suffering, because it is at this point that Feeling may give rise to passionate emotion of various types, and it is, therefore, here that one may be able to break that fatuous concatenation. If, in receiving a sense impression, one is able to pause and stop at the phase of Feeling, and make it, in its very first stage of manifestation, the object of Bare Attention, Feeling will not be able to originate Craving or other passions. It will stop at the bare statements of 'pleasant', 'unpleasant' or 'indifferent', giving Clear Comprehension time to enter and to decide about the attitude or action to be taken. Furthermore, if one notices, in Bare Attention, (the conditioned arising of feeling, its gradual fading away and giving room to another feeling, one will find from one's own experience that there is no necessity at all for being carried away by passionate reaction, which will start a new concatenation of suffering.

This decisive role of Feeling in the mental continuum will make it understandable why the Contemplation of Feeling has in the Buddhist Scriptures[12] a place of similar importance within (the sphere of mind as the Contemplation of the Four Material Elements has in regard to the body. Also in the methodical Satipaṭṭhāna meditation (as described in Chapter 5), as soon as the meditator has come to a stage of smooth progress with the bodily objects of mindfulness, the meditation master will ask him to pay attention to the feelings of satisfaction and dissatisfaction that may arise in him during and in connection with the practice. Also one who practises without a teacher may do likewise as soon as he notices that his attention to the basic bodily objects is well established.

These satisfactions and dissatisfactions are of course rather complex states of mind and not pure 'feelings' (as defined above). But by directing *bare attention* to them, they will be divested of their emotional components and of their egocentric reference; they will appear as mere pleasant or unpleasant sensations, and will thus no longer be able to carry the meditator away into states of excessive elation or dejection which will deflect him from the path of progress.

An undue stress on the 'feeling'-aspect of reality marks the so-called emotional natures. By them, the pleasurable or unpleasant features of an experience are repeatedly and passionately dwelt upon, and thereby magnified. This will often lead to an exaggerated view of the situation and an extreme reaction to it, be it one of elation or dejection, overrating or deprecating, etc. But apart from markedly emotional types, even when feeling is just as uncontrolled as is the case with the average man, it will also tend to produce habitual overstatements, with all the dissatisfaction and disappointment they entail. Often one may hear people exclaim: 'This or that is my only happiness!' or 'This or that would be the death of me!' But the still voice of Mindfulness speaks: 'It is a pleasant feeling, like many others too—and nothing else!' or 'It is an unpleasant feeling, like many others too—and nothing else!' Such an attitude will contribute much to an inner balance and contentedness, which are needed so greatly among the vicissitudes of life.

Another innate weakness of the world of feeling as far as it is uncontrolled by reason and wisdom, is its extreme and uncritical *subjectivity*. Uncontrolled feeling does not in the least question the values that it attaches so lavishly to persons and things; it does not admit that other evaluations of the same object are possible at all; it easily disregards or hurts the feelings—i.e. the emotional values—of others, all this owing to its being so naively self-centred. Here, too, Right Mindfulness provides the remedy, by extending detached observation also to the 'feelings' of others, and comparing them with one's own, in accordance with the 'Instructions for Practice' given in the Discourse.

In the text of the Contemplation of Feeling as formulated in the Discourse, there is first the simple statement of the general quality of the feeling just arisen, i.e. pleasant, unpleasant or indifferent. Then follows the same statement combined with a qualification as to the worldly or lofty nature of these three kinds of feelings. Such bare discriminative statements will prove to be very helpful to a gradual refinement of the emotional life and to an increase of noble and elimination of ignoble feelings. The curt and simple, but repeated registering of the nature of feelings just arisen, will have a greater influence on the emotional life than an emotional or rational counter-pressure by way of eulogy, deprecation, condemnation or persuasion. Experience shows that emotional persons are less susceptible to the arguments or emotional reactions of others than to repeated suggestion through brief, simple and definite statements—impressing them by the strength and assurance of the inner conviction with which they were made. The same principle will work with our own emotions too. The simple device of Bare Attention, i.e. of making those bare statements given in the Discourse, will prove a very apt method for rendering that elusive world of emotions more susceptibe to guidance and control. This will be particularly important when, in daily life, in the encounters with one's own emotions and those of others, a quick, simple, but effective dealing with them is required.

III. The Contemplation of the State of Mind (*Cittānupassanā*)

Here too, mind is placed in front of the clear mirror of Bare Attention. The object of observation is here the condition and the level of mind, or consciouness, in general, as it presents itself at the given moment. For that purpose, the relevant passage of the Discourse gives various examples of contrasting states of mind of a beneficial or harmful, developed or undeveloped nature, e.g. mind with and without lust, hatred or delusion, mind concentrated and unconcentrated. Exceptions are only two terms—the shrunken and distracted mind—where two states of mind, both of harmful, but opposite nature, are contrasted.

On the level of general mind-training, the chief benefit of the contemplation of the State of Mind lies in its being an effective way of self-examination leading to an increasing measure of self-knowledge. Here again there is a bare registering of the state of mind, either in retrospection or whenever possible and desirable, by the immediate confrontation with one's present mood or state of mind. This method of allowing the simple facts of observation to speak and make their impact on the mind, will be more wholesome and efficacious than a method of introspection that enters into inner arguments of self-justifications and self-accusations, or into an elaborate search for 'hidden motives'. These latter methods of self-examination may (though not necessarily must) lead to serious defects or obstacles in character development, varying with different types of people. Some may become awkwardly self-conscious, unsure of themselves, incapable of healthy spontaneous reactions and behaviour; for others it may result in constant inner conflicts, feelings of guilt or inferiority (which, however, are sometimes enjoyed); others who believe that they have succeeded in their self-justification, may become completely enwrapped in their conceit. And all of them may succumb to the self-complacency and self-righteousness of those who pride themselves in taking the 'spiritual path of self-introspection'. All these risks are absent or greatly reduced, in the sober and unobtrusive method of bare registering which, through regular application, can easily become a natural function of mind, free from artificiality and egocentric concern.

Such self-examination makes for honesty towards oneself which is indispensable for inner progress and for mental health.

In most cases man carefully avoids looking too closely into his own mind, lest the sight of his own faults and shortcomings may disturb his complacency or do serious damage to his self-esteem. But if on certain occasions, he cannot but notice his faults, he tends to gloss over that unpalatable truth as hurriedly as he can. By such an attitude he will make himself unable to check the reappearance and the growth of these undesirable traits.

On the other hand, man's good qualities too, particularly those which are still weak, should receive full notice when they appear, it will encourage their development. This express attention to, and recollection of, one's good traits is likewise often neglected.

Both omissions are made good by the Contemplation of the State of Mind.

In the methodical meditative practice, the Contemplation of the State of Mind will help to assess one's progress or failures (e.g. mind concentrated or not). Furthermore, the bare statements made in this contemplation will be of assistance in coping with interruptions and other disturbances during meditation. If there is, for instance, anger about a disturbing noise, the bare statement 'mind with anger' will often be able to dissolve the feeling of irritation, replacing an emotionally restless state by the unemotional state of self-examination. Such a procedure will also divert the attention from the original disturbance (the noise) and change the direction of mind from those external objects to internal ones.

Here, as in other instances, we have seen how the single and simple device of bare attention brings in its wake several benefits, in various fields of application.

IV The Contemplation of Mental Contents (*Dhammānupassanā*)

By the regular practice of this last of the four contemplations, the mental objects (*dhammā*—having here this specific meaning), i.e. the contents of thought, will gradually assume the thought-forms of the *Dhamma,* in the sense of the Buddha's teaching of actuality and liberation. For that purpose, the five exercises given in this section of the Discourse furnish a sufficient selection of such thought-forms or doctrinal terms which are in accordance with true vision, and will give to the mind a natural slant towards the goal of deliverance. They should be absorbed as much as possible into the thought-patterns of daily life, and should replace those concepts which cannot stand the scrutiny of Right Understanding, and are too closely associated with notions and purposes alien to the Way of Mindfulness.

The *first* exercise deals with the five principal Mental Hindrances (*nīvarana*), and the *fourth* with the seven Factors of Enlightenment (*bojjhaṅga*); in other words, these two exercises deal with qualities to be abandoned and qualities to be acquired, respectively. Other qualities to be abandoned are indicated in the *third* exercise (on the six Sense Bases), under the term of Fetters (*saṁyojana*).

The first parts of the *first* and of the *fourth* exercise belong to the practice of Bare Attention. The content of these passages is briefly as follows: if one of the Mental Hindrances or a Factor of Enlightenment is present or absent in the meditator, he should be fully aware of that fact. To Bare Attention belongs likewise the following part of the *third* exercise: '. . . and what fetter arises dependent on both (e.g. eye and forms) that he knows well'.

All the aforementioned three passages giving a bare statement of the present condition of consciousness, are, properly speaking, parts of the Contemplation of the State of Mind. Here they serve as the indispensable preparation for the second phase of all these three exercises. In that second phase, purposeful and thoroughly examining Clear Comprehension is employed in the following tasks: (1) to avoid, to overcome temporarily and to annihilate finally the respective Hindrances and Fetters, (2) to produce and develop the Factors of Enlightenment. For both these tasks, the negative one and the positive, an intimate knowledge of the conditions which are conducive to the arising and non-arising of the respective states of mind is indispensable. In the Discourse, this enquiry into the conditions is mentioned in a general way thus: 'In what manner the arising of the non-arisen (Hindrance, Fetter, Factor of Enlightenment) comes to be, that he knows well . . ."

Some of the principal conditions for the arising or non-arising of these mental factors will be found in the explanatory notes to the respective sections of the Discourse (29, 31, 33); they are described in greater detail in Buddhaghosa's Commentary on the Discourse.[13]

But a theoretical knowledge of these 'conditions' is not enough. It is by actually observing, within oneself, the Hindrances, Fetters or Enlightenment Factors, that one will gradually gather information about the outer and inner circumstances which favour or obstruct the arising and non-arising of these qualities. These circumstances may vary with different individuals, and often one will not be fully aware that there are typical situations which are particularly conducive to the arising or non-arising of those positive and negative qualities. A repeated and observant acquaintance with them will help one to avoid unfavourable situations and to bring about favourable ones. This will prove to be of considerable assistance on the road of progress.

These three exercises (the first, the fourth, and the third in its second phase) pertain to mind knowledge and mind development.

The *second, third* (in its first phase) and the *fifth* exercise, dealing with the five Categories of Clinging (*upādāna-kkhandha*), the six Sense Bases (*āyatana*) and the four Noble Truths (*sacca*) circumscribe actuality in its entirety—each in its particular way, and from a different angle.

These three exercises will enable the meditator to bring his daily experiences, which are habitually referred to a non-existing abiding self, into conformity with the true nature of actuality which does not contain anything static or perpetual, be it personal or impersonal. Conventional language (*vohāra* or *sammuti*), based on the belief in an abiding personality, is here converted into the 'ultimate' or factual terms (*paramattha*) of the Dhamma. In that way, the single experiences of life can be brought into relationship with the Dhamma as a whole, and can be assigned their proper places within the system of the doctrine.

For such application of the Contemplation of Mental Contents, the Commentary gives an example which becomes all the more impressive as it is regularly repeated there. After explaining in full each exercise given in the Discourse, the Commentary always brings it into relationship with the four Noble Truths. For instance: 'Here the Truth of Suffering is the mindfulness which lays hold of in-and-out-breathing. The Craving that foreruns that mindfulness and causes it is the Truth of Origination. The non-occurrence of both is the Truth of Cessation. The Pure Path of understanding Suffering, of abandoning Origination, of taking Cessation as the object, is the Way of Truth.'

This is a very striking illustration of the way how the Contemplation of Mental Contents can and should be applied in daily life: wherever circumstances allow one to attend mindfully and thoughtfully to any occurrence, big or small, one should relate it to the Four Truths. In this manner, one will be able to come closer to the postulate that *life should become one with the spiritual practice and practice become full-blooded life*. Thus the world of common experience that is so 'talkative' where physical and mental grasping or rejecting is concerned, but quite mute as to the language of liberating insight, will become more and more 'articulate' and evocative as to the eternal voice of the Dhamma.

The three Contemplations of feeling, state of mind and mental contents dealing with the mental part of man, converge, as does the Contemplation of the Body, in the central conception of the Dhamma: *Anattā,* Not-self. The whole Discourse on the Foundations of Mindfulness may be regarded as a comprehensive theoretical and practical instruction for the realization of that liberating truth of *Anattā,* having the two aspects of egolessness and voidness of substance. The guidance provided by Satipaṭṭhāna will bring about not only a deep and thorough understanding of that truth, but also, by visible demonstration through the several exercises, that immediate visualization of it which alone imparts life-transforming and life-transcending power.

FOUR

Culture of Mind

Culture of Mind and Culture of Heart

Satipaṭṭhāna, the training in Right Mindfulness, is culture of mind in its highest sense. But from the Discourse, and also from the preceding exposition, some readers may perhaps receive the first impression that it is a rather coldly intellectual, dry and prosy teaching, being indifferent to ethics, and neglecting the culture of the heart. Though we hope that the warm life pulsating within the sober frame of Satipaṭṭhāna will not have remained unnoticed, a few words about that objection shall be added.

The seeming deficiency as to the consideration of ethics is explained by the fact that, on many other occasions, the Buddha has spoken with the greatest emphasis of morality as the indispensable basis for any higher mental development. This fact, well known to all followers of the Master, did not require to be mentioned again in a Discourse devoted to a special subject. But to meet any doubts or objections, a few additional remarks, to that purpose, are added here.

Morality, regulating the relations between an individual and his fellowmen, must, in this world of ours, be supported and protected by precepts, rules and law, and it must also be rationally explained by common sense and philosophy. But morality's safest roots lie in a true *culture of the heart.* In the Buddha's teaching, this culture of the heart has a prominent place, and finds an ideal expression in the four *Sublime States* or *Divine Abodes of the Mind* (*brahma-vihāra*): Loving-kindness, Compassion, Sympathetic Joy and Equanimity.[14] Selfless and boundless loving-kindness is the basis of the other three qualities as well as of any effort for ennobling the mind. Therefore, in the Satipaṭṭhāna method too, a primary task of Mindfulness is to watch that no deed, word or thought offends against the spirit of unbounded loving-kindness (*mettā*). The cultivation of it should never be absent from the path of the disciple. 'Maintain this mindfulness (of loving-kindness)!' says the classical Mettā Sutta, the 'Song of Loving- kindness'.

Furthermore it was said by the Buddha, again connecting loving-kindness with Satipaṭṭhāna:

' "I shall protect myself": with that thought the Foundations of Mindfulness should be cultivated. "I shall protect others": with that thought the Foundations of Mindfulness should be cultivated. By protecting oneself one protects others; by protecting others one protects oneself.

'And how does one, by protecting oneself, protect others? By repeated practice (of mindfulness), by its meditative development, and by frequent occupation with it.

'And how does one, by protecting others, protect oneself? By patience, by a non-violent life, by loving-kindness and compassion.'

—Saṁyutta-Nikāya 47, 19

The Message of Self-Help

In the beginning of this exposition, the Way of Mindfulness was called a 'message of help'. Now, after all that has been said in these pages, it may be more exactly described as a 'message of self-help'. Self-help, in fact, is the only effective help. Though the help offered or given by others, through instruction, advice, sympathy, practical assistance or material generosity, can be of decisive importance for the individual in need of it, yet it will always require a good share of 'self-help'—willing acceptance and proper utilization—for becoming an effective, *actual* help.

> *'By self alone is evil done, by self one is defiled;*
> *By self is evil left undone, by self alone one is purified.*
> *Pure and impure on self alone depend;*
> *No one can make another pure.'*
>
> —Dhammapada, v. 165

> *'The effort you yourself must make,*
> *The Perfect Ones point out the Way'.*
>
> —ibid., v. 276

But quite apart from clearly showing the *way* of help, the message that there *is* help at all must of itself be regarded as truly glad tidings by a world that has become entangled all over in ties of its own making. Mankind has good reasons to despair of any help because too often attempts have been made to loosen the fetters in one place or another, with the only result that, just by that action, the fetters cut still deeper into the flesh somewhere else. But there *is* help and it has been found by the Buddhas and those of their disciples who attained to the consummation of the teaching. By men 'whose eyes are not completely covered by dust', these Enlightened Ones will not be mistaken for those who offer only partial, symptomatic and therefore ineffective help. The true Helpers will be recognized through the singular harmony and balance, consistency and naturalness, simplicity and depth, appearing in their teachings as well as in their life. These great Helpers will be recognized by the warm smile of understanding, compassion and assurance that glows on their lips and inspires a confidence that will grow beyond all doubt.

This smile of assurance on the Buddha's face says: 'You too can attain! Open are the doors to the Deathless!' Soon after the Buddha had entered through these doors of Enlightenment, he proclaimed:

'Like me victorious saints will be,
Who have attained to the defilements' end'.

The Buddha's 'showing the way' to the exalted goal was not made with cold indifference; it was not merely a casual pointing of the finger to the road, nor was it a mere 'piece of paper', with an intricate 'map' provided by some abstruse scripture that was thrust into the hands of those in need of an experienced guide and helper. The pilgrims were not merely left to their own poor devices (as far as they knew any) to wend their way with emaciated bodies and confused minds. The Buddha's 'showing of the way' included the pointing to the *provisions* needed for that long journey—provisions which, in fact, the pilgrims carry with them without being aware of it, in their dumb stupor. Emphatically did the Buddha proclaim again and again that man is in full possession of all the resources needed for self-help. The most simple and most comprehensive way in which he spoke about these resources is this method of Satipaṭṭhāna. Its essence may be compressed into the two words: 'Be mindful!' That means: *Be mindful of your own mind!* And why? Mind harbours all: the world of suffering and its origin, but also Ill's final cessation and the path to it. Whether the one or the other will be predominant depends again on our own mind, on the direction that the flux of mind receives through this very moment of mind-activity that faces us just now!

Satipaṭṭhāna, always dealing with this crucial present moment of mind activity, must necessarily be a teaching of *self-reliance.* But self-reliance has to be gradually developed, because men, knowing not how to handle the tool of mind, have become used to leaning on others and on habit; and, owing to that, this splendid tool, the human mind, has, in fact, become unreliable through neglect. Therefore the road to self-mastery which Satipaṭṭhāna shows, begins with very simple steps which even the most diffident of men may take.

Satipaṭṭhāna, in that simplicity which befits a teaching claiming to be the Only Way, starts, in fact, with very little: with one of the most elementary functions of mind, *attention,* or initial mindfulness. This is indeed so very near and familiar that every man, if he only would, may easily base on it his first steps of self-reliance. And quite as familiar are the first objects of that attention: they are *the tasks and little activities of everyday life.* What Mindfulness does with them, is: to take them out of their habitual grooves and sort them out for closer inspection and improvement.

The visible *improvements in the work of everyday life,* effected by careful attention, thoroughness and circumspection, will give additional encouragement to the quest for self-help.

There will be noticeable *improvements in the mind's condition,* while the quietening influence of self-possessed action and thought will infuse a well-being and happiness where once dissatisfaction, ill-humour and irritability may have ruled.

If, in that way, the burden of daily life has been eased to some extent, it will be a tangible proof of the Satipaṭṭhāna-method's capacity to relieve suffering. This initial result, however, will accord with the Dhamma only so far as it is said to be 'beneficial in the beginning' (*ādi-kalyāna*). Higher results—the benefits of the middle and of the end of the road—are to follow and have to be aspired for.

In the course of further practice the *little things of everyday life* will become teachers of great wisdom, revealing gradually their own immense dimension of depth. If one gradually learns to understand their language, profound aspects of the Dhamma will come into the range of one's direct experience, and thereby confidence in one's own mind and in the power of its hidden resources will grow.

Receiving such direct instruction from life itself, one will gradually learn to dispose with unnecessary mental ballast and unnecessary complications of thought. Seeing how life wins clarity and ease under the selecting and controlling influence of Right Mindfulness, one will gradually learn to deal with unnecessary complications in one's practical life too, caused by the thoughtless perpetuation of habits and wants.

Satipaṭṭhāna restores *simplicity* and *naturalness* to a world that grows more and more complicated, problematic and reliant on artificial devices. It teaches these virtues of simplicity and naturalness primarily for the sake of their own inherent merits, but also for easing the task of spiritual self-help.

Certainly this world of ours is complex in its very nature, but it need not grow infinitely in its complexity, and it need not be as complicated and perplexing as the unskilfulness, ignorance, unrestrained passion and greed of men have made it. All these qualities making for increasing complication of life, can be effectively countered by mental training in Right Mindfulness.

Satipaṭṭhāna teaches man how to cope with all this confusing complexity of his life and its problems: in the first instance, by endowing him with *adaptability* and pliancy of mind, with quickness of apt response in changing situations, with the 'skilfulness in applying the right means' (i.e. Clear Comprehension of Suitability). As to the *irreducible* minimum of life's complexity, that too may, to a reasonable extent, well be mastered with the help of Right Mindfulness. It teaches, for that purpose: how to keep one's affairs, both worldly and ethical, tidy and without arrears and debts; how to use and to keep the reins of control; how to *co*-ordinate the numerous facts of life, and how to *sub*-ordinate them to a strong and noble purpose.

As to the complications *capable* of reduction, Satipaṭṭhāna holds up the ideal of *simplicity of wants.* To stress this ideal today is most urgent in view of the dangerous modern tendency artificially to create, to propagandize, and 'condition' for, ever new wants. The results of that tendency as appearing in social and economic life, belong to the secondary causes of war, while the root of that tendency—Greed—is one of its primary causes. For the material and spiritual welfare of humanity it is imperative to check that development. And as to our particular subject, spiritual self-help—how can man's mind become self-reliant if it keeps on surrendering itself to that endless and weary toil of continuously increasing imaginary needs entailing a growing dependency on others? Simplicity of life should be cultivated for the sake of its own inherent beauty as well as for the sake of the freedom it bestows.

Let us glance now at the avoidable *inner* complications, or at least a few of them. Here Satipaṭṭhāna teaches how to control and to improve man's principal tool, the mind, and it shows the right purpose for its use.

A frequent source of the growth of inner and outer complications is unnecessary and uncalled-for *interference.* But one who is truly mindful will first mind his own mind's business. The desire to interfere will be effectively curbed by acquiring the habit of Bare Attention, which is in direct contrast to interference. Clear Comprehension, the guide to circumspect action, will then carefully examine the purpose and suitability of an intended interfering activity, and will mostly advise to drop it.

Many inner complications are caused by *extreme attitudes* of the mind and by an unwise handling of the various pairs of opposites operating in life. Surrendering to extreme attitudes of any description will limit one's freedom of action and thought, and the capacity of true understanding; it reduces independence and the chances of effective practical and spiritual self-help. By ignorance of the laws governing the pairs of opposites or by taking sides with either of the extremes in their eternal conflict, one will become a helpless pawn in their recurrent movements. Satipaṭṭhāna as an expression of the Buddha's Middle Path is a way leading above and beyond extremes and opposites. It corrects one-sided development by filling out deficiencies and reducing excess. It instils a sense of proportion, and aspires to harmony and balance without which there cannot be lasting self-reliance and effective self-help.

As an example, two opposite types of character may be mentioned as they were formulated and further elaborated, by C. G. Jung: the introvert ('turned inward') and the extravert ('turned outward') which partly cover such other opposites as the contemplative and the active, the solitary and the sociable type, etc. The character as a Middle Path, is so deeply ingrained in Satipaṭṭhāna that this method is, in fact, capable of attracting as well as compensating both types.

Beginners in meditation will often be painfully conscious of the sometimes considerable disparity in the condition of their minds during ordinary life and during the limited period given to spiritual practice. Through Satipaṭṭhāna that gap is reduced and finally closed by a gradual merging of life and practice, which will be of benefit to both. Many, discouraged by the disparity spoken of above, and by the failure of their efforts, have left the road of mental culture and spiritual self-help, and have surrendered to creeds teaching that man can only be saved by grace. This is not likely to occur to the disciple of the Satipaṭṭhāna Method of self-reliance and self-help.

Another source of inner complications is the powerful and unpredictable influence of *subconsciousness*. But through Bare Attention a natural, close and more 'friendly' contact with it will result, due to the growing familiarity with the most subtle vibrations of body and mind, and supported by the attitude of 'waiting and listening' that avoids all coarse and harmful meddling with the subconscious realm. In that way, and by the slowly and steadily pervading light of Mindfulness, the subconsciousness will become more 'articulate' and more amenable to control, i.e. capable of being co-ordinated with, and helpful to, the governing tendencies of the conscious mind. By reducing the element of the unpredictable and of the unmanageable emerging from the subconscious, self-reliance will receive a safer basis.

In its spirit of self-reliance, Satipaṭṭhāna does not require any elaborate *technique* or external devices. The daily life is its working material. It has nothing to do with any exotic cults or rites nor does it confer 'initiations' or 'esoteric knowledge' in any way other than by self-enlightenment.

Using just the conditions of life it finds, Satipaṭṭhāna does not require complete *seclusion* or *monastic life*, though in some who undertake the practice, the desire and the need for these may grow. Occasional periods of seclusion, however, are helpful for initiating methodical and strict practice, and for stepping up the progress in it. Western society, too, should provide opportunities for such periodical seclusion in suitable environment. Apart from their value for strict meditative practice, the atmosphere of such 'Houses of Stillness' will be a source of physical and mental regeneration from the effects of urban civilization.

Satipaṭṭhāna is a way of *self-liberation*. Being based on the Law of Kamma, i.e. self-responsibility for one's actions, Satipaṭṭhāna, in its ultimate aim and in its complete practice, is incompatible with a belief in vicarious salvation, in a saving divine grace, or in mediation by priests.

Satipaṭṭhāna is free from *dogmas,* from reliance on 'divine revelations', or any external authority in matters spiritual. Satipaṭṭhāna relies only on first-hand knowledge as furnished by the direct vision of one's own experience. It teaches how to purify, extend and deepen this mainspring of true knowledge—direct experience. The Word of the Buddha is accepted and cherished by the disciple of Satipaṭṭhāna, as the detailed travelling directions given by one who has already gone the whole length of the Way, and therefore deserves confidence. But it becomes a mental property of the disciple only according to the degree of verification by his own experience.

This character of Satipaṭṭhāna as a message of self-reliance and self-help is documented in the words of the Buddha himself, spoken during the very last days of his life, a fact that gives to them a particular emphasis:

> *'Therefore, Ananda, be ye islands unto yourselves! Be ye a refuge unto yourselves! Betake yourselves to no external refuge! The Truth (Dhamma) be your island, the truth be your refuge! Take no other refuge! And how is this done?*
>
> *'Therefore, Ananda, a monk dwells contemplating the body, in the body—contemplating the feelings, in the feelings—contemplating consciousness, in consciousness—contemplating mind objects, in mind objects, ardent, clearly comprehending and mindful, having overcome, in the world, hankering and dejection.*
>
> *'And whosoever, Ananda, either now or after I am dead, shall be an island unto themselves, a refuge unto themselves, shall betake themselves to no external refuge, but holding fast to the truth as their*

island and refuge, taking refuge in nothing else— it is they, Ananda, among my Bhikkhus, who shall reach the very topmost height—but they must be anxious to learn'.

—Mahā-parinibbāna-sutta

The serious student will appreciate the cogency of that last sentence.

For the rest, it was tersely and rightly said that, after a disciple has received information about the Way and the Goal, there are only two rules for his successful spiritual practice: 'Begin!' and 'Go on!'

FIVE

The Burmese Satipaṭṭhāna Method

Though the distinguishing features of Satipaṭṭhāna meditation seem so simple and obvious after one has heard or read about them once, yet the prevailing notions about the way of practice have largely remained rather vague. Even in some Buddhist countries, the true understanding and the actual practice have been lagging far behind a mainly devotional attitude and an intellectual appreciation. It was in Burma, in this twentieth century, that a deep-reaching change was effected in that situation by monks who, by their searching spirit, clearly outlined again the singular features of the Way of Mindfulness. Through their own energetic meditative effort they removed for others many obstacles to the correct understanding and practice of the Only Way. And there were many in Burma, and soon also in other countries, who followed them with earnest endeavour.

It was at the beginning of this century that a Burmese monk, U Narada by name, bent on actual realization of the teachings he had learnt, was eagerly searching for a system of meditation offering a direct access to the Highest Goal, without encumbrance by accessories. Wandering through the country, he met many who were given to strict meditative practice, but he could not obtain guidance satisfactory to him. In the course of his quest, coming to the famous meditation-caves in the hills of Sagaing in Upper Burma, he met a monk who was reputed to have entered upon those lofty Paths of Sanctitude (*ariya-magga*) where the final achievement of Liberation is assured. When the Venerable U Narada put his question to him, he was asked in return: 'Why are you searching outside of the Master's word? Has not the Only Way, Satipaṭṭhāna, been proclaimed by Him?'

U Narada took up this indication. Studying again the text and its traditional exposition, reflecting deeply on it, and entering energetically upon its practice, he finally came to understand its salient features. The results achieved in his own practice convinced him that he had found what he was searching for: a clear-cut and effective method of training the mind for highest realization. From his own experience he developed the principles and the details of the practice which formed the basis for those who followed him as his direct or indirect disciples.

In order to give a name to the Venerable U Narada's method of training in which the principles of Satipaṭṭhāna are applied in such a definite and radical way, we propose to call it here the *Burmese Satipaṭṭhāna Method*; not in the sense that it was a Burmese invention but because it was in Burma that the practice of that ancient Way had been so ably and energetically revived.

The pupils of the Venerable U Narada spread the knowledge of his method in Burma as well as in other Buddhist countries, and many were greatly benefited by it in their progress on the Path. The Venerable U Narada Mahāthera, widely known in Burma as the Jetavan (or Mingun) Sayadaw, passed away on the 18th March 1955, aged 87. Many believe that he attained to final Deliverance (Arahatta).

It is a cause of deep gratification that, in present-day Burma, the practice of, and instruction in, Satipaṭṭhāna is flourishing and to a remarkable extent bearing results, thus providing a striking contrast to the waves of materialism surging throughout the world. Satipaṭṭhāna is to-day a strong force in the religious life of Burma. There are numerous training centres in the country, where many thousands have undergone courses of strict Satipaṭṭhāna practice. These courses are attended by monks and lay people alike. It was a sign of mature wisdom that the Government of Burma, under the leadership of Prime Minister U Nu, soon after the country achieved independence, encouraged and supported these centres of meditation, appreciating that minds that had been trained there will be an asset to the country in any walk of life.

Prominent among the teachers of Satipaṭṭhāna to-day is the Venerable Mahasi Sayadaw (U Sobhana Mahāthera) who, through his personal instruction in meditation courses, and through his books and lectures, has contributed much to the development of the practice in Burma. Many thousands have been benefited by his wise and experienced guidance. Men and women, young and old, poor and rich, learned and simple folk have taken up the practice with great earnestness and enthusiasm. And results are not lacking.

Primarily thanks to the efforts of the Venerable Mahāsi Sayadaw and his pupils, the practice of this method of meditation has spread to Thailand and Ceylon, and preparations are being made for a meditation centre in India.

Instructions for the Methodical Practice of Satipaṭṭhāna as Taught in Burma

General Remarks

In the following pages, information will be given about a course of strict meditative practice according to the Satipaṭṭhāna method. The course was held at the 'Thathana Yeiktha',[15] at Rangoon (Burma), under the guidance of the Venerable Mahāsi Sayadaw[16] (U Sobhana Mahāthera).

A course of practice at this meditation centre lasts usually one to two months. After that period the meditators are expected to continue the practice at their own abodes, in adaptation to their individual conditions of life. During the course of strict practice the meditators do not engage themselves in reading and writing, or any other work than that of meditation and the routine activities of the day. Talk is limited to the minimum. The lay meditators, at that institution, observe, for the duration of their stay there, the Eight Precepts (*aṭṭhanga-sīla*) which include, e.g. abstinence from taking solid food (and certain liquids, as milk, etc.) after twelve o'clock, noon.

A brief written statement on practical meditation, even if limited to the very first steps as is done here, cannot replace personal guidance by an experienced teacher who alone can give due consideration to the requirements and the rate of progress of the individual disciple. The following notes are therefore meant only for those who have no access to an experienced meditation master. The fact that their number will be very great, in the West as well as in the East, has induced the writer to offer these notes, with all their inherent shortcomings, as a practical supplement to the main body of the book.

It is a fundamental principle of the Satipaṭṭhāna method that the disciple should take his very first steps on the firm ground of his own experience. He should learn to see things as they are, and he should see them for himself. He should not be influenced by others giving him suggestions or hints about what he *may* see or is expected to see. Therefore, in the aforementioned course of practice, no theoretical explanations are given, but only the bare instructions about what to do and not to do, at the start of the practice. When, after some initial practice, mindfulness becomes keener, and the meditator becomes aware of features in his object of mindfulness which were hitherto unnoticed, the meditation master may, in individual cases, decide not merely to say (as usual), 'Go on!' but indicate briefly the direction to which the disciple's attention may be turned with benefit. It is one of the disadvantages of a written statement that even these indications cannot be given, as they necessarily depend on the progress of the individual meditator at the start of his practice. Yet, if the instructions given here are closely followed, the meditator's own experience will become his teacher and will lead him safely onwards, though it has to be admitted that progress is easier under the direction of an experienced meditation master.

Soberness, self-reliance and an observant, watchful attitude are the characteristics of this meditative practice. A true Satipaṭṭhāna Master will be very reticent in his relationship with those whom he instructs; he will avoid seeking to 'impress' them by his personality and making 'followers' of them. He will not have recourse to any devices that are likely to induce autosuggestion, hypnotic trance or a mere emotional exultation. Those who employ such means, for themselves or for others, should be known to be on a path averse to the Way of Mindfulness.

In taking up this practice, one should not expect 'mystical experiences' or cheap emotional satisfaction. After one has made one's earnest initial aspiration, one should no longer indulge in thoughts of future achievements or hanker after quick results. One should rather attend diligently, soberly and exclusively to those very simple exercises which will be described here. At the outset, one should even regard them just as purposes in themselves, i.e. as a technique for strengthening mindfulness and concentration. Any additional significance of these exercises will naturally unfold itself to the meditator, in the course of his practice. The faint outlines of that significance which appear at the horizon of the meditator's mind, will gradually grow more distinct and finally become like commanding presences to him who moves towards them steadily.

The method outlined here falls into the category of Bare Insight (*sukkha vipassanā*), that is the exclusive and direct practice of penetrative insight, without the previous attainment of the meditative absorptions (*jhāna*).[17] The method aims, in its first stage, at a discernment of bodily and mental processes (*nāma-rūpa-pariccheda*) in one's own personality by one's own experience. An increasingly keen awareness of the nature of these processes, and a strengthened concentration (up to the degree of Access- or Neighbourhood Concentration; (*upacāra-samādhi*) will result in a deepening insight into the Three Characteristics of existence—Impermanence, Suffering and Egolessness—gradually leading to the attainment of the Stages of Sanctity (*magga-phala*), that is to final Liberation. The approach to that final goal leads through the Seven Stages of Purification (*satta visuddhi*) which are treated in Buddhaghosa's *Path to Purification.*

Preliminaries: Physical Posture

The Western mode of sitting, on a chair with legs hanging, is rather unfavourable for one who wishes to sit in meditation for increasingly longer periods of time, without discomfort and without frequently shifting the body. When seated on a chair the beginner in self-control may easily yield to any slight wish to shift legs or body even before benumbedness of limbs calls for it; or he may keep legs or body too rigid and tense for physical and mental ease. In postures with legs bent, however, the rump rests on a broad and firm basis, the body forming a triangle. When legs are crossed or linked, it is not so easy to shift on the seat and there is little necessity for it. With practice one can maintain such a posture for long periods.

The best-known Yoga posture, with fully crossed legs, the *padmāsana* or lotus posture, is rather difficult for most Westerners. Though it is advantageous for meditations aiming at full mental absorption (*jhāna*) it is of less importance for the Satipaṭṭhāna practice. We shall, therefore, not describe it here, but turn to the description of two easier postures.

In the *vīrāsana* ('hero's posture') the bent left leg is placed on the ground and the right leg upon it, with the right knee resting on the left foot, and the right foot on the left knee. There is no crossing, only a bending of legs in this posture.

In the *sukhāsana* ('the comfortable posture') both bent legs are placed on the ground evenly. The heel of the left foot rests between the legs; the toes are between the knee bend of the right leg which provides, as it were, the outer frame of the left leg. Since there is no pressure on the limbs whatsoever, this posture is the most comfortable one, and is, therefore, recommended in the Burmese meditation centre aforementioned.

For comfort in either of these postures it is essential that the knees rest firmly and without strain on their support (the floor, the seat, or on the other leg). The advantages of a posture with legs bent are so considerable for an earnest meditator that it will be worth his effort to train himself in any such posture. But if these postures come not easily to him, it is advisable to allow for posture training a separate period of time which may be used to one's best ability, for reflection, contemplation or Bare Attention. For the sake of such posture training, however, one should not delay or disturb one's determined attempt to achieve and sustain a higher degree of mental concentration, and for that purpose one may use, for the time being, a mode of sitting that is comfortable, dealing as best as one can with the disadvantages mentioned before. One may, then, sit on a straight-backed chair of a height that allows the legs to be placed on the floor without strain.

When sitting with legs bent, one may place a pillow, a folded cloth or blanket under the lower back, bringing it level with the legs. The body should be kept erect but not rigidly stiff or tense. The head should be slightly bent forward and the gaze should gently (not rigidly) rest where it naturally falls at that position of the head. One may place at that spot any small and simple object for focussing one's glance on it; preferably a geometrical shape like a cube or cone, without a shining or light-reflecting surface, and without anything else that may divert thoughts. Such a device is, of course, not a necessity.

Female meditators in the East do not sit in either of the postures with legs bent as described above, nor with legs crossed. They kneel on ample-sized, well-stuffed cushions, sitting on their heels, the hands resting on the knees.

As to the mode of sitting, the meditator will have to use his own discretion, and apply to his individual case the 'clear comprehension of suitability'.

Clothing should be loose, for instance at the waist. Before one starts with the meditation one should make sure that muscles are relaxed, for instance, neck, shoulders, face, hands, etc.

Eating

In the countries of Theravāda Buddhism, those who take up a strict course of full-time practice in a meditation centre, usually observe, among other rules, the sixth precept of the monk, that is they abstain from solid food and nourishing liquids after mid-day. For those, however, who work all day, this will hardly be practicable though it will be feasible for periods of meditation during a weekend or holidays. In any case, however, for one who wishes to take up in earnest regular meditative practice, it will be very desirable that he should be moderate in eating. It was not without reason that the Buddha recommended repeatedly 'moderation in eating' to those devoted to meditation. Experience will confirm the benefits of it to those who are determined to make actual progress in meditation and are not satisfied with casual attempts.

Preliminaries: The Mental Attitude

The aim of the meditative practice to be described here, is the highest which the teaching of the Buddha offers. Therefore, the practice should be taken up in a mental attitude befitting such a high purpose. The Buddhist meditator may begin with the recitation of the Threefold Refuge, keeping in mind the true significance of that act.[18] This will instil confidence in him, which is so important for meditative progress: confidence in the peerless Teacher and Guide, the *Buddha*; confidence in the liberating efficacy of his Teaching (*Dhamma*), and in particular the Way of Mindfulness; confidence aroused by the fact that there have been (those who have realized the Teaching in its fullness: the Community of Saints (*ariya-sangha*), the Accomplished Ones (*arahats*). Such conviction will fill him with joyous confidence in his own capacity and will give wings to his endeavour. In such a spirit, the follower of these Three Ideals should start his meditation practice with the quiet but determined aspiration (to attain the highest, not in a distant future but in this very life.

'I shall be going now the Path trodden by the Buddhas and the Great Holy Disciples. But an indolent person cannot follow that Path. May my energy prevail! May I succeed'!'

But also the non-Buddhist will do well to consider that, in following even partly the Way of Mindfulness, he enters ground that is hallowed to the Buddhist, and therefore deserving of respect. Such courteous awareness will help him in his own endeavours on the Way.

It will bring firmness to his steps on the Way if he makes a solemn aspiration like the following ones or any other that he may formulate for himself:

For mind's mastery and growth effort must be made
If once you see the need. Why not make it now?
The road is clearly marked.
May what I win bring weal to me and to all beings!

Mind brings all happiness and woe. To conquer woe
I enter now the Path of Mindfulness.
May what I win bring weal to me and to all beings!

The Programme of Practice

I. Training in General Mindfulness

During a course of strict training the time of practice is the whole day, from morning to night. This does not mean that the meditator should all that time attend exclusively to a single, that is the primary subject, of meditation with which we shall deal below. Though he should certainly devote to it as much of the day and night as he possibly can, there will of course be pauses between the single spells of the main practice; and for beginners these pauses will be fairly frequent and of longer duration. But also during these intervals, be they long or short, the guiding rope of mindfulness must not be dropped or allowed to slacken. Mindfulness of all activities and perceptions should be maintained throughout the day to the greatest possible extent: beginning with the first thought and perception when awakening, and ending with the last thought and perception when falling asleep. This general mindfulness starts with, and retains as its centre piece, the Awareness of the four Postures (*iriyāpatha-manasikāra*), i.e. going, standing, sitting and lying down. That means, one has to be fully aware of the posture presently assumed, of any change of it (including the preceding intention to change it), of any sensation connected with the posture, e.g. pressure, i.e. touch consciousness (*kāya-viññāṇa*), and of any noticeable feelings of pain or ease ('Contemplation on Feeling'). For instance, when lying down for the night and waking up in the morning, one should be aware of one's reclining posture and of touch ('lying down, touching').

The meditator may not be able at once to attend mindfully to all or even a greater part of the activities and impressions of the day. He therefore may start with the postures alone and gradually extend the scope of mindfulness to all routine activities, as dressing, washing, eating, etc. This extension will come naturally when, after the first few days of full-time practice, the mind becomes calmer, observation keener and mindfulness more alert.

One example may illustrate how mindfulness may be applied correctly to a series of activities: a wish arises to clean the mouth in the morning, and one is aware of that wish (thought-conscious: 'he knows mind and mental objects'); one sees the glass and water jug, at some distance (visual consciousness); one goes towards that place (posture-conscious); stops there (posture-conscious); stretches the hand towards the jug ('acting with clear comprehension when bending and stretching'); one grasps the jug (touch-conscious), etc.

While performing these activities, one should also notice the arising of any pleasant or unpleasant feelings ('Contemplation of Feeling'), of stray thoughts interrupting the flow of mindfulness (Mind Contemplation: 'unconcentrated mind'), of lust (e.g. when eating; Mind Contemplation: 'mind with lust'; Mind-object Contemplation: Hindrance of Sense Desire, or Fetter arising through tongue and flavours), etc. In brief, one should be aware of all ocurrences, bodily and mental, as they present themselves. In that way, one will attend to all four objects, or Contemplations, (of Satipaṭṭhāna, during the day of practice.

Such a detailed application of Mindfulness involves a considerable slowing-down of one's movements which can be maintained only in periods of strict practice, and not, or only rarely, during everyday life. The experience, and the effects, of that slowing-down practice will, however, prove wholesome and useful in many ways.

In attending to those routine activities of the day, mindfulness need not be directed to all minute phases of them (as it should be with the principal subjects). By doing so, the slowing- down would be too great. It will be sufficient if mindfulness goes watchfully along with these activities, noticing only those details which present themselves without effort.

The initial purpose of this general application of Mindfulness is the strengthening of awareness and concentration to an extent enabling the meditator to follow the unceasing flow of variegated mental and bodily impressions and activities, for an increasingly long period and without a break of attention or without an *unnoticed* break. It will count as 'uninterrupted mindfulness', if the meditator is not carried away by his stray thoughts, but if breaks of attention are noticed at once when they occur, or soon after. For the beginner, the standards of 'general mindfulness' will be satisfied by that procedure.

II. The Main Practice with Selected Subjects

After one has attended mindfully to the various routine activities of the morning, one sits down on the meditation seat, being aware of one's preceding intention to sit down, the single phases of the act, and then of 'touching' and 'sitting'. Now one turns one's attention to the regular *rising and falling movement of the abdomen,* resulting from the process of breathing. The attention is directed to the slight sensation of pressure caused by that movement, and not so visually observing it. This forms the *primary object* (*mūl' ārammaṇa*) of mindfulness, in the course of practice described here. It has been introduced into the practice by the Venerable U Sobhana Mahāthera (Mahāsi Sayadaw) as it was found to be very effective.

It should be well understood that one must not think *about* the movement of the abdomen, but keep to the bare noticing of that physical process, being aware of its regular rise and fall, in all its phases. One should try to retain that awareness without break, or without *unnoticed* break, for as long a period as possible without strain. The insight at which the method aims, will present itself to the mind spontaneously, as the natural result, or the maturing fruit, of growing mindfulness. The Meditation Master said: 'The knowledge will arise by itself' (*ñāṇam sayam eva uppajjissati*). It will come in the degree in which, through sharpened awareness, features of the observed processes appear which were hitherto unnoticed. Insight arrived at in this way will carry the conviction conveyed by one's own indubitable experience.

Though it is the breathing which causes the abdominal movement, the attention directed to the latter must not be regarded as a variety of the 'Mindfulness of Breathing' (*ānāpānasati*). In the practice described here the object of mindfulness is not the breath but just the rise and fall of the abdomen as felt by the slight pressure.

In the case of beginners, the abdominal movement is not always clearly noticeable at once and sometimes may remain distinct only for short recurring periods. This is nothing unusual and will improve in the course of diligent practice. As a help in making the movement of the abdomen perceptible more often and for a longer stretch, one may lie down; by doing so it will become more distinct. One may also place one's hand on the abdomen for tracing the movement first in that way; it will then be easier to keep track of it even when the hand is removed. If one feels it helpful, one may well continue the exercise in a reclining position, provided one can keep off sleepiness and lassitude. But, in between, one may try it repeatedly in the sitting posture.

Whenever the awareness of the abdominal movement ceases or remains unclear, one should not strain to 'catch' it, but should turn one's attention to '*touching*' and '*sitting*'. This should be done in the following way. From the many points of contact, or better, perceptions of touch, that are present in the apparently uniform act of sitting—e.g. at the knees, thighs, shoulders, etc.—six or seven may be chosen. The attention should turn to them successively, travelling, as it were, on that prescribed route, ending with the awareness of the sitting posture, and starting again with the same series: touching—touching—touching—sitting; touching—touching—touching—sitting. One should dwell on the single perception just for the length of these two-syllable words (spoken internally, and later to be abandoned when one has got into the time rhythm). It should be noted that the object of mindfulness is here the respective sensation, and not the places of contact in themselves, nor the words 'touching-sitting'. One may change, from time to time, the selection of 'touches'.

This awareness of 'touching-sitting' is, as it were, a 'stand-by' of the awareness of the abdominal movement, and is one of the secondary objects of the main practice. It has, however, a definite value of its own for achieving results in the domain of Insight.

When, while attending to 'touching-sitting', one notices that the abdominal movement has become clearly perceptible again, one should return to it, and continue with that primary object as long as possible.

If one feels tired, or, by sitting long, the legs are paining or benumbed, one should be aware of these feelings and sensations. One should keep to that awareness as long as these feelings and sensations are strong enough to force attention upon them and to disturb the meditation. Just by the act of noticing them quietly and continuously, i.e. with Bare Attention, these feelings and sensations may sometimes disappear, enabling one to continue with the primary object. In the awareness of the disturbing sensations one stops short at the bare statement of their presence without 'nursing' these feelings and thus strengthening them by what one adds to the bare facts, i.e. by one's mental attitude of self-reference, excessive sensitivity, self-pity, resentment, etc.

If, however, these unpleasant sensations, or tiredness, persist and disturb the practice, one may change the posture (noticing the intention and the act of changing), and resort to *mindfully walking up and down.* In doing so, one has to be aware of the single phases of each step. The sixfold division of these phases as given, e.g. in the Commentary to the Discourse, will be too elaborate for the beginner. It is sufficient to notice three (A) or two (B) phases. For fitting into a two-syllable rhythm it is suggested to formulate them as follows: A. 1. lifting, 2. pushing, 3. placing; B. 1. lifting, 2. placing, of the foot. Whenever one wishes to walk somewhat quicker, one may use the twofold division; otherwise the threefold one is preferable as affording a closer sequence of mindfulness, without a gap.

This practice of mindful walking is, particularly for certain types of meditators, highly recommendable both as a method of concentration and as a source of Insight. It may therefore be practised in its own right, and not only as a 'change of posture' for relieving fatigue. In the Discourses of the Buddha we meet a frequently recurring passage, saying: 'By day, and in the first and third watches of the night, he purifies his mind from obstructing thoughts, while *walking up and down or sitting*.'

If walking up and down is taken up as a practice in its own right, it is desirable to have for that purpose a fairly long stretch of ground, either in the house (a corridor or two adjoining rooms) or outdoors, since turning around too often may cause disturbance in the continuous flow of mindfulness. One should walk for a fairly long time, even until one feels tired.

During the entire day of practice, stray thoughts, or an unmindful 'skipping' of steps (in walking), phases or sequences of the abdominal movements, or of parts of any other activities, should be clearly noticed. One should pay attention to the fact whether these breaks in attention have been noticed at once after occurring, or whether, and how long, one was carried away by stray thoughts, etc., before resuming the original object of mindfulness. One should aim at noticing these breaks at once, and then returning immediately to one's original object. This may be taken as a measure of one's growing alertness. The frequency of these breaks will naturally decrease when, in the course of the practice, mental quietude and concentration improve. Growing competence in this practice of immediate awareness of breaks of attention will be a valuable help in the strenghtening of one's self-control, and in checking mental defilements (*kilesa*) as soon as they arise. Its importance for one's progress on the Path and one's mental development in general is evident.

One should not allow oneself to be irritated, annoyed or discouraged by the occurrence of distracting or undesirable thoughts, but should simply *take these disturbing thoughts themselves as (temporary) objects of one's mindfulness,* making them thus a part of the practice (through the Contemplation of the State of Mind). Should feelings of irritation about one's distracted state of mind arise and persist, one may deal with them in the very same way; that is, take them as an opportunity for the Contemplation of Mind-objects: the Hindrance of aversion, or of restlessness and worry. In this context the Meditation Master said: Since a multiplicity of thought-objects is unavoidable in ordinary life, and such defilements as lust, aversion, etc., are sure to arise in all unliberated minds, it is of vital importance to face these variegated thoughts and defilements squarely, and to learn how to deal with them. This is, in its own way, just as important as acquiring an increased measure of concentration. One should, therefore, not regard it as 'lost time' when one is dealing with these interruptions of the methodical practice.

The same method should be applied to interruptions from outside. If there is, for instance, a disturbing noise, one may take brief notice of it as 'sound'; if it was immediately followed by annoyance about the disturbance, one should register it, too, as 'mind with anger'. After that, one should return to the interrupted meditation. But if one does not succeed at once in doing so, the same procedure should be repeated. If the noise is loud and persistent and keeps one from attending to the subject of meditation, one may, until the noise ceases, continue to take it as an object of mindfulness, namely as one of the six sense-bases, within the frame of the Contemplation of Mind-objects (see p. 135): 'He knows the ear and sound, and knows the fetter (annoyance) arising dependent on both . . .' In the fluctuations of sound one can observe 'rise and fall'; in its intermittent occurrence, its origination and disappearance, and its conditioned nature will become clear.

In that way, *disturbances of the meditative practice can be transformed into useful objects of the practice;* and what appeared inimical, can be turned into a friend and teacher.

Nevertheless, when the mind has been quieted or the outer disturbances have disappeared, one should return to the primary subject of meditation, since it is the sustained cultivation of it that will make for quicker progress.

Three to four hours of continuous mindfulness, i.e. without unnoticed breaks, are regarded as the minimum for a beginner undergoing a course of strict practice. This, of course, does not mean that three or four hours are sufficient for the whole day of practice. If one has 'lost the thread' of mindfulness, be it after, or before, that minimal period, one should take it up again and again, and continue with the practice of sustained concentration, as long as possible

Quiet sustained effort, without too much regard to bodily discomfort, is recommended, particularly during a course of strict practice. Often, when disregarding the first appearance of fatigue, one will discover behind it new resources of energy, a 'second-wind'. On the other hand, one should not go to extremes, and should allow oneself rest when effort ceases to be useful. These intervals of rest will also form parts of the practice (with less intense focussing) if one keeps mindful. The more natural and relaxed the flow of one's mindfulness is, or becomes, in following the continual arising and disappearing of its selected or variegated objects, the less fatigue will be caused by it.

When alertness grows one may also give particular attention to one's thoughts or moods of satisfaction or dissatisfaction, even if very subtle. They are the seeds of stronger forms of attraction and aversion, and of feelings of pride or inferiority, elation or depression. It is therefore important to get acquainted with them, to notice them and to stop them early. One should also avoid futile thoughts of the past or the future, as Satipaṭṭhāna is concerned with the present only.

The primary and secondary objects dealt with here (i.e. abdominal movement, touching-sitting, walking) are retained throughout the whole practice, i.e. during a strict course and afterwards, without anything being added in the way of new devices, etc. If there is persistent application to them, these simple exercises are capable of leading gradually to the highest results. Main emphasis rests on the primary object, i.e. the movement of the abdomen.

Sundry Remarks

In view of its importance, it is here again emphasized that the objects of mindfulness are here the bodily and mental processes themselves, as they occur. One should, during the practice, not be side-tracked into discursive thoughts or feelings *about* them. If such thoughts or feelings arise, one should deal with them as recommended here, and should then return to the original object of mindfulness.

Yet, a certain reservation may be made. In the successful progress of the practice it may happen that the meditator's mind is suddenly flood-lit by a quick succession of thoughts, illuminating for him strikingly certain parts of the Dhamma or sayings of the Master; or strong emotion may arise: happiness and rapture, a confidence in, or veneration for, the Buddha, etc. These will be experiences of great intellectual and emotional satisfaction (which one should objectively know as such, at least retrospectively). In such moments, the meditator will judge for himself how much room he may allow, with advantage, to these thoughts and feelings. Though they may be of great value to his general progress, and should certainly not be suppressed by force, the meditator should know that they are just by-products of the practice in which he is engaged. After the waves of those thoughts and feelings have subsided, he should return to the primary and secondary objects, and, with their help, push on to higher achievement, in the field of Insight.

As remarked earlier (p. 91), the main exercises should first be practised for their own sake, as devices for the strengthening of mindfulness and concentration. One should first become thoroughly familiar with the processes underlying those exercises, and should not be intent on 'quick results', other than the growth of mindfulness. The other results, in the field of Insight, will appear in due course. Any premature intellectual straining at achieving them will only interfere with the quietude and singleness of mind required for attending successfully to the primary and secondary objects. At the beginning of the practice it is therefore advisable to disregard, for the time being, the few hints on results in Insight which had to be included here, but are not given in oral instruction.

The situation is similar with the practice of *general* (all-day) mindfulness, outside the hours devoted to the primary and secondary objects. The first purpose of it is to create a *generally* high level of keen awareness by which, what we may call the 'peak hours' of mindfulness (i.e. the attention to the main exercises) will be greatly benefited. It puts the mind in proper poise and gives it heightened efficiency for the 'decisive attack' to be launched at those 'peak hours'. But beneficial influence will be noticeable also in the reverse direction: results achieved in concentration and Insight during the 'peak hours' will strengthen the concentration and the penetrative power of mindfulness during the periods of general awareness. It may well happen that important results of Insight will appear first, not in connection with the primary object, but on some other occasion during the day of practice.

In view of the valuable reciprocal support of all-day mindfulness and application to the main exercises, it is desirable that a determined practice of Satipaṭṭhāna should start with a number of weeks exclusively devoted to it, in the way described here. In order to get gradually accustomed to such a strict mental discipline, one may begin with a day or two (weekend), extend it to a week, and increase the period up to one's opportunity to do so. Such a time of strict training will be a strong impetus to a regular continuation of the practice during one's normal life.

If one's circumstances of life are such that even on days of strict practice, social contact cannot be entirely avoided, one may, for that time, deliberately and mindfully put aside the practice and be satisfied with an attitude of general mindfulness (e.g. Clear Comprehension in speaking). After one has regained one's privacy, one should, in the same deliberate and mindful way, resume the practice, 'just as one takes up again a piece of luggage that one has temporarily put down' (Commentary).

In the living conditions of a modern city, however, it may sometimes be difficult, or even impossible, to make suitable arrangements for a period of strict practice, even with the limitations and adjustments suggested. The question was therefore put to the Meditation Master whether, and to what extent, progress may be expected if the practice is restricted to the short time of leisure allowed by the daily routine, without a preceding period of strict training. The reply was that some of the Meditation Master's lay pupils had practised in that manner, while pursuing their professions, and had partly obtained good results. But progress, as far as the specific Buddhist aspect of the practice is concerned, will be slower and more difficult, and will also depend on the capacities and persistence of the individual. Very regular practice is imperative, under such circumstances, even if the time at one's disposal is short. Such restricted practice too, will bestow beneficial results for a general development of mind, as indicated in the main body of this book; and these results, again, will be conducive to further progress.

For such a restricted way of practice, and also for its continuation *after* strict training, the programme outlined here will have to be adapted to circumstances. (1) The place of general (all-day) mindfulness will have to be taken by aspiring to a maximum level of mindfulness, circumspection and restraint, during the whole day, adapted to the demands of professional and domestic life. Again, during working hours, one will be able, even for seconds, to direct one's attention to the postures or to breathing; and the work itself will be benefited by it (see p. 91). (2) To the practice with the primary and secondary objects one should devote all time available for privacy, at the early morning hours and at night. When beginning with systematic practice, one may, for a short time and to the extent possible, dispense with any other private pursuits (including reading, etc.), and restrict social contact to the minimum. This may serve as a substitute for the initial period of strict and exclusive practice.

When pursuing the practice of Mindfulness in one's normal environment, one should do it as unobtrusively as possible, for spiritual as well as practical reasons. The practice of Mindfulness and Clear Comprehension should show itself in its fruits, and not in any outward behaviour that may appear unusual to others. One may make the choice of one's regular exercises accordingly, and reserve other practices for occasions affording privacy.

The Place of the Methodical Practice of Satipaṭṭhāna within the System of Buddhist Meditation

1. The system of Buddhist meditation divides into two great parts: (*a*) the Development of Tranquillity (*samatha-bhāvanā*) and (*b*) the Development of Insight (*vipassanā-bhāvanā*).

> (*a*) The *Development of Tranquillity* aims at the full concentration of mind, attained in the meditative Absorptions (*jhāna*). These Absorptions are gained, in different degrees, by the systematic practice of any of the 38 traditional 'subjects of meditation, conducive to Tranquillity' (*samatha-kammaṭṭhāna*). Through the high degree of mental unification and stillness attained in these Absorptions, the fivefold sense perception is temporarily obliterated, and conceptual and discursive thought, being weak in the first stage of Absorption, is completely absent in the following stages. From the latter fact alone it can be gathered that, in the Buddha's teaching, the Development of Tranquillity or the meditative

Absorptions, are only means to an end, and cannot lead, by themselves, to the highest goal of liberation which is attainable only through Insight. After rising from these states of Absorption, the meditator is therefore advised to continue his meditation with the Development of Insight.

(*b*) *The Development of Insight.* Here the mental phenomena present in the Absorption and the bodily processes on which they are based, are analysed and viewed in the light of the Three Characteristics (see p. 24 f.). That procedure, adopted in Buddhist meditation, serves as a safeguard against the speculative or phantastic interpretation of meditative experience. The degree of concentration, attainable in, and necessary for, the successful practice of Insight is called Access- or Neighbourhood-Concentration (*upacāra-samādhi*). Here, thought-conception and discursive thinking retain their full strength, but owing to the mental concentration achieved, they are not easily diverted to a multiplicity of objects, but pursue steadily and efficiently the course set for them.

It is the combined practice of Tranquillity and Insight which is most frequently described in the Buddhist scriptures. But we meet also, and not at all rarely, with a method which, in later terminology, is called the practice of Bare Insight (*sukkha-vipassanā*), i.e. the direct and exclusive meditative practice of it without a previous attainment of the Absorptions. The Satipaṭṭhāna Method described here, and the directions of practice outlined in the preceding pages, belong to that category of Bare Insight.

Though the term 'Bare Insight' (*sukkha-vipassanā*) does not occur in the canonical Collection of Discourses of the

Buddha (*Sutta-Piṭaka*), there are numerous texts in that Collection which are illustrative of that method of meditation, that is instructions and instances where the penetrative insight into reality is followed by the entry into the stages of holiness, without prior attainment of the Absorptions. Some of such texts are included in the Third Part of this volume (see Texts 52, 53).

Leaving aside characters who, by nature, strongly incline to that approach of Bare Insight, there is no doubt that the method to be preferred is that in which the attainment of the Absorptions precedes the systematic practice of Insight. In the Absorptions, the mind attains a very high degree of concentration, purity and calm, and reaches deep down into the subconscious sources of intuition. With such a preparation, the subsequent period of Insight--practice is likely to bring quicker and steadier results. Therefore he who has good reason to believe that he is able to make fairly quick progress on the road, is certainly well advised to select a 'primary subject of meditation' (*mūla-kammaṭṭhāna*) that is conducive also to the attainment of the Absorptions, e.g. the Mindfulness on Breathing.

Yet, we have to face the fact that, in this hectic and noisy age of ours, the natural quietude of mind, the capacity for higher degrees of concentration, and the requisite external conditions to cultivate both, have greatly decreased, compared with the days of old. This holds good not only for the West, but also, though in a lesser degree, for the East, and even for a not inconsiderable section of Buddhist monkhood. The principal conditions required for cultivating the Absorptions are seclusion and noiselessness; and these are very rare commodities nowadays. In addition, environment and education have produced an increasing number of those types who will naturally be more attracted by, and adapted to, the direct Development of Insight.

Under such circumstances, it would amount to a neglect of promising roads of progress if one were to insist rigidly on an exclusive approach through the Absorptions, instead of making use of a method emphatically recommended by the Buddha himself: a method which is more easily adaptable to the current inner and outer conditions, and yet leads to the aspired goal. To make use of it will be a practical application of the Clear Comprehension of Suitability.

While repeated failures to make progress on the road of Tranquillity (sometimes due to unfavourable external conditions) will tend to discourage the meditator, the comparatively quick initial results obtainable through the Development of Insight will mean encouragement and a powerful stimulus to unremitting effort. In addition, if Access-Concentration (p. 109) has once been gained through the meditative development of Insight, the chances of attaining to the *full* concentration of the Absorptions are considerably enhanced for those who aspire after it.

These reasons of practicability referred to here, will certainly have contributed to the fact that Satipaṭṭhāna has obtained such a strong hold on the minds of many in modern Burma. The single-minded application to the Way of Mindfulness and the enthusiastic propagation of it, by Burman devotees, are based on the conviction conveyed by personal experience. The emphasis which the practice of Satipaṭṭhāna receives in Burma, and in the pages of this book, is, however, not meant to be a discouragement or disparagement of other methods or devices. Satipaṭṭhāna would not be the Only Way if it could not encompass them all.

The method described in the preceding 'Instructions', is based on the first Satipaṭṭhāna, the Contemplation of the Body (*kāyānupassanā*). The bodily processes selected here as principal objects of Mindfulness serve for the systematic development of Insight throughout the whole practice, from the first steps of the beginner up to the summit of the highest goal. The other three Contemplations of Satipaṭṭhāna (feeling, state of mind, and mental contents) are not taken up in a systematic way but are attended to whenever their objects occur, either in connection with the primary and secondary objects or within the range of general (all-day) mindfulness. In that way the whole field of Satipaṭṭhāna is covered.

When mental objects appear in close connection with one of the bodily objects, it will be less difficult to discern their subtle nature. Owing to their subtlety, they are not taken separately as objects for the systematic development of Insight, as this promises success only in the case of those meditators who have attained to the Absorptions (*jhāna*).

The emphasis on the Contemplation of the Body is supported by utterances of the Buddha in his Discourses, as well as by the commentarial tradition.

It was said by the Enlightened One:

'Whosoever, O monks, has developed and frequently practiced Mindfulness of the Body, included for him therein are all beneficial things conducive to wisdom'
(Majjh. 119, Kāyagatāsati Sutta)

'If the body is unmastered (by meditation; abhāvito*), the mind will be unmastered; if the body is mastered, the mind is mastered'*
(Majjh. 36, Mahā-Saccaka Sutta)

The 'Path of Purification' (*Visuddhi Magga*) says:

'If, after having attended to the corporeal processes, one takes up the mental processes, and they do not present themselves clearly, the meditator should not

> abandon the practice, but should again and again comprehend, consider, take up and define just the corporeal processes. If the corporeal becomes to him fully distinct, unconfused and clear, the mental processes which have that corporeal process as object, will become clear by themselves'.
>
> 'Since mental processes will become clear only to one who has grasped the corporeal with full clarity, any endeavour in grasping the mental processes should be made only by thoroughly grasping the corporeal, not otherwise. . . . If one proceeds thus, the practice of one's subject of meditation (*kammaṭṭhāna*) will come to growth, development and maturity'.

A few explanatory words will be appropriate here, concerning the 'primary object' (abdominal movement), introduced by the Venerable U Sobhana Mahāthera. It may be objected that this practice is not found in the Satipaṭṭhāna Sutta, nor in other texts. But it shares that circumstance with many other physical and mental processes which likewise are not expressly mentioned in the scriptures, but belong nevertheless to the all-comprehensive domain of mindfulness. Our 'primary object' may, however, well be included in the passage of the Discourse, saying, 'Just as his body is disposed, so he understands it', or, alternatively, in the section of the Six Sense Bases, 'he understands the organ of touch and tactual objects'. Certainly, all objects of touch when they occur and are noticed, should be covered by the wide net of mindfulness. By an eminent monk of our days it was rightly said: 'All conditional phenomena (*sankhārā*), bodily or mental, are legitimate objects of the Insight practice'.

How that exercise came to be introduced, together with the spirit in which it is offered by the Meditation Master, has been very aptly expressed by a lay disciple in Burma. 'This exercise has not been "invented" by the Meditation Master, it was not arbitrarily or deliberately "devised". It was rather so that the bodily processes concerned did not escape his attention'. Having found attention to it helpful, he cultivated it and recommended it to others. It has no 'mystic significance', but is just a simple and sober fact of our bodily existence like many others. But, by patient application, one may make it reveal what it has to tell, and give it a chance to kindle the flame of penetrative Insight.

This exercise has a number of definite advantages which will find confirmation through actual practice: (1) The abdominal movement is an automatic process and is constantly present; it need not be produced deliberately and thus offers itself easily for detached and sustained observation, (2) being a movement it gives opportunity for numerous observations conducive to Insight, e.g. of the incessant rise and fall, 'birth and death', of that process. It shares these two advantages with 'Mindfulness of Breathing'; and in fact, these two seem to be the only bodily processes which possess these characteristics and, at the same time, are suitable objects for meditative observation (which for instance the heart beat is not). A third advantage particular to the abdominal movement is that it is, and remains, rather 'coarse' in its impact, which is a definite advantage for observations conducive to Insight; while breathing, in the advanced stages of the meditative practice, tends to become more and more subtle and hardly noticeable. To one who has practised Insight meditation or understands its aims, these three advantages of the awareness of the abdominal movement should be quite sufficient to convince him that it is eminently suitable for the purpose intended.

SIX

Mindfulness of Breathing (Ānāpāna-sati)

Instructions for the Practice

There may be, however, those who, for various reasons, prefer to choose the breath as the primary object of mindfulness, be it for the prior attainment of the Absorptions or for the direct development of Insight. For their benefit, brief instructions on 'Mindfulness of Breathing' (*ānāpāna-sati*) are added here. They are based on the respective section in the Satipaṭṭhāna-Sutta. An alternative method of practice, starting with the counting of the breaths, is described in *The Path of Purification* (Visuddhi Magga).

We have mentioned before that, for Mindfulness of Breathing, the Lotus Posture with fully crossed legs is preferable though it is not of absolute necessity. We have also given a warning not to interfere with the breath in any way: in Buddhist practice, there should be no holding or stopping of the breath, no deliberate deepening nor attempts to force it into a definite time rhythm. The only task here is to follow the natural flow of the breath mindfully and continuously, without a break or without unnoticed break. The point where one should fix one's attention is the nostrils against which the breathing air strikes, and one should not leave that point of observation because here one can easily check the entry and exit of the breath. One should, for instance, not follow the breath on its way down the body and back since this will deflect attention by diverting it to the several stages of the breath's journey. There may be fluctuations as to where the impact of the breath is felt distinctly: it may change between both nostrils; there may also be definite individual differences according to the length of nose or width of nostrils. Beyond noticing these fluctuations and differences one should not be further concerned with them but attend to the breath itself wherever it becomes most distinct in succession.

Though mindfulness is kept at its post of observation, yet there is, caused through the slight pressure of the air, a more or less distinct awareness of the breath's passage through the body; but directed attention should not be given to it. Just as the eye though focussed on a definite object, will also comprise in its field of vision some neighbouring objects, so also has mindfulness a certain extension of its range beyond its chosen centre. There is a very apt simile for it in the ancient Buddhist literature: if a man saws a log of wood his attention will be concentrated on the 'point of contact' of the saw's teeth and the log; but he will also be aware of the coming and going of the saw beyond that point, without, however, paying any particular attention to it.

A beginner often makes the mistake of being too tense or self-conscious when first turning his attention to the breath. If he does it, as it were, with an inner jerk or as if pouncing upon a prey, he will be quite out of touch with the delicate respiratory process. After concluding the initial contemplation or aspiration, the meditator should calmly turn his attention to the natural flow of the breath and go along with it, participating in its regular rhythm. No emphatic act of will ('Now I will catch the breath!') is required; it will only obstruct.

In the relevant section of the Discourse (see p. 126), it is first said: 'Breathing in a long (short) breath he knows "I breathe in a long (short) breath."' This does not mean that one should deliberately lengthen (deepen) or shorten the breath but that one should just notice whether it is relatively longer or shorter at the time of observation. The meditator will quite naturally become aware of these differentiations in the respiratory process, and of many other details too, when once he gets used to direct watchful attention to breathing. It is the same as with any other perception, for instance that of a visible object; closer and sustained observation will reveal many facts unnoticed by a superficial glance.

Through regular and diligent practice, the meditator should first make himself capable of sustained attention to the flow of breath for an increasingly longer period of time, without a break or (at the beginning) without unnoticed break. When he can maintain concentration for twenty minutes with comparative ease, he will be able to notice still more details of the process observed. The fact will now become more marked that even the fleeting moment of a single breath has an extension in time, a distinct beginning, middle and end of the movement. This observation will herald a further development in the practice.

The meditator might now notice that his mindfulness is not equally clear and keen during all three phases of a breath's duration. Slow natures, for instance, after attending to the end phase of a breath might miss the first phase of the next breath, being not quick enough to rally to it immediately. Or through anxiety not to miss the beginning of the next breath one may have unwittingly skipped the end phase of the preceding breath. This may serve as an illustration to a warning of wide application found in the Buddhist scriptures: 'not to lag behind nor to overshoot the mark'.

Noticing those subtle differences in the alertness and clarity of attention may well be regarded as a successful step in the development of mindfulness and concentration. Through these observations the meditator will also gain useful self-knowledge which will help him to adjust his mental disposition as required for a well-balanced effort that avoids both slackness and tenseness.

Along with noticing the fluctuations in the application of mindfulness there will arise in the meditator the wish and the effort to remedy the deficiency. He will endeavour to keep his mindfulness at an even level throughout all three phases of a breath's duration. When succeeding in it, the meditator will have practised according to the third exercise in the Discourse: 'Conscious of the *whole* (breath-) body, I shall breathe in—breathe out'.

The twofold effort—of watching without interruption the sequence of breaths and of paying equal attention to all phases of the breath—may have left traces of tension or vibration in the breathing process and in the observing mind, which will be noticed when alertness grows. Again, implicit in that observation, there will be the wish and effort to bring still greater calmness to the respiratory and mental process involved. This is the fourth and last stage of practice as mentioned in the Discourse: 'Calming the bodily function (of breathing), I shall breathe in—breathe out'.[19]

It may, however, require persevering practice until all these stages will become a fairly secure possession of the meditator and can be entered upon with comparative ease. If this has been achieved further progress may be expected.

It is also at this point of Calming the Breath where the two main strands of Buddhist meditation (Samatha and Vipassanā) temporarily part.

If the meditator aspires to the attainment of the *Absorptions* (*jhāna*) through the deepening of Tranquillity (*samatha*), he should continue the process of Calming and make the breath still more fine and subtle and its flow smoother. Though he should make sure that his mindfulness covers all three phases of the breath, he should not pay to them any particular attention. Any discriminating observation or examination will be only an obstruction here. When aiming at Absorption one should, as it were, float along with the undulating flow of the breath. Continuing diligently with that practice, concentration of mind will grow and in due time there may appear a simple mental image (*nimitta*), like a star, etc., heralding full absorption. But complicated and varying images or visions are not a sign of progress; they should be soberly noticed and dismissed.

In full- or half-day practice aiming at Absorption, mindfulness should be present throughout, but this only in a very general way, without attention to details. Walking, for instance, should be done mindfully but without dissection into phases as done in the practice of Insight. Through a close scrutiny of details the mind will become too much engaged and interested in a multiplicity of objects while here the aim should be the unification and tranquillity of the mind.

But if, after having come to the stage of Calming, the meditator wishes to go the direct road of *Insight*, he should give marked attention to the single phases of the breath, in particular to the beginning and the end; and all those secondary and general objects of mindfulness should be carefully attended to, as explained earlier (see page 100). It is thus only a slight shift in the focussing of attention which will make all the difference between the methods of Jhānic development and that of Insight.

When, in Insight-practice, the meditator has achieved some skill up to the stage of Calming, he will, in due course, become aware of the fact that two processes are involved here: the physical process (*rūpa*) of breathing or abdominal movement, and the mental process (*nāma*) of knowing it. Though theoretically this is quite evident, the mind, before having attained skill in concentration, will be too much concerned with the *object* of attention for being conscious of its own activity. If the awareness of these two processes has become strong through repetition, they will present themselves regularly as a pairwise progression of physical and mental phenomena: breathing, knowing; breathing, knowing. . . .

When continuing the effort, there will come a time when the end phase of the single breath or the abdominal movement will stand out very strongly while the other phases revert in the background. The dividing line between the end of one breath or movement and the beginning of the next will become very marked, and the fact of cessation will impress itself deeply upon the meditator's mind. At this point again, further progress may be expected.

These two stages—the pairwise progression and the predominance of the end phase—will be natural developments of the meditation. They cannot be 'willed' while the process observed is going on, as this would mean a break in attention. These observations will be the lawful outcome of diligent practice. In oral instruction, the meditation master will not speak about stages not yet attained by the disciple but in this written statement it had to be done in order to offer a few road marks or criteria of progress, to a meditator who is without a personal teacher. Though the guidance by an experienced teacher is preferable an earnest meditator may well make good progress in his lone effort if he is watchful and critical concerning his practice.

H1: NOTES

1. For instance, birth, sickness, old age and death, sex and family life; search for food, for love and power, etc.

2. See, in Buddhist psychology (Abhidhamma), the term *āvajjana,* lit. 'turning towards (the object)'. It is the first in a series of several moments of consciousness required for a single act of perception.

3. On the place of memory, in Buddhist psychology, see the author's *Abhidhamma Studies,* p. 39 (Colombo 1949, Frewin & Co.).

4. The reservation *'comparatively* bare' has been added because, according to the penetrative scrutiny applied by the Abhidhamma, even the earliest stage of bare presentation of sense data carries a subtle flavour from earlier similar impressions.

5. The name of this third kind of Clear Comprehension, *gocara-sampajañña,* may well have been chosen as an allusion to the well-known passage quoted here.

6. The states of consciousness producing the 'perfect act' of the Saint, are called in the Abhidhamma *kriya-javana,* i.e. the mere functional 'act-impulsions' or 'act-motives' in the mind of the Saint, which have no longer the quality of effect-producing Kamma.

7. See page 126. For details of the practice, see Chapter 6 and Part Three, text 39.

8. For details opf practice, see Chapter 6 and Part Three, text 39.

9. That is the state of the Once-returner (*sakadāgami*) and the Non-returner (*anāgāmi*).

10. Detailed instructions for the practice of that meditation are given in Ch. XI of the *Visuddhi-Magga* (transl. by Ñanamoli Thera: *The Path of Purification,* Colombo 1956).

11. See *Visuddhi-Magga* (transl., p. 399).

12. See Part Three, texts 48–51.

13. *The Way of Mindfulness,* p. 119 ff.

14. See *The Four Sublime States,* by Nyanaponika Thera (Buddhist Publication Society, Kandy, Ceylon).

15. Pronounced 'Yeeta'.

16. 'Sayadaw', a Burmese word, is a respectful way of addressing senior or learned Buddhist monks, and means 'great teacher'.

17. See page 87.

18. See *The Threefold Refuge,* by Ñaṇamoli Thera (a free tract of the Buddhist Publication Society, Kandy).

19. Some of the preceding remarks concerning 'Mindfulness of Breathing' apply also to mindfulness directed to the abdominal movement; in particular those about the three phases of a single movement.

Part Two

THE BASIC TEXT

The Greater Discourse on the Foundations of Mindfulness

Mahā-Satipaṭṭhāna-Sutta

Being the 22nd Text of the Collection of Long Discourses of the Buddha (Dīgha-Nikāya) with Notes

Namo Tassa Bhagavato Arahato Sammā-Sambuddhassa

The Foundations of Mindfulness

Thus have I heard. At one time the Blessed One was living among the Kurus, at Kammāsadamma, a market-town of the Kuru people.

There the Blessed One addressed the monks thus: 'Monks', and they replied to him 'Venerable Sir'. And the Blessed One spoke as follows:

This is the sole way, monks[1], for the purification of beings, for the overcoming of sorrow and lamentation, for the destroying of pain and grief, for reaching the right path, for the realization of Nibbāna, namely the four Foundations of Mindfulness.

What are the four? Herein (in this teaching) a monk dwells practising body-contemplation on the body,[2] ardent, clearly comprehending and mindful, having overcome covetousness and grief concerning the world; he dwells practising feeling-contemplation on feelings, ardent, clearly comprehending and mindful, having overcome covetousness and grief concerning the world; he dwells practising mind-contemplation on the mind,[3] ardent, clearly comprehending and mindful, having overcome covetousness and grief concerning the world; he dwells practising mind-object-contemplation on mind-objects, ardent, clearly comprehending and mindful, having overcome covetousness and grief concerning the world.

I. The Contemplation of the Body

1. Mindfulness of Breathing

And how, monks, does a monk dwell practising body-contemplation on the body?

Herein, monks, a monk having gone to the forest, to the foot of a tree, or to an empty place, sits down cross-legged, keeps his body erect and his mindfulness alert.[4] Just mindful he breathes in and mindful he breathes out.

Breathing in a long breath, he knows 'I breathe in a long breath'; breathing out a long breath, he knows 'I breathe out a long breath'; breathing in a short breath, he knows 'I breathe in a short breath'; breathing out a short breath, he knows 'I breathe out a short breath'. 'Conscious of the whole (breath-) body, I shall breathe in', thus he trains himself. 'Conscious of the whole (breath-) body, I shall breathe out', thus he trains himself. 'Calming the bodily function (of breathing), I shall breathe in', thus he trains himself; 'Calming the bodily function (of breathing), I shall breathe out', thus he trains himself.[5]

As a skilful turner or his apprentice, making a long turn, knows 'I am making a long turn', or making a short turn, knows 'I am making a short turn', just so the monk breathing in a long breath, knows 'I breathe in a long breath'; breathing out a long breath, knows 'I breathe out a long breath'; breathing in a short breath, knows 'I breathe in a short breath'; breathing out a short breath, knows 'I breathe out a short breath'. 'Conscious of the whole (breath-) body, I shall breathe in'; 'Conscious of the whole (breath-) body, I shall breathe out'. 'Calming the bodily function (of breathing), I shall breathe in', thus he trains himself; 'Calming the bodily function (of breathing), I shall breathe out', thus he trains himself.

Thus he dwells practising body-contemplation on the body internally, or externally, or both internally and externally.[6] He dwells contemplating origination-factors[7] in the body, or he dwells contemplating dissolution-factors[8] in the body, or he dwells contemplating both origination- and dissolution-factors[9] in the body. Or his mindfulness that 'there is a body'[10] is established in him to the extent necessary for knowledge and mindfulness.[11] Independent[12] he dwells, clinging to nothing in the world.

2. The Postures of the Body

And again, monks, a monk when going, knows 'I am going'; when standing, he knows 'I am standing'; when sitting, he knows 'I am sitting'; when lying down, he knows 'I am lying down'; or he knows any other position of the body.

Thus he dwells practising body-contemplation on the body internally, or externally, or both internally and externally. He dwells contemplating origination-factors in the body, or he dwells contemplating dissolution-factors in the body, or he dwells contemplating both origination- and dissolution-factors in the body.[13] Or his mindfulness that 'there is a body' is established in him to the extent necessary for knowledge and mindfulness. Independent he dwells, clinging to nothing in the world. Thus indeed, a monk dwells practising body-contemplation on the body.

3. Mindfulness with Clear Comprehension

And again, monks, a monk in going forward and in going back, applies clear comprehension;[14] in looking straight on and in looking elsewhere, he applies clear comprehension; in bending and in stretching (his limbs), he applies clear comprehension; in wearing the robes and carrying the almsbowl, he applies clear comprehension; in eating, drinking, chewing and savouring, he applies clear comprehension; in obeying the calls of nature, he applies clear comprehension; in walking, standing, sitting, falling asleep, waking, speaking and being silent, he applies clear comprehension.

Thus he dwells practising body-contemplation on the body internally . . . (*as before*). . . .

Thus indeed, a monk dwells practising body-contemplation on the body.

4. The Reflection on the Repulsiveness of the Body

And again, monks, a monk reflects upon this very body, from the soles of his feet up and from the crown of his head down, enclosed by the skin and full of impurities, thinking thus: 'There are in this body: hair of the head, hair of the body, nails, teeth, skin, flesh, sinews, bones, marrow, kidneys, heart, liver, pleura, spleen, lungs, intestines, mesentery, gorge, faeces, bile, phlegm, pus, blood, sweat, solid fat, tears, liquid fat, saliva, mucus, synovic fluid, urine'.[15]

As if there were a double-mouthed provision bag filled with various kinds of grain such as hill-paddy, paddy, green-gram, cow-pea, sesamum, husked rice; and a man with sound eyes, having opened it, should examine it thus: 'This is hill-paddy, this is paddy, this is green-gram, this is cow-pea, this is sesamum, and this is husked rice." Just so, monks, a monk reflects on this very body, from the soles of his feet up and from the crown of his head down, enclosed by the skin and full of impurities: 'There are in this body: hair of the head . . . urine.'

Thus he dwells practising body-contemplation on the body internally . . . (*as before*). . . .

Thus indeed, a monk dwells practising body-contemplation on the body.

5. The Reflection on the Material Elements

And again, monks, a monk reflects upon this very body however it be placed or disposed, with regard to its primary elements: 'There are in this body the earth element, the water element, the fire element and the air element'.[16]

As if a skilful butcher or his apprentice, having slaughtered a cow and divided it into portions were sitting at the junction of four high-roads, just so a monk reflects upon this very body however it be placed or disposed, with regard to its primary elements: 'There are in this body the earth element, the water element, the fire element and the air element'.

Thus he dwells practising body-contemplation on the body internally . . . (*as before*). . . .

Thus indeed, a monk dwells practising body-contemplation on the body.

6. The Nine Cemetery Contemplations

1. And again, monks, as if a monk sees a body one day dead, or two days dead, or three days dead, swollen, blue, and festering, discarded in the charnel-ground, he then applies (this perception) to his own body thus: 'Truly, this body of mine too is of the same nature, it will become like that and will not escape from it'. Thus he dwells practising body-contemplation on the body internally. . . .

2. And again, monks, as if a monk sees a body discarded in the charnel-ground, being devoured by crows, hawks, vultures, herons, dogs, leopards, tigers, jackals or by various kinds of worms, he then applies (this perception) to his own body thus: 'Truly, this body of mine too is of the same nature, it will become like that and will not escape from it'. . . .

3. And again, monks, as if a monk sees a body discarded in the charnel-ground: reduced to a skeleton held together by the tendons, with some flesh and blood adhering to it . . .

4. Reduced to a skeleton held together by the tendons, blood-besmeared, fleshless . . .

5. Reduced to a skeleton held together by the tendons, without flesh and blood, he then applies (this perception) to his own body thus: 'Truly, this body of mine too is of the same nature, it will become like that and will not escape from it'. . . .

6. And again, monks, as if a monk sees a body discarded in the charnel-ground and reduced to loose bones scattered in all directions—here bones of the hand, there bones of the foot, shin bones, thigh bones, pelvis, spine and skull. . . .

7. And again, monks, as if a monk sees a body discarded in the charnel-ground: reduced to bleached bones of shell-like colour . . .

8. Reduced to bones more than a year old, lying in a heap . . .

9. Reduced to rotted bones, crumbling to dust, he then applies (this perception) to his own body thus: 'Truly, this body of mine too is of the same nature, it will become like that and will not escape from it'.

Thus he dwells practising body-contemplation on the body internally, or externally, or both internally and externally. He dwells contemplating origination-factors in the body, or he dwells contemplating dissolution-factors in the body, or he dwells contemplating both origination- and dissolution-factors in the body. Or his mindfulness that 'there is a body' is established in him to the extent necessary for knowledge and mindfulness. Independent he dwells, clinging to nothing in the world.

Thus indeed, monks, a monk dwells practising body-contemplation on the body.

II. The Contemplation of Feelings

And how, monks, does a monk dwell practising feeling-contemplation on feelings?

When experiencing a pleasant feeling, the monk knows: 'I experience a pleasant feeling'; when experiencing a painful feeling, he knows: 'I experience a painful feeling'; when experiencing a neutral feeling, he knows: 'I experience a neutral feeling'. When experiencing a pleasant worldly feeling, he knows: 'I experience a pleasant worldly feeling'; when experiencing a pleasant unworldly feeling, he knows: 'I experience a pleasant unworldly feeling'; when experiencing a painful worldly feeling, he knows: 'I experience a painful worldly feeling'; when experiencing a painful unworldly feeling, he knows: 'I experience a painful unworldly feeling'; when experiencing a neutral worldly feeling, he knows: 'I experience a neutral worldly feeling'; when experiencing a neutral unworldly feeling, he knows: 'I experience a neutral unworldly feeling'.[17]

Thus he dwells practising feeling-contemplation on feelings internally, or externally, or both internally and externally. He dwells contemplating origination-factors in feelings, or he dwells contemplating dissolution-factors in feelings, or he dwells contemplating both origination- and dissolution-factors in feelings.[18] Or his mindfulness that 'there are feelings' is established in him to the extent necessary for knowledge and mindfulness. Independent he dwells, clinging to nothing in the world.

Thus indeed, monks, a monk dwells practising feeling-contemplation on feelings.

III. The Contemplation of Mind

And how, monks, does a monk dwell practising mind-contemplation on the mind?[3]

Herein a monk knows the mind with lust, as with lust; the mind without lust as without lust; the mind with hate as with hate; the mind without hate as without hate; the mind with delusion as with delusion; the mind without delusion as without delusion; the shrunken state of mind as the shrunken state;[19] the distracted state of mind as the distracted state;[20] the developed state of mind as developed;[21] the undeveloped state of mind as undeveloped;[22] the surpassable mind as surpassable;[23] the unsurpassable mind as unsurpassable;[24] the concentrated mind as concentrated; the unconcentrated mind as unconcentrated; the freed mind as freed;[25] the mind not freed as not freed.

Thus he dwells practising mind-contemplation on the mind internally, or externally, or both internally and externally. He dwells contemplating origination-factors in the mind, or he dwells contemplating dissolution-factors in the mind, or he dwells contemplating both origination- and dissolution-factors in the mind.[26] Or his mindfulness that 'there is mind' is established in him to the extent necessary for knowledge and mindfulness. Independent he dwells, clinging to nothing in the world.

Thus indeed, monks, a monk dwells practising mind-contemplation on the mind.

IV. The Contemplation of Mind-Objects

And how, monks, does a monk dwell practising mind-object-contemplation on mind-objects?[3]

1. The Five Hindrances

Herein a monk dwells practising mind-object-contemplation on the mind-objects of the five hindrances.[27] And how does he practise mind-object-contemplation on the mind-objects of the five hindrances?

Herein, monks, when *sense-desire*[28] is present in him, the monk knows, 'There is sense-desire in me', or when sense-desire is absent, he knows, 'There is no sense-desire in me'. He knows how the arising of non-arisen sense-desire comes to be; he knows how the rejection of arisen sense-desire comes to be; and he knows how the non-arising in the future of the rejected sense-desire comes to be.

When *anger* is present in him, the monk knows, 'There is anger in me', or when anger is absent, he knows, 'There is no anger in me'. He knows how the arising of non-arisen anger comes to be; he knows how the rejection of arisen anger comes to be; and he knows how the non-arising in the future of the rejected anger comes to be.

When *sloth and torpor* are present in him, the monk knows, 'There is sloth and torpor in me', or when sloth and torpor are absent, he knows, 'There is no sloth and torpor in me'. He knows how the arising of the non-arisen sloth and torpor comes to be; he knows how the rejection of the arisen sloth and torpor comes to be; and he knows how the non-arising in the future of the rejected sloth and torpor comes to be.

When *agitation and worry* are present in him, the monk knows, 'There are agitation and worry in me', or when agitation and worry are absent, he knows, 'There are no agitation and worry in me'. He knows how the arising of the non-arisen agitation and worry comes to be; he knows how the rejection of the arisen agitation and worry comes to be; and he knows how the non-arising in the future of the rejected agitation and worry comes to be.

When *doubt* is present in him, the monk knows, 'There is doubt in me', or when doubt is absent, he knows, 'There is no doubt in me'. He knows how the arising of the non-arisen doubt comes to be; he knows how the rejection of the arisen doubt comes to be; and he knows how the non-arising in the future of the rejected doubt comes to be.[29]

Thus he dwells practising mind-object contemplation on mind-objects internally, or externally, or both internally and externally. He dwells contemplating origination-factors in mind-objects, or he dwells contemplating dissolution-factors in mind- objects, or he dwells contemplating both origination- and dissolution-factors in mind-objects.[29] Or his mindfulness that 'there are mind-objects' is established in him to the extent necessary for knowledge and mindfulness. Independent he dwells, clinging to nothing in the world.

Thus indeed, monks, a monk dwells practising mind-object-contemplation in the mind-objects of the five hindrances.

2. The Five Aggregates of Clinging

And again, monks, a monk dwells practising mind-object-contemplation on the mind-objects of the five Aggregates of Clinging. And how does he practise mind-object-contemplation on the mind-objects of the five Aggregates of Clinging?[30]

Herein a monk thinks: 'Thus is material form, thus the arising of material form, thus the passing away of material form; thus is feeling, thus the arising of feeling, thus the passing away of feeling; thus is perception, thus the arising of perception, thus the passing away of perception; thus are mental formations, thus the arising of mental formations, thus the passing away of mental formations; thus is consciousness, thus the arising of consciousness, thus the passing away of consciousness.'

Thus he dwells practising mind-object-contemplation on mind-objects internally, or externally, or both internally and externally. He dwells contemplating origination-factors in mind-objects, or he dwells contemplating dissolution factors in mind-objects, or he dwells contemplating both origination- and dissolution-factors in mind-objects.[31] Or his mindfulness that 'there are mind-objects' is established in him to the extent necessary for knowledge and mindfulness. Independent he dwells, clinging to nothing in the world.

Thus, indeed, monks, a monk dwells practising mind-object-contemplation on the mind-objects of the five Aggregates of Clinging.

3. The Six Internal and the Six External Sense-Bases

And again, monks, a monk dwells practising mind-object-contemplation on the mind-objects of the six internal and the six external sense-bases. And how does he practise mind-object- contemplation on the mind-objects of the six internal and the six external sense-bases?

Herein, monks, a monk knows the *eye*, knows *visible forms*, and knows the fetter[32] that arises dependent on both (the eye and forms); he knows how the arising of the non-arisen fetter comes to be; he knows how the rejection of the arisen fetter comes to be; and he knows how the non-arising in the future of the rejected fetter comes to be.

He knows the *ear* and *sounds* . . . the *nose* and *smells* . . . the *tongue* and *flavours* . . . the *body* and *tactual objects* . . . the *mind* and *mind-objects*, and knows the fetter arising dependent on both; he knows how the arising of the non-arisen fetter comes to be; he knows how the rejection of the arisen fetter comes to be; and he knows how the non-arising in the future of the rejected fetter comes to be.

Thus he dwells practising mind-object-contemplation on mind-objects internally, or externally, or both internally and externally. He dwells contemplating origination-factors in mind-objects, or he dwells contemplating dissolution-factors in mind-objects, or he dwells contemplating both origination- and dissolution-factors in mind-objects.[33] Or his mindfulness that 'there are mind-objects' is established in him to the extent necessary for knowledge and mindfulness. Independent he dwells, clinging to nothing in the world.

Thus indeed, monks, a monk dwells practising mind-object-contemplation on the mind-objects of the six internal and the six external sense-bases.

4. The Seven Factors of Enlightenment

And again, monks, a monk dwells practising mind-object-contemplation on the mind-objects of the seven factors of enlightenment. And how does he practise mind-object-contemplation on the mind-objects of the seven factors of enlightenment?[34]

Herein, monks, when the enlightenment-factor of *mindfulness* is present in him, a monk knows, 'The enlightenment-factor of mindfulness is in me'; or when the enlightenment-factor of mindfulness is absent, he knows, 'The enlightenment-factor of mindfulness is not in me'. And he knows how the arising of the non-arisen enlightenment-factor of mindfulness comes to be; and how perfection in the development of the arisen enlightenment-factor of mindfulness comes to be.

When the enlightenment-factor of *investigation of reality*[35]—*energy*—*rapture*—*tranquillity*—*concentration*—*equanimity* is present in him, a monk knows, 'The enlightenment-factor of equanimity is in me'; or when the enlightenment-factor of equanimity is absent he knows, 'The enlightenment-factor of equanimity is not in me'. And he knows how the arising of the non-arisen enlightenment factor of equanimity comes to be; and how perfection in the development of the arisen enlightenment-factor of equanimity comes to be.

Thus he dwells practising mind-object-contemplation internally, or externally, or both internally and externally. He dwells contemplating origination-factors in mind-objects, or he dwells contemplating dissolution-factors in mind-objects, or he dwells contemplating both origination- and dissolution-factors in mind-objects.[36] Or his mindfulness that 'there are mind-objects' is established in him to the extent necessary for knowledge and mindfulness. Independent he dwells, clinging to nothing in the world.

Thus indeed, monks, a monk dwells practising mind-object-contemplation on the mind-objects of the seven factors of enlightenment.

5. The Four Noble Truths

And again, monks, a monk dwells practising mind-object-contemplation on the mind-objects of the four Noble Truths. And how does he practise mind-object-contemplation on the mind-objects of the four Noble Truths?

Herein, monks, a monk knows according to reality, 'This is suffering'; he knows according to reality, 'This is the origin of suffering'; he knows according to reality, 'This is the cessation of suffering'; he knows according to reality, 'This is the path leading to the cessation of suffering'.

And what, monks, is the *Noble Truth of Suffering?*

Birth is suffering; old age is suffering; death is suffering; sorrow, lamentation, pain, grief and despair are suffering; not to get what one wishes, is suffering; in short, the five Aggregates of Clinging are suffering.

What, now, is birth? The birth of beings belonging to this or that order of beings, their being born, their origination, their conception, their springing into existence, the manifestation of the Aggregates, the acquisition of the sense-bases—this is called birth.

And what is old age? Old age is the ageing of beings belonging to this or that order of beings, their getting frail, decrepit, grey and wrinkled; the failing of their vital force, the wearing out of their sense faculties—this is called old age.

And what is death? The departing and vanishing of beings out of this or that order of beings, their destruction, disappearance, death, the completion of their life period, dissolution of the Aggregates, the discarding of the body—this is called death.

And what is sorrow? The sorrow arising through this or that loss or misfortune which one encounters, the sorrowing, the sorrowful state of mind, the inward sorrow, inward woe—this is called sorrow.

And what is lamentation? Whatsoever, through this or that loss or misfortune which one encounters, is wail and lament, wailing and lamenting, the state of wail and lamentation—this is called lamentation.

And what is pain? The bodily pain and bodily unpleasantness, the painful and unpleasant feeling produced by bodily contact—this is called pain.

And what is grief? The mental pain and mental unpleasantness, the painful and unpleasant feeling produced by mental contact—this is called grief.

And what is despair? Distress and despair arising through this or that loss or misfortune which one encounters, the state of distress and desperation—this is called despair.

And what is the 'Suffering of not getting what one wishes'? In beings subject to birth the wish arises: 'O, that we were not subject to birth! O, that no new birth were before us!' And in beings subject to old age, disease, death, sorrow, lamentation, pain, grief and despair, the wish arises: 'O, that we were not subject to these things! O, that these things were not before us!' But this cannot be got by mere wishing; and not to get what one wishes, is suffering.

And what is (the meaning of the statement) 'In short, the five Aggregates of Clinging'? They are the Aggregates of material form, feeling, perception, mental formations and consciousness. This is what is called 'in short, the five Aggregates of Clinging are suffering'.

This, monks, is the Noble Truth of Suffering.

And what, monks, is the *Noble Truth of the Origin of Suffering?*

It is that craving which gives rise to fresh rebirth, and, bound up with pleasure and lust, finds ever fresh delight, now here, now there—to wit, the Sensual Craving, the Craving for (Eternal) Existence and the Craving for Non-Existence.

But where does this craving arise and take root? Wherever in the world there are delightful and pleasurable things, there this craving arises and takes root.

Eye, ear, nose, tongue, body and mind, are delightful and pleasurable: there this craving arises and takes root.

Visual forms, sounds, smells, tastes, bodily impressions and mind-objects, are delightful and pleasurable: there this craving arises and takes root.

Eye-consciousness, ear-consciousness, nose-consciousness, tongue-consciousness, body-consciousness, and mind-consciousness . . . (the corresponding sixfold) contact—the feeling born of that sixfold contact—the sixfold will (for visual forms, etc.)—the sixfold craving—the sixfold thought-conception (concerning visual forms, etc.)—the sixfold discursive thought: these are delightful and pleasurable: there this craving arises and takes root.

This, monks, is the Noble Truth of the Origin of Suffering.[37]

And what, monks, is the *Noble Truth of the Cessation of Suffering?*

It is the complete fading away and extinction of this very craving, its forsaking and giving up, the liberation and detachment from it.

But where may this craving be abandoned, where may it be extinguished?

Wherever in the world there are delightful and pleasurable things, there this craving may be abandoned, there it may be extinguished.

Eye, ear, nose, tongue, body and mind, are delightful and pleasurable: there this craving may be abandoned, there it may be extinguished.

Visual forms, sounds, smells, tastes, bodily impressions and mind-objects, there this craving may be abandoned, there it may be extinguished.

Eye-consciousness, ear-consciousness, nose-consciousness, tongue-consciousness, body-consciousness and mind-consciousness . . . (the corresponding sixfold) contact—the feeling born of that sixfold contact—the sixfold will—the sixfold craving— the sixfold thought-conception—the sixfold discursive thought: these are delightful and pleasurable; there this craving may be abandoned, there it may be extinguished.

This, monks, is the Noble Truth of the Cessation of Suffering.[38]

And what, monks, is the *Noble Truth of the Path leading to the Cessation of Suffering*?

It is that Noble Eightfold Path, namely, Right Understanding, Right Thought, Right Speech, Right Action, Right Livelihood, Right Effort, Right Mindfulness, Right Concentration.

And what, monks, is Right Understanding? To understand suffering, to understand the origin of suffering, to understand the cessation of suffering, to understand the path leading to the cessation of suffering: this is Right Understanding.

And what is Right Thought? Thoughts free from lust, thoughts free from ill-will, thoughts free from cruelty: this is Right Thought.

And what is Right Speech? To abstain from lying, from tale-bearing, from harsh speech, from vain talk: this is Right Speech.

And what is Right Action? To abstain from killing, from taking what is not given, from adultery: this is Right Action.

And what is Right Livelihood? When the noble disciple, avoiding a wrong way of livelihood, gets his livelihood by a right way of living: this is Right Livelihood.

And what is Right Effort? Herein a monk rouses his will to avoid the arising of evil, unsalutary states, he makes effort, stirs up his energy, applies his mind to it and strives. For overcoming the evil, unsalutary states that have arisen, he rouses his will, makes effort, stirs up his energy, applies his mind to it and strives. For arousing of salutary states that have not yet arisen, he rouses his will, makes effort, stirs up his energy, applies his mind to it and strives. For maintaining the salutary states that have arisen, for not neglecting them but bringing them to growth, full maturity and perfect development, he rouses his will, makes effort, stirs up his energy, applies his mind to it and strives: this is Right Effort.

And what is Right Mindfulness? Herein a monk dwells practising body-contemplation on the body—practising feeling-contemplation on feelings—practising mind-contemplation on the mind—practising mind-object-contemplation on mind-objects, ardent, clearly comprehending and mindful, having overcome covetousness and grief concerning the world: this is Right Mindfulness.

And what is Right Concentration? Herein a monk detached from sensual objects, detached from unsalutary things, enters into the *first absorption,* born of detachment, accompanied by thought-conception and discursive thought, and filled with rapture and joy. After the subsiding of thought-conception and discursive thought, and by gaining inner tranquillity and oneness of mind, he enters into a state free from thought-conception and discursive thought, the *second absorption,* which is born of Concentration and filled with rapture and joy. After the fading away of rapture, he dwells in equanimity, mindful, clearly aware; and he experiences in his person that feeling of which noble ones say 'Happy is the man of equanimity and mindfulness'; thus he enters the *third absorption.* After the giving up of pleasure and pain, and through the disappearance of previous joy and grief, he enters into a state beyond pleasure and pain, into the *fourth absorption,* which is purified by equanimity and mindfulness. This is Right Concentration.

This, monks, is the Noble Truth of the Path leading to the Cessation of Suffering.

Thus he dwells practising mind-object-contemplation on mind-objects internally, or externally, or both internally and externally. He dwells contemplating origination-factors in mind-objects, or he dwells contemplating dissolution-factors in mind-objects, or he dwells contemplating both origination- and dissolution-factors in mind-objects.[39] Or his mindfulness that 'there are mind-objects' is established in him to the extent necessary for knowledge and mindfulness. Independent he dwells, clinging to nothing in the world.

Thus indeed, monks, a monk dwells practising mind-object contemplation on the mind-objects of the four Noble Truths.

Verily, monks, whosoever practises these four Foundations of Mindfulness in this manner for seven years, one of two results may be expected in him: Highest Knowledge[40] here and now, or, if there be yet a remainder of clinging, the state of non-return.[41]

Let alone seven years, monks. Should any person practise these four Foundations of Mindfulness in this manner for six years . . . five years . . . four years . . . three years . . . two years . . . for one year, then one of two results may be expected in him: Highest Knowledge here and now, or, if there be yet a remainder of clinging, the state of non-return.

Let alone one year, monks. Should any person practise these four Foundations of Mindfulness in this manner for seven months . . . six months . . . five months . . . four months . . . three months . . . two months . . . a month . . . for half-a-month, then one of two results may be expected in him: Highest Knowledge here and now, or, if there be yet a remainder of clinging, the state of non-return.

Let alone half-a-month, monks. Should any person practise these four Foundations of Mindfulness in this manner for seven days, one of two results may be expected in him: Highest Knowledge here and now, or, if there be yet a remainder of clinging, the state of non-return.

Because of this it was said: 'This is the sole way, monks, for the purification of beings, for the overcoming of sorrow and lamentation, for the destroying of pain and grief, for reaching the right path, for the realization of Nibbana, namely the four Foundations of Mindfulness.'

Thus spoke the Blessed One. Glad in heart, the monks welcomed the words of the Blessed One.

Notes

1. *Monks* (Pali: *bhikkhave*; Sing.: *bhikkhu*). A bhikkhu is one who has received the Higher Ordination (*upasampadā*) in a Buddhist monastic order (*sangha*) that is based on the acceptance of the Code of Discipline (*vinaya*). In this context, however, the Commentary says: '*Bhikkhu* is given here as an example for those dedicated to the practice of the Teaching. . . . Whosoever undertakes that practice . . . is here comprised under the term *bhikkhu*.'

2. The repetition in the phrases 'practising body-contemplation on the body', 'feeling-contemplation on feelings', etc., is meant to impress upon the meditator the importance of remaining aware whether, in the sustained attention directed upon a single chosen subject, one is still keeping to it, and has not strayed into the field of another Contemplation. For instance, when contemplating any bodily process, a meditator may unwittingly be side-tracked into a consideration of his *feelings* connected with that bodily process. He should then be clearly aware that he has left his original subject, and is engaged in the Contemplation of Feeling. See p. 21.

3. In Part One of this book, the Pali terms for 'mind' (*citta*) and 'mind-objects' (*dhammā*) have been given a somewhat freer rendering by 'state of mind' and 'mental contents' respectively, in order to bring out their significance more clearly.

4. Literally, 'setting up mindfulness in front'.

5. For an explanation of these exercises see p. 116.

6. *Internally:* contemplating his own breathing; *externally,* contemplating another's breathing; *internally and externally:* contemplating his own and another's breathing alternately, with uninterrupted attention. See p. 2.

7. The origination-factors (*samudaya-dhammā*), that is the conditions of the origination of the breath-body, are: the body in its entirety, the nasal apertures and mind.

8. The dissolution-factors (*vaya-dhammā*) are: the dissolution of the body and the nasal apertures, and the ceasing of mental activity.

9. The contemplation of both, alternately.

10. That is to say; only bodily processes exist, without a soul, self or abiding substance. The corresponding phrase in the following Contemplations should be understood accordingly.

11. *Knowledge* is here the fourfold Clear Comprehension (see p. 37); *Mindfulness* is Bare Attention. The meditator should endeavour to keep within the domain and purpose proper to this method of practice. He should not be side-tracked by reflections, emotions, or mental images evoked by the Contemplations; on arising they should be briefly noticed and dismissed.

12. Independent of craving and wrong views.

13. All Contemplations of the Body, excepting that of Breathing, have as factors of origination: ignorance, craving, kamma, food, and the general characteristic of originating; and as factors of dissolution: disappearance of ignorance, craving, kamma, food, and the general characteristic of dissolving.

14. See p. 37.

15. With the later addition of 'brain in the skull', these 32 parts of the body form a frequent subject of meditation in Buddhist countries. For details of the meditative practice. See *The Path of Purification,* Ch. VIII, 8.

16 . These 'elements' (*dhātu*) are the primary qualities of matter, explained by Buddhist tradition as solidity (earth), adhesion (water), caloricity (fire) and motion (wind or air). See *The Path of Purification,* Ch. XI.

17. An explanation of the worldly (*sāmisa*) and unworldly (*nirāmisa*) types of the three feelings is given in the 137th Discourse of the Majjhima-Nikaya (Middle Length Sayings). There the worldly feelings are called 'bound up with the home life'; and the unworldly feelings 'bound up with renunciation'. Unworldly pleasant feeling is, for instance, the happiness resulting from meditation and from the insight into the impermanency of existence. Unworldly painful feeling is, for instance, the painful awareness of one's imperfections and of one's tardy progress on the path of deliverance. Unworldly neutral feeling is the equanimity acquired by insight.

18. The origination-factors for feeling are: ignorance, craving, kamma, sense-impression (*phassa*) and the general characteristic of originating; the dissolution-factors are: 'the disappearance of the former four, and the general characteristic of dissolving'.

19. This refers to rigidity of mind and indolence; included are also states like lethargy, slowness of response, hesitation, inner tension due to repression, etc.

20. This refers to a restless state of mind, and includes agitation, flightiness, desire for change, etc.

21. The consciousness of the meditative Absorptions of the fine-material and immaterial sphere (*rūpa*-and *arūpa-jhāna*).

22. The ordinary consciousness of the sensuous state of existence.

23. The consciousness of the sensuous state of existence, having other mental states superior to it.

24. The consciousness of the fine-material and immaterial spheres, having no mundane states superior to it.

25. Temporarily freed from the defilements either through the meditative development of Insight freeing from single evil states by force of their opposites; or through the Absorptions (*jhānas*).

26. For Mind, or Consciousness, the origination-factors are: ignorance, craving, kamma, body-and-mind (*nāma-rūpa*), and the general characteristic of originating; the dissolution-factors are: the disappearance of the former four, and the general characteristic of dissolving.

27. These five Hindrances (*nīvaraṇa*) are the chief obstructions to the development of mind. They must be temporarily suspended for the attainment of the Absorptions and also of the Access Concentration (*upacāra-samādhi*) required for the full development of Insight. See *The Five Mental Hindrances,* by Nyanaponika Thera (Kandy 1961, Buddhist Publication Society).

28. This refers to the desire for any of the five sense-objects.

29. The factors of origination are here the conditions productive of the Hindrances, such as wrong reflection on attractive objects, etc.; the dissolution-factors are those conditions which remove the Hindrances, e.g. right reflection.

30. Pali: *upādāna-kkhandha.* These five Groups constitute the so-called personality. By making them objects of clinging (*upādāna*), existence in form of repeated births and deaths is perpetuated.

31. The origination- and dissolution-factors for the Group of Material Form are the same as those for the bodily posture (Note 13); for Feeling, Perception and Mental Formations, as in Note 18; for Consciousness, as in Note 26.

32. The ten principal Fetters (*saṁyojana*) as given in the Discourse Collections (Sutta-Piṭaka) are: 1. personality belief, 2. scepticism, 3. belief in purification through external observances, rules and rites, 4. sensual lust, 5. ill-will, 6. craving for fine-material existence, 7. craving for immaterial existence, 8. conceit, 9. restlessness, 10. ignorance. These ten Fetters of the mind may arise through uncontrolled perception by any of the six senses. Their 'non-arising in the future' comes to be by attaining to the four Stages of Sanctity, as Stream-entry (*Sotāpatti*), etc. See *The Word of the Buddha,* by Nyanatiloka (Kandy 1959, Buddhist Publication Society), pp. 35ff.—The explanation given in the Commentary to the Discourse, refers to a slightly different list of Fetters used in the Abhidhamma, the Philosophical Collection of the Buddhist Canon.

33. Origination-factors of the ten physical sense-bases are ignorance, craving, kamma, food, and the general characteristic of originating; dissolution-factors: the general characteristic of dissolving, and the disappearance of ignorance, etc. The

origination- and dissolution-factors of the mind-base are the same as those of consciousness (see Note 26); the factors of the mind-object base are the same as those of feeling (see Note 18).

34. For a detailed explanation see *The Seven Factors of Enlightenment,* by Piyadassi Thera (Kandy, Buddhist Publication Society).

35. *Dhamma-vicaya.* According to the commentators, the term *dhamma* does not signify, in this context, the Buddha's teaching but refers to the mental and physical phenomena (*nāma-* and *rūpa-dhammā*) as presented to the meditator's mind, by the first enlightenment-factor 'Mindfulness'.

36. Just the conditions conducive to the origination and dissolutions of the Factors of Enlightenment comprise the origination- and dissolution-factors here.

37. Here the Truth of Suffering is explained, not in the customary wording but in terms of the actual Satipaṭṭhāna practice. Impressively and repeatedly, mindfulness lays bare the roots of suffering when encountering the diverse manifestations of craving in the sixfold sense-experience and in the mental functions connected and concerned with that experience. This part of the Discourse may also be taken as an illustration to parts of the section on the Six Sense-bases, and in particular, of the statement: 'He knows how the arising of the non-arisen fetter comes to be'. This text further exemplifies the repeated statement 'He contemplates origination-factors. . . .'

38. The Third Truth is here likewise explained in terms of the actual observation how craving ceases in the several instances mentioned. Such observations can be made when

the origination of craving has been mindfully noticed (see above). This act of mindful noticing will necessarily stop the continued flow of craving; because detached observation and craving cannot go together. This section illustrates the statement 'He knows how the rejection of the arisen fetter comes to be'. Repeated awareness of craving's cessation in individual instances, will give a foretaste of the Final Cessation or Nibbāna, and that experience will strengthen the conviction that this aim is capable of achievement.

39. The origination- and dissolution-factors of the Truths should be understood as the arising and passing away of Suffering, or Craving; and as the factors productive of the development of the Path, or inhibiting it. The Truth of Cessation is not to be included in this contemplation since Nibbāna has neither origination nor dissolution.

40. *Aññā,* i.e. the knowledge of final emancipation, or Sainthood (*arahatta*).

41. That is, the non-returning to the world of sense-existence. This is the last stage before the attainment of the final goal of Sainthood.

PART THREE

FLOWERS OF DELIVERANCE

An Anthology of Texts Dealing with Right Mindfulness, Translated from the Pali and Sanskrit with Notes

". . . if with such flowers of deliverance he is decked, this stainless one will never be reborn."

—Theragāthā v. 100 (Text 20)

The sources of the texts translated here are indicated in a list appearing at the end of this Part Three. The list follows the numbering of the texts.

From the Pali Canon

Nature and Aim of Satipaṭṭhāna

1. The Sole Way

Once the Enlightened One dwelt at Uruvela, on the bank of the Nerañjara river, under the Fig Tree of the Goat-herds. And while he thus dwelt alone and secluded, the following thought arose in him:

'This is the sole way for the purification of beings, for the overcoming of sorrow and lamentation, for the destroying of pain and grief, for reaching the right path, for the realization of Nibbāna, namely the four Foundations of Mindfulness.

'What are the four? Herein a monk may dwell practising body-contemplation on the body . . . practising feeling-contemplation on feelings . . . practising mind-contemplation on mind . . . practising mind-object contemplation on mind-objects, ardent, clearly comprehending and mindful, having overcome covetousness and grief concerning the world.[5]

And Brahma Sahampati cognized in his mind the thoughts of the Exalted One, and just as a strong man may stretch his bent arm or bend his stretched arm, so quickly departed he from the Brahma world and appeared before the Exalted One. Arranging his upper garment over one shoulder, he saluted the Exalted One with folded hands and addressed him thus:

'So it is, Exalted One! So it is, Blessed One! This is the sole way for the purification of beings . . . namely the four Foundations of Mindfulness. . . .'

Thus spoke Brahma Sahampati. And after these words he further said:

> 'He sees the only way that ends rebirth,
> Compassion-moved he knows the noble path
> By which before the Sorrow's Sea was crossed,
> Will be in future, and is crossed just now.'

According to this text, the Buddha's first conception of the liberating Way of Mindfulness dates back to the time immediately after his Englightenment. According to an early scripture, the Mahā Vagga *of the* Vinaya-Piṭaka *(the Code of Discipline), the Buddha spent the first seven weeks after his Enlightenment in the close vicinity of the Bodhi Tree. In the fifth and seventh week he stayed under a tree known as the Goat-herds' Fig Tree* (ajapāla-nigrodha) *because herdsmen used to sit under it. It is this place and time to which the words of the above text refer.*

2. Be Your Own Refuge

The last Season of the Rains before the Buddha's decease, was spent by him in a little village called Beluva. There a serious illness befell him. But moved by the wish that the monks living in other places should have one last opportunity of seeing him before his death, he suppressed his illness by an effort of will. He rose from his sick bed and sat down at a shady place. There his faithful attendant for many years, the venerable Ānanda, approached him and gave vent to his joy at the Master's recovery, saying that he had consoled himself with the thought that the Master would not pass away before he had given instruction concerning the Community of Monks. But the Buddha said: 'What is it, Ānanda, that the Community of Monks expects from me? The teaching, Ānanda, has been proclaimed by me without making any distinction between esoteric and exoteric. The Perfect One knows not the closed fist of secretive teachers in regard to his teaching. Who thinks, "I shall lead the Community of Monks, and it should follow me," it is such a one who may wish to give some last instructions concerning the Community of Monks.'

After a few more words, he made that solemn and weighty utterance which, in the context briefly sketched here, carries a particular emphasis and significance:

Be your own island, Ānanda, be your own refuge! Do not take any other refuge! Let the Teaching be your island, let the Teaching be your refuge; do not take any other refuge!

'And how, Ānanda, does a monk take himself as an island, himself as refuge, as without any other refuge? How is the Teaching his island and refuge, and nothing else?

'Herein a monk dwells practising body-contemplation on the body . . . feeling-contemplation on feelings . . . mind-contemplation on the mind . . . mind-object contemplation on mind-objects, ardent, clearly comprehending and mindful, having overcome covetousness and grief concerning the world.

'In that way, Ānanda, will a monk be his own island and refuge, without any other; in that way will he have the Teaching as his island and refuge, and nothing else.

'And all those, Ānanda, who either now or after my death, will dwell being their own island, their own refuge, without any other; having the Teaching as island and refuge, and nothing else—it is they among my bhikkhus who will reach the utmost height if they are willing to train themselves.'

According to tradition, this episode occurred about ten months before the passing away of the Buddha. Within these ten months also fell the death of his two chief disciples, Sāriputta and Mahā-Moggallāna. When the death of Sāriputta was reported to the Buddha, he again gave the above exhortation.

Thus the texts 1 and 2 show that Satipaṭṭhāna stood at the beginning and end of the Buddha's career.

3. Continuance of the Teaching

Once the venerable Ānanda and the venerable Bhadda lived at Pataliputta, in the Cock Monastery. In the evening, after the venerable Bhadda had risen from his seclusion, he betook himself to the venerable Ānanda, and after he had exchanged friendly and polite greetings, he spoke to him:

'What, brother Ānanda, is the cause, what is the reason if, after the decease of the Perfect One, the Good Law does not continue for long? And what, brother Ānanda, is the cause, what is the reason if, after the decease of the Perfect One, the Good Law continues for long?'

—'Well said, brother Bhadda, well said! Pleasing is your wisdom, pleasing your insight, excellent is your question!

'If, brother, the four Foundations of Mindfulness are not cultivated and not practised regularly, then the Good Law will not continue for long after the decease of the Perfect One. But, brother, if the four Foundations of Mindfulness are cultivated and practised regularly, then the Good Law will continue for long after the decease of the Perfect One.'

4. A Great Man

At Sāvatthi, the venerable Sāriputta betook himself to the Exalted One, saluted him respectfully and sat down at one side. Thus seated he addressed the Exalted One as follows:

' "A great man, a great man"—thus people speak. In how far, Lord, is a man great?'

—'With a liberated mind, Sāriputta, I declare, is one a great man. With a mind not liberated is he not a great man.

'How then, Sāriputta, is the mind liberated? In that case, Sāriputta, a monk dwells practising body-contemplation on the body . . . feeling-contemplation on feelings . . . mind-contemplation on the mind . . . mind-object on mind-objects, ardent, clearly comprehending and mindful, having overcome covetousness and grief concerning the world.

'Thus, Sāriputta, is the mind liberated. And with a liberated mind, I declare, is one a great man. But with a mind not liberated is he not a great man.'

5. Marvellous and Wonderful

You may, Ānanda, also keep in mind this marvellous and wonderful quality of the Perfect One: knowingly arise feelings in the Perfect One, knowingly they continue, knowingly they cease; knowingly arise perceptions in the Perfect One, knowingly they continue, knowingly they cease; knowingly arise thoughts in the Perfect One, knowingly they continue, knowingly they cease. This, Ānanda, you may also keep in mind as a marvellous and wonderful quality of the Perfect One.

6. The Resort

'Five sense faculties, O Brahmin, have different domains, different fields, and they do not take part in the domain and field of each other. What five?

'The sense faculties of seeing, hearing, smelling, tasting and of touch. For these five sense faculties having different domains and different fields, not partaking in the domains and fields of each other, for them, O Brahmin, mind is the resort,[1] and the mind partakes in their field.'

—'But for the mind, venerable Gotama, what is the resort?'

—'For the mind, Brahmin, mindfulness is the resort.'

—'And for mindfulness, venerable Gotama, what is the resort?'

—'For mindfulness, Brahmin, deliverance is the resort.'

—'For deliverance, venerable Gotama, what is the resort?'

—'For deliverance, Brahmin, Nibbāna is the resort.'

—'But for Nibbāna, venerable Gotama, what is the resort?'

—'You have now overstepped the range of questioning, Brahmin. The term of your questioning cannot be conceived. For it is for entering into Nibbāna that the Holy Life is being lived; it has Nibbāna as its goal, Nibbāna as its end.'

7. The Practice for All

Once the Exalted One dwelt among the Kosala people, in Sālā, a village of the Brahmins. There he addressed the monks as follows: 'Those who are new monks, not long gone forth, who have come but recently to this teaching and discipline, they should be encouraged, introduced to and established in the cultivation of the four Foundations of Mindfulness. Which four?

'Come, O brethren, practise body-contemplation on the body, ardent and clearly comprehending, single-minded, with a serene heart and a collected and concentrated mind, for knowing the body as it truly is.

'Practise feeling-contemplation on feelings . . . for knowing feelings as they truly are; practise mind-contemplation on the mind . . . for knowing the mind as it truly is; practise mind-object contemplation on mind-objects, ardent and clearly comprehending, single-minded, with a serene heart and a collected and concentrated mind, for knowing mind-objects as they truly are.

'Also those monks who are in the Higher Training[2] but have not yet attained to the goal and strive after the Highest Peace—they, too, dwell ardent and clearly comprehending, single minded, with a serene heart and a concentrated and collected mind, practising body-contemplation on the body, for the full understanding of the body; practising feeling-contemplation of feelings, for the full understanding of feelings; practising mind-contemplation on the mind, for the full understanding of the mind; practising mind-object contemplation on mind-objects, for the full understanding[3] of mind-objects.

'Also those monks who are Holy Ones (Arahats), taint-free; who have lived the Holy Life to the end, have accomplished their task, laid down the burden, attained to the goal, destroyed the fetters of existence, and are liberated in perfect wisdom—they, too, dwelt ardent and clearly comprehending, single-minded, with a serene heart and a concentrated and collected mind, practising body-contemplation on the body, being unfettered by the body; practising feeling-contemplation on feelings, being unfettered by the feelings; practising mind-contemplation on the mind, being unfettered by the mind; practising mind-object contemplation on mind-objects, being unfettered by the mind-objects.

'And also those who are new monks, not long gone forth, who have come but recently to this teaching and discipline—they, too, should be encouraged, introduced to and established in the cultivation of the four Foundations of Mindfulness.'

8. Satipaṭṭhāna, the Standard of Attainment

Once the venerable Sariputta spoke to the venerable Anuruddha: 'People speak of *one in Higher Training*,[2] brother Anuruddha. In how far is one engaged in Higher Training?'

—'With partial development of the four Foundations of Mindfulness, brother, is one in Higher Training.'

'People speak of *one beyond Training*;[4] brother Anuruddha. In how far has one gone Beyond Training?'

—'With perfect development of the four Foundations of Mindfulness, brother, has one gone Beyond Training.'

9. A Weighty Word

Once the venerable Anuruddha and the venerable Sāriputta lived near Vesalī, at Ambapāli's grove. In the evening, after the venerable Sāriputta had risen from his seclusion, he betook himself to the venerable Anuruddha. After he had exchanged with him friendly and polite greetings, he spoke to him thus:

'Radiant are your features, brother Anuruddha; bright and pure of complexion is your face. What might be the mind's abode in which the venerable Anuruddha often dwells?'

—'With my mind firmly established in the four Foundations of Mindfulness, do I now often dwell, brother.

'A monk, brother, who is an Arahat, taint-free; who has lived the Holy Life to the end, has completed his task, laid down the burden, attained to the goal, destroyed the fetters of existence, and is liberated in perfect wisdom—he frequently dwells with a mind firmly established in the four Foundations of Mindfulness.'

—'A gain is it for us, brother, a great gain that we have heard that weighty word from the mouth of the venerable Anuruddha.'

10. Unflinching

Once the venerable Anuruddha lived at Sāvatthi, in the house near the Salalā Tree. There he addressed the monks as follows:

'This river here, the Ganges, brethren, flows to the East, is bent toward the East, directed toward the East. Now suppose a large group of people approaches, carrying mammoties and baskets, and they say: "We shall make this river, the Ganges, flow to the West, bend it toward the West, direct it toward the West." What do you think, brethren: can this large group of people actually make the Ganges flow toward the West, bend it toward the West, direct it toward the West?'

—'Verily not, brother.'

—'And why not?'

—'The Ganges, to be sure, brother, flows to the East, is bent toward the East, is directed toward the East. Impossible it is to make it flow to the West, to bend and direct it toward the West, whatever fatigue and pain this large group of people might undergo'

—'Similarly, brethren: if a monk who has cultivated and frequently practised the four Foundations of Mindfulness, is surrounded by kings and ministers, by his friends, acquaintances and relatives and, offering treasure, they entreat him: "Come, my dear man! What do you want with these yellow robes? Why do you go about with a shaven head? Come, return to the lay life where you may enjoy your treasure and do good deeds!" But, brethren, that a monk who has cultivated and frequently practised the four Foundations of Mindfulness, should give up the training and return to a lower state, this is not possible. And why not? There is no possibility that a mind turned for a long time toward detachment, bent toward detachment, directed toward detachment, should return to a lower state.'

11. The Deathless

There are four Foundations of Mindfulness, monks. Which are the four?

Herein a monk practises body-contemplation on the body, ardent, clearly comprehending and mindful, having overcome covetousness and grief concerning the world. While he thus practises body-contemplation on the body, any desire for the body is abandoned in him. Through the abandonment of desire the Deathless is realized.

He practises feeling-contemplation on feelings, ardent, clearly comprehending and mindful, having overcome covetousness and grief concerning the world. While he thus practises feeling-con- templation on feelings, any desire for feelings is abandoned in him. Through the abandonment of desire the Deathless is realized.

He practises mind-contemplation on the mind, ardent, clearly comprehending and mindful, having overcome covetousness and grief concerning the world. While he thus practises mind-contemplation on the mind, any desire for the mind is abandoned in him. Through the abandonment of desire the Deathless is realized.

He practises mind-object contemplation on mind-objects, ardent, clearly comprehending and mindful, having overcome covetousness and grief concerning the world. While he thus practises mind-object contemplation on mind-objects, any desire for mind-objects is abandoned. Through the abandonment of desire the Deathless is realized.

12. Taints

There are three taints,[5] O monks: the taint of sensuality, the taint of desire for renewed existence, and the taint of ignorance.

For eliminating these three taints, O monks, the four Foundations of Mindfulness should be cultivated.

13. Past and Future

For the giving up and overcoming of those theories which are concerned with past and future, the four Foundations of Mindfulness should be cultivated, O monks.

14. For One's Own Sake

For one's own sake, monks, vigilant mindfulness should be made the mind's guard and this for four reasons:

'May my mind not harbour lust for anything inducing lust!' —for this reason vigilant mindfulness should be made the mind's guard, for one's own sake.

'May my mind not harbour hate toward anything inducing hate!'—for this reason vigilant mindfulness should be made the mind's guard, for one's own sake.

'May my mind not harbour delusion concerning anything inducing delusion!'—for this reason vigilant mindfulness should be made the mind's guard, for one's own sake.

'May my mind not be infatuated by anything inducing infatuation!'—for this reason vigilant mindfulness should be made the mind's guard, for one's own sake.

When now, monks, a monk's mind does not harbour lust for lust-inducing things, because he is free from lust; when his mind does not harbour hate toward hate-inducing things, because he is free from hate; when his mind does not harbour delusion concerning anything inducing delusion, because he is free from delusion; when his mind is not infatuated by anything inducing infatuation, because he is free from infatuation—then such a monk will not waver, shake or tremble, he will not succumb to fear, nor will he adopt the views of other recluses.[6]

15. Right Protection

Once the Blessed One dwelt in the Sumbha country, in a town of the Sumbha people, called Sedaka. There he addressed the monks as follows:

'Long ago there lived an acrobat who worked with a bamboo pole. Putting up his bamboo pole, he spoke to his girl-apprentice Medakathalikā: "Come, dear Medakathalikā, climb the pole and stand on my shoulders!"—"Yes, master" said she and did as told. And the Acrobat said: "Now, dear Medakathalikā, protect me well, and I shall protect you. Thus watching over each other, protecting each other, we shall show our skill, make for us a living, and shall safely get down from the bamboo pole."

'But Medakathalikā, the apprentice, said: "Not so, Master! You, O master, should protect yourself; and I, too, shall protect myself. So self-guarded, self-protected we shall show our skill, earn for us a living, and shall safely get down from the bamboo pole."

'This is the right way' said the Blessed One and spoke further as follows:

'It is just as the apprentice said: "I shall protect myself," in that way the Foundations of Mindfulness should be practised. "I shall protect others," in that way the Foundations of Mindfulness should be practised. Protecting oneself one protects others; protecting others one protects oneself.

'And how does one, in protecting oneself, protect others? By the repeated and frequent practice of meditation.[7]

'And how does one, in protecting others, protect oneself? By patience and forbearance, by a non-violent and harmless life, by loving-kindness and compassion.[8]

'"I shall protect myself," in that way the Foundations of Mindfulness should be practised. "I shall protect others," in that way the Foundations of Mindfulness should be practised. Protecting oneself, one protects others; protecting others, one protects oneself.'[9]

16. The Sick Householder

The householder Sirivaḍḍha of Rājagaha, a follower of the Teaching, was stricken by a grave disease, and he sent a request to the venerable Ānanda to come and see him. Following that request, the venerable Ānanda betook himself to the sick man's house and spoke to Sirivaḍḍha, the householder, as follows:

'Is your condition tolerable, householder, can you bear up? Are the pains lessening and not increasing? Do you feel an improvement, not a worsening?'

—'No, Lord, my condition is not tolerable; it is hard to bear. The pains increase and do not lessen; a deterioration may be expected, not an improvement.'

—'Hence, householder, you should train yourself thus: "I will practise body-contemplation on the body . . . feeling contemplation on feelings . . . mind-object contemplation on mind-objects, ardent, clearly comprehending and mindful, having overcome covetousness and grief concerning the world." '

—'These four Foundations of Mindfulness, Lord, taught by the Exalted One, can be found with me, and I live in accordance with these teachings: because I dwell, O Lord, practising body-contemplation on the body . . . mind-object contemplation on mind-objects, ardent. . . .

'And concerning those five lower fetters,[10] explained by the Exalted One, I do not see a single one of them, O Lord, which I have not discarded.'

—'A gain is this for you, householder, a great gain! The fruition of the state of Non-returning,[11] householder, has been declared by you.'

17. A Sick Monk

Once, while the venerable Anuruddha lived near Sāvatthi, he fell ill and was in pain, suffering from a grave disease. On that occasion, several monks went to the venerable Anuruddha and spoke to him thus:

'What might be the state of mind dwelling in which painful bodily sensations are unable to perturb the mind of the venerable Anuruddha?'

—'It is a state of mind, brethren, that is firmly grounded in the four Foundations of Mindfulness; and due to that, painful bodily sensations cannot perturb my mind.'

18. The Thera Uttiya

When illness came, my mindfulness arose:

'Illness has called: there is no time for indolence!'

19. From Constraint to Freedom

E'en in constraints of life the teaching can be found
That to Nibbāna leads, the end of ill:
It's found by those who win to mindfulness;

Their hearts attain to perfect concentration.

20. Flowers of Deliverance

Full trained and firm in right endeavour,
With mindfulness one's very own domain—
If with such flowers of deliverance one is decked,
This stainless one will never be reborn.

21. Awareness of the Present

Do not hark back to things that passed,
And for the future cherish not fond hopes:
The past was left behind by thee,
The future state has not yet come.

But who with vision clear can see[12]
The present which is here and now,
Such wise one should aspire to win
What never can be lost nor shaken.[13]

22. Accumulations

'A heap of unwholesomeness,' speaking thus of the five Hindrances one will speak of them correctly. For, indeed, they are entire an accumulation of unwholesomeness. Which are the five? Sense desire, ill will, sloth and torpor, restlessness and worry, sceptical doubt.

'A heap of wholesomeness,' speaking thus of the four Foundations of Mindfulness one will speak of them correctly. For, indeed, they are entire an accumulation of wholesomeness.

23. The Gift of Friendship

Those for whom you have sympathy, O monks, those who deem it fit to listen to you—friends and companions, kinsmen and relatives—they should be encouraged, introduced to and established in the four Foundations of Mindfulness.

24. All-Helpful

Mindfulness, I declare, O monks, is helpful everywhere.

The First Steps

25. Obstacles

Without giving up six things, O monks, will it not be possible to dwell practising body-contemplation on the body . . . feeling-contemplation on feelings . . . mind-contemplation on the mind . . . mind-object contemplation on mind-objects. Which are these six?

To be fond of activity; to be fond of talking; to be fond of sleeping; to be fond of company; lack of sense-control; immoderate eating.

26. Gradual Progress

Once the Exalted One dwelt near Saketa in the deer park of Añjana-vana. At that time the Wanderer Kundaliya, an ascetic, went there, and after exchanging friendly and polite greetings with the Exalted One, he sat down at one side. Sitting at one side he spoke to the Exalted One thus:

'I am accustomed to visit the parks of monasteries, Sir, and to go to meetings. After a meal, having finished my breakfast, I have the habit of going from monastery to monastery, from park to park. There I meet some ascetics and Brahmans who engage in discussions just because they think it beneficial to argue and criticize. Now, what does the venerable Gotama consider to be beneficial?'

—'It is the fruit of deliverance by knowledge[14] that the Perfect One considers to be beneficial.'

—'Now, venerable Gotama, by the cultivation and frequent practice of which things can the fruit of deliverance by knowledge be accomplished?'

—'The seven Factors of Enlightenment, if cultivated and frequently practised, will accomplish the fruit of deliverance by knowledge.'

—'And which things, cultivated and frequently practised, will accomplish the seven Factors of Enlightenment?'

—'The four Foundations of Mindfulness, if cultivated and frequently practised, will accomplish the seven Factors of Mindfulness.'

—'And which things, cultivated and frequently practised, will accomplish the four Foundations of Mindfulness?'

—'Threefold good conduct.'[15]

—'And which things, cultivated and frequently practised, will accomplish the threefold good conduct?'

—' Sense-control. '

27. The Beginning

Sāvatthi. Once the venerable Bāhiya went to the Exalted One, saluted him respectfully and sat to one side. Sitting on one side, he spoke to the Exalted One thus:

'It will be good, Lord, if the Exalted One can explain to me the teaching in brief so that, after having listened to the instruction, I may live alone, secluded, earnest and resolute.'

'Well, Bāhiya, you should first purify the beginning of all salutary things. And what is the beginning of all things salutary? Virtue that has been well purified, and correct understanding. When your virtue is very pure and your understanding correct, then, Bāhiya, supported and aided by virtue, you may cultivate the four Foundations of Mindfulness.

'If, Bāhiya, thus supported and aided by virtue, you will cultivate the four Foundations of Mindfulness, whichever night may come and whichever day may dawn for you, you may expect only growth in things salutary, not deterioration.'

And the venerable Bāhiya, gladdened and satisfied by the words of the Exalted One, saluted him respectfully and went away.

And the venerable Bāhiya lived now alone and secluded, earnest, ardent and resolute. And the goal for the sake of which noble sons go forth from home to homelessness, that highest perfection of the Holy Life he soon came to know directly, in this very life, realizing it for himself; 'Ceased has rebirth, fulfilled is the Holy Life, the task is done, nothing further remains after this,' this he knew.

Thus the venerable Bāhiya had become one of the Arahats.

28. The Purpose of the Moral Rules

'Those salutary rules of morality proclaimed by the Exalted One, for what purpose, brother Ānanda, has he proclaimed them?'

—'Well said, brother Bhadda, well said! Pleasing is your wisdom, pleasing your insight, excellent is your question!

'Those salutary rules of morality proclaimed by the Exalted One, were proclaimed by him for the sake of cultivating the four Foundations of Mindfulness.'

General Directions for the Practice

29. The Instruction to Bāhiya

Thus, Bāhiya, should you train yourself: 'In what is seen there must be only the seen; in what is heard there must be only the heard; in what is sensed (as smell, taste or touch) there must be only what is sensed; in what is thought there must be only what is thought.[16]

30. Directed and Undirected Meditation

Sāvatthi. One morning, after the venerable Ānanda had dressed he took bowl and robe and went to a nunnery. Having arrived there he sat down on a prepared seat. The nuns approached and, having respectfully saluted the venerable Ānanda, they sat at one side and spoke to him thus:

'There are many nuns here, venerable Ānanda, who, well established in the four Foundations of Mindfulness, have experienced a great result gradually increasing.'

—'So it is, sisters. So it is, sisters. From any monk or nun whose mind is well established in the four Foundations of Mindfulness, it may be expected that they will experience a great result, gradually increasing.'

And the venerable Ānanda, having instructed, encouraged, aroused and gladdened the nuns by a talk on the Dhamma, went away. He then went for alms food in Sāvatthi, and having returned from the alms round, after his meal, he betook himself to the Exalted One. Having respectfully saluted the Master, he sat at one side and told of his visit to the nunnery. And the Exalted One spoke thus:

'So it is, Ānanda. So it is, Ānanda. Verily, from any monk or nun whose mind is well established in the four Foundations of Mindfulness, it may be expected that they will experience a great result, gradually increasing.

'What are those four? Herein a monk dwells practising body-contemplation on the body, ardent, clearly comprehending and mindful, having overcome covetousness and grief concerning the world. While he thus dwells practising body-contemplation on the body, there arises within him, with the body as object, bodily excitation or mental sluggishness; or his mind is distracted by outward things. That monk, Ānanda, should then direct his thoughts to any confidence-inspiring object.[17] Having done so, joy will arise in him. In a joyful mind, rapture will arise. In an enraptured mind, inner tranquillity will appear. He who is tranquil within, will feel happiness; and a happy mind wins concentration. Now, he thinks: "The purpose for which I directed the mind (elsewhere), is now fulfilled. Should I not now turn away from it?" And he turns away,[18] and no longer reflects and considers.[19] "I am now free from reflecting and considering, mindful within, and happy," thus he knows.

'Further, Ānanda, a monk dwells practising feeling-contemplation on feelings . . . mind-contemplation on the mind—mind-object contemplation on mind-objects. While he thus dwells, there arises in him, with feelings . . . the state of mind . . . or mind-objects as object, bodily excitation or mental sluggishness; or his mind is distracted by outward things. That monk, Ānanda, should then direct his thoughts to any confidence-inspiring object. Having done so, joy will arise in him. In a joyful mind, rapture will arise. In an enraptured mind inner tranquillity will appear. He who is tranquil within, will feel happiness; and a happy mind wins concentration. Now he thinks: "The purpose for which I directed the mind (elsewhere), is now fulfilled. Should I not now turn away from it?" And he turns away, and no longer reflects and considers. "I am now free of reflecting and considering, mindful within and happy," thus he knows.

'This, Ānanda, is directed meditation.[20]

'And what, Ānanda, is undirected meditation?[21]

'If, Ānanda, a monk's mind need not be directed outward,[22] he knows: "My mind is not outward-directed." And he further knows: "In the earlier and later (stages of the practice) I am without impediments, free, undeflected."[23] And he further knows: "I dwell practising body-contemplation on the body, feeling- contemplation on feelings, mind-contemplation on the mind, mind-object contemplation on mind-objects, ardent, clearly comprehending and mindful, having overcome covetousness and grief concerning the world. And I am happy."

'This, Ānanda, is undirected meditation.

'Thus, Ānanda, have I shown to you the directed meditation and the undirected meditation. What a master can do for his disciples, wishing them well, out of compassion and sympathy, that I have done for you. Here, Ānanda, are trees and secluded cells! Practice meditation, Ānanda! Be not neglectful, lest you regret it afterwards! This is my injunction to you.'

Thus spoke the Exalted One. Glad in heart rejoiced the venerable Ānanda in the words of the Blessed One.

Explanations of the Discourse

31. Contemplating Origination Factors

I shall show you, monks, the origination and cessation in the four Foundations of Mindfulness. Listen to my words!

What now, monks, is the origination of the body? Through the origination of nutriment there is origination of the body. Through the cessation of nutriment there is cessation of the body.

Through the origination of sense impression[24] there is origination of feelings. Through the cessation of sense impression there is cessation of feelings.

Through the origination of mind-and-body (*nāma-rūpa*) there is origination of consciousness.[25] Through the cessation of mind-and-body there is cessation of consciousness.

Through the origination of attention there is origination of mind-objects.[26] Through the cessation of attention there is cessation of mind-objects.

32. He Dwells Internally . . . *I*

The Brahma Sanaṁkumāra addressed the Tāvatiṁsa Gods thus:

'What do the revered Tāvatiṁsa Gods think about it? Has not the Exalted One who is the knower, the seer, the Holy One and Fully Enlightened, well proclaimed the four Foundations of Mindfulness, for attaining what is salutary? And what are these four? Herein a monk practises body-contemplation on the body *internally*. While he thus dwells he is well concentrated and serene. When he is thus well concentrated and serene he evokes knowledge and vision concerning the body of others, *external* to himself. (And so in regard to feelings, state of mind, and mind-objects.)'

33. He Dwells Internally . . . *II*

How does a monk dwell practising body-contemplation on the body *internally*? Herein a monk reflects upon his own body, from the soles of his feet upward and from the crown of his head downward, enclosed by the skin and full of impurities, thinking thus: "There are in this body: hair of the head . . . synovic fluid, urine." He then practises with this object, develops it, attends to it frequently and firmly establishes it in his mind. Having done so, he then turns his mind to a body external to himself.

And how does a monk dwell practising body-contemplation on the body *externally*? Herein a monk reflects upon a body external to himself: 'There are in *his* body: hairs of the head . . . .' He then practises with that object, develops it, attends to it frequently and firmly establishes it in his mind. Having done so, he turns his mind to the body internally and externally.

And how does a monk dwell practising body-contemplation on the body both *internally and externally*? Herein a monk reflects upon a body internally and externally: 'There are in this body: hairs of the head . . . .' Thus a monk dwells practising body-contemplation on the body, both internally and externally. (And so in regard to feelings, the state of mind, and mind-objects.)

34. The Sevenfold Contemplation of the Four Satipaṭṭhānas

How does one dwell practising body-contemplation on the body?

Herein a certain person contemplates the corporeal phenomenon 'earth' (*paṭhavī-kāya*) (1) as impermanent and not as permanent; (2) as painful and not as pleasurable; (3) as not-self and not as a self; (4) he turns away and is not delighted by it; (5) he is dispassionate and does not crave; (6) he causes cessation of it and not origination; (7) he relinquishes and does not grasp. Contemplating it as impermanent, he abandons the notion of permanency; contemplating it as painful, he abandons the notion of pleasure; contemplating it as not-self, he abandons the notion of a self; by turning away he abandons delight; by being dispassionate he abandons greed; by causing cessation he abandons origination; by relinquishing he abandons grasping.

In that sevenfold manner he practises body-contemplation.

The body is the 'foundation'[27], not 'mindfulness'; but mindfulness is 'foundation' as well as 'mindfulness'. With that mindfulness and with that knowledge[28] he contemplates the body. Hence it is called 'the Foundation of Mindfulness consisting of practising body-contemplation on the body' (*kāye kāyānupassanā-satipaṭṭhāna*).

Again, a certain person contemplates as impermanent and not as permanent the corporeal phenomena water, heat, air, hair of the head and of the body, the upper and lower skin, flesh, blood, sinews, bones, marrow. He contemplates them as painful . . . (*continue as above up to:*) Hence it is called 'the Foundation of Mindfulness consisting of practising body-contemplation on the body'.

How does one dwell practising feeling-contemplation on feelings?

Herein a certain person contemplates as impermanent and not as permanent, the pleasant, unpleasant and neutral feelings; the feelings born of visual impressions, sound-impressions, smell-impressions, taste-impressions, touch-impressions and mind-impressions. He contemplates them as painful and not as pleasurable; as not-self and not as a self; he turns away and is not delighted by them; he is dispassionate and does not crave; he causes cessation and not origination; he relinquishes and does not grasp. Contemplating them as impermanent, he abandons the notion of permanency; contemplating them as painful, he abandons the notion of pleasure; contemplating them as not-self, he abandons the notion of a self; by turning away he abandons delight; by being dispassionate he abandons greed; by causing cessation he abandons origination; by relinquishing he abandons grasping.

In that sevenfold manner he practises feeling-contemplation.

Feeling is the 'foundation', not 'mindfulness'; but mindfulness is 'foundation' as well as 'mindfulness'. With that mindfulness and that knowledge he contemplates feelings. Hence it is called 'the Foundation of Mindfulness consisting of practising feeling-contemplation on feelings.'

How does one dwell practising mind-contemplation on the mind?[20]

Herein a certain person contemplates as impermanent and not as permanent the lustful state of mind and the lust-free state of mind; the hating state of mind and the hate-free state of mind... (*continue as in the Discourse*); he contemplates as impermanent and not as permanent, visual consciousness, auditory consciousness, olfactory consciousness, gustatory consciousness, tactile consciousness and mind-consciousness. And each of them he further contemplates as painful and not as pleasurable; as not-self and not as a self; he turns away and is not delighted by them; he is dispassionate and does not crave; he causes cessation and not origination; he relinquishes and does not grasp. Contemplating them as impermanent, he abandons the notion of permanency; contemplating them as painful, he abandons the notion of pleasure; contemplating them as not-self, he abandons the notion of a self; by turning away he abandons delight; by being dispassionate he abandons greed; by causing cessation he abandons origination; by relinquishing he abandons grasping.

In that sevenfold manner he practises mind-contemplation.

Mind is the 'foundation', not 'mindfulness'; but mindfulness is 'foundation' as well as 'mindfulness'. With that mindfulness and that knowledge he contemplates the mind. Hence it is called 'the Foundation of Mindfulness consisting of practising mind-contemplation on the mind'.

How does one dwell practising mind-object contemplation on mind-objects?

Herein a certain person contemplates as impermanent and not as permanent, the other phenomena, excepting the body, excepting feelings, excepting mind (i.e. consciousness).[30] He contemplates them as painful and not as pleasurable; as not-self and not as a self; he turns away and is not delighted by them; he is dispassionate and does not crave; he causes cessation and not origination; he relinquishes and does not grasp. Contemplating them as impermanent, he abandons the notion of permanency; contemplating them as painful, he abandons the notion of pleasure; contemplating them as not-self, he abandons the notion of a self; by turning away he abandons delight; by being dispassionate he abandons greed; by causing cessation he abandons origination; by relinquishing he abandons grasping.

In that sevenfold manner he practises mind-object contemplation.

Mind-objects are the 'foundation', not 'mindfulness'; but mindfulness is 'foundation' as well as 'mindfulness'. With that mindfulness and that knowledge he contemplates mind-objects. Hence it is called 'the Foundation of Mindfulness consisting of practising mind-object-contemplation on mind-objects'.

35. The Contemplation of the Body

If the body is not mastered (by meditation; *abhāvita*), the mind cannot be mastered. If the body is mastered, mind is mastered.

36. There is one thing, monks, that, cultivated and regularly practised, leads to a deep sense of urgency, . . . to the Supreme Peace . . . to mindfulness and clear comprehension, . . . to the attainment of right vision and knowledge, . . . to happiness here and now, . . . to realizing deliverance by wisdom and the fruition of Holiness (*arahatta-phala*): it is mindfulness of the body.

37. The Discourse on Mindfulness of the Body

Thus have I heard. Once the Exalted One dwelt at Sāvatthi, in the Jeta Grove, in Anāthapiṇḍika's monastery. At that time, a number of monks having returned from the alms round, after the meal, had gathered in the assembly hall. Among them this conversation took place: 'It is wonderful, brethren, it is extraordinary how the Exalted One, the knower, the seer, the Holy One, fully enlightened, has described this Mindfulness of the Body as being of great fruit, of great advantage.' Here this conversation of the monks was interrupted. The Exalted One having risen from his seclusion in the evening, went to the assembly hall and sat down on a seat prepared for him. Thus seated he addressed the monks: 'Talking about what, monks, are you seated here? What was the conversation that you have interrupted?'

—'Having returned from the alms-round, after our meal, we had gathered in the assembly hall, and this conversation arose among us: "It is wonderful, brethren, it is extraordinary how the Exalted One, the knower, the seer, the Holy One, fully enlightened has described this Mindfulness of the Body as being of great fruit, of great advantage." It is this conversation, Lord, that we had interrupted when the Exalted One came.'

—'How then, monks, is Mindfulness of the Body of great fruit, of great advantage, if cultivated and regularly practised?

(*Mindfulness of Breathing*) 'Herein, monks, a monk having gone to the forest, to the foot of a tree, or to an empty place, sits down cross-legged, keeps his body erect and his mindfulness alert. Just mindful he breathes in and mindful he breathes out. Breathing in a long breath, he knows 'I breathe in a long breath' . . . (*continue as in the Discoure, up to:*) 'Calming the bodily function (of breathing), I shall breathe out', thus he trains himself.

'In him who thus lives earnest, ardent and resolute, worldly memories and inclinations will fade away, and through their fading his mind will become firm within, will be calm, harmonious and concentrated. In that way, monks, cultivates a monk Mindfulness of the Body.

Here follow, as given in the Discourse, the sections on The Postures of the Body, on Mindfulness and Clear Comprehension, Repulsiveness of the Body, and the Cemetery Contemplations, each followed by the above paragraph: 'In him who thus lives earnest . . .

(*The Meditative Absorptions*) 'Furthermore, monks, a monk detached from sense-objects, detached from unsalutary ideas, enters into the *first absorption* that is born of detachment, accompanied by thought-conception and discursive thinking, and filled with rapture and joy. With that rapture and joy born of detachment, he saturates and imbues, permeates and pervades this body so that not a single spot of his entire body remains unpervaded by the rapture and joy born of detachment.

If a skilful barber or his apprentice were to pour soap powder on a metal dish and mix it with water repeatedly added; then the ball of soapy lather would be full of moisture, pervaded with moisture, inside and outside, without dripping.

Similarly it is with that monk: with the rapture and joy born of detachment he saturates and imbues, permeates and pervades this body so that not a single spot of his entire body remains unpervaded by the rapture and joy born of detachment.

In him who thus lives earnest, ardent and resolute, worldly memories and inclinations will fade away, and through their fading his mind will become firm within, will be calm, harmonious and concentrated. In that way, monks, cultivates a monk Mindfulness of the Body.

Further, monks: after the stilling of thought-conception and discursive thinking, he gains the inner tranquillity and harmony of the *second absorption* that is free of thought-conception and discursive thinking, born of concentration and filled with rapture and joy. With that rapture and joy born of concentration, he saturates and imbues, permeates and pervades this body so that not a single spot of his entire body remains unpervaded by that rapture and joy born of concentration.

If there were a deep lake, with spring water welling up from within, and there were no inflow of water neither from East nor West, neither from North nor South; nor would rains fill it with their showers now and then; but the cool spring within the lake would saturate and imbue, permeate and pervade it with its cool waters so that not a single spot of the lake remains unpervaded by the cool spring water—similarly it is with that monk: with the rapture and joy born of concentration, he saturates and imbues, permeates and pervades this body so that not a single spot of his entire body remains unpervaded by that rapture and joy born of concentration.

In him who thus lives . . .

Further, monks: after the fading away of rapture the monk dwells in equanimity, mindful and clearly aware, and he experiences a happiness in this body, of which the Noble Ones say: 'Happily lives he who dwells in equanimity and is mindful!'— that *third absorption* he wins. With that rapture-free happiness he saturates and imbues, permeates and pervades this body so that not a single spot of his entire body remains unpervaded by that rapture-free happiness.

If there were, in a lotus pond, blue, red or white lotus blossoms born in the water, grown in the water, nurtured in submersion, (then these lotus plants are from the tip to the roots saturated and imbued, permeated and pervaded by the cool water so that not a single spot of these lotus plants remains unpervaded by the water. Similarly it is with that monk: with rapture-free happiness he saturates and imbues, permeates and pervades this body so that not a single spot of his entire body remains unpervaded by that rapture-free happiness.

In him who thus lives . . .

Further, monks: with the abandoning of pleasure and pain, and with the previous disappearance of joy and grief, he enters upon and dwells in the *fourth absorption* which is beyond pleasure and pain, and has purity of mindfulness due to equanimity. He sits pervading this very body with a pure and lucid mind so that not a single spot of his entire body remains unpervaded by that pure and lucid mind.

Suppose a man, seated, were wrapped in a white cloth that covers his head, so that there were not a single spot of his body that is not covered by the white cloth. Similarly it is with that monk: he sits pervading this very body with a pure and lucid mind so that not a single spot of his entire body remain unpervaded by that pure and lucid mind.

In him who thus lives earnest, ardent and resolute, worldly memories and inclinations will fade away, and through their fading his mind will become firm within, will be calm, harmonious and concentrated. In that way, monks, cultivates a monk Mindfulness of the Body.

Whosoever, monks, has cultivated and regularly practised Mindfulness of the Body, included in it are for him all beneficial things conducive to wisdom.

If someone were to conceive in his mind the great ocean, included in it are for him all those little rivers that have flowed into the ocean. Similarly it is with anyone who has cultivated and regularly practised Mindfulness of the Body: included in it are for him all beneficial things conducive to wisdom. But in a monk by whom Mindfulness of the Body has not been cultivated, not regularly practised, in him, O monks, Māra will find entry, will obtain a hold.

If, monks, a man were to throw a heavy stone ball into a heap of wet clay, what do you think, monks, will not that heavy ball of stone find entry into that heap of wet clay, will it not obtain a hold in it?—Certainly, Lord.—Similarly, monks, whosoever has not cultivated, not regularly practised Mindfulness of the Body, in him Māra will find entry, will obtain a hold.

If, monks, there were a dry, sapless piece of wood, and a man came with the upper kindling stick, thinking 'I shall make fire, I shall produce a flame': what do you think, monks, will that man be able to do it?—Certainly, Lord.—Similarly, monks, whosoever has not cultivated, not regularly practised Mindfulness of the Body, in him Māra will find entry, will obtain a hold.

If, monks, there were a water pot, empty of water, placed on a stand, and a man came with a load of water: what do you think, monks, will that man be able to pour that water into the pot?— Certainly, Lord.—Similarly, monks, whosoever has not cultivated, not regularly practised Mindfulness of the Body, in him Māra will find entry, will obtain a hold.

But whosoever, monks, has cultivated and regularly practised Mindfulness of the Body, in him Māra will not find entry, will not obtain a hold. If, monks, a man were to throw a light skein of thread against a door plank made of solid heart wood:

what do you think, monks, could this light skein of thread find entry into the door plank made of solid heart wood, could it obtain a hold in it?—Certainly not, Lord.—Similarly, monks, whosoever has cultivated and regularly practised Mindfulness of the Body, in him Māra cannot find entry, cannot obtain a hold.

If there were a fresh piece of wood, full of sap, and a man came with the upper kindling stick, thinking 'I shall make fire, I shall produce a flame': what do you think, monks, will that man be able to do it?—Certainly not, Lord.—Similarly, monks, whosoever has cultivated and regularly practised Mindfulness of the Body, in him Māra cannot find entry, cannot obtain a hold.

If there were a full water pot, placed on a stand, filled to the brim with water so that crows could drink from it, and a man came with a load of water: what do you think, monks, will that man be able to pour the water into that pot?—Certainly not, Lord.—Similarly, monks, whosoever has cultivated and regularly practised Mindfulness of the Body, in him Māra cannot find entry, cannot obtain a hold.

Whosoever, monks, has cultivated and regularly practised Mindfulness of the Body, to whatever state realizable by direct knowledge he may bend his mind for reaching it by direct knowledge, he will then acquire proficiency in that very field.

If there were a full water pot, placed on a stand, filled to the brim with water so that crows could drink from it, and a strong man were to tilt it more and more, would then the water flow out? —Certainly, Lord.—Similarly, monks, whosoever has cultivated and regularly practised Mindfulness of the Body, to whatever state realizable by direct knowledge he may bend his mind for realizing it by direct knowledge, he will then acquire proficiency in that very field.

If there were, on level ground, a square tank bounded by a dam, filled to the brim with water so that crows could drink from it, and a strong man were to open the dam more and more, would then the water flow out?—Certainly, Lord.—Similarly, monks, whosoever has cultivated and regularly practised Mindfulness of the Body, to whatever state realizable by direct knowledge he may bend his mind for realizing it by direct knowledge, he will then acquire proficiency in that very field.

Suppose, at the junction of four main roads, on level ground, a chariot with noble horses were standing, harnessed in readiness, furnished with a goad stick; and a skilled charioteer, a master of horse training, mounting the chariot, taking the reins in his left hand and the goad in his right, were to drive along where he wanted. Similarly, monks, whosoever has cultivated and regularly practised Mindfulness of the Body, to whatever state realizable by direct knowledge he may bend his mind for realizing it by direct knowledge, he will then acquire proficiency in that very field.

If, monks, Mindfulness of the Body has been cultivated and regularly practised, made a vehicle (of progress) and a firm possession of the mind; has been consolidated, strengthened and perfected, then ten blessings may be expected. What ten?

The disciple overpowers passion[31] and dissatisfaction,[32] and is not overpowered by dissatisfaction; again and again, he subdues the recurring dissatisfaction. He overpowers fear and anxiety, and is not overpowered by them; again and again he subdues the recurring fears and anxieties. He endures cold and heat, hunger and thirst, wind and scorching sun, gadflies, mosquitoes and serpents; patiently he endures disagreeable, unpleasant words, and bodily pains that arise, which are severe, piercing, disagreeable, unpleasant, of a fatal nature. The four Absorptions that purify the mind, these states of happiness found in the present, he attains at will, without difficulty and strain. He becomes endowed with various supernormal powers: being one he becomes many; having become many, he again becomes one; he appears and disappears; unhindered he goes through walls, fences and mountains as through the air; he submerges and emerges in the earth as in water; without sinking he walks on the water as on the earth; cross-legged he flies through the air like a winged bird; he touches and strokes with his hand the sun and the moon, those great and powerful luminaries; even up to the Brahma world he yields power over his body.—With the Divine Ear, purified and superhuman, he hears sounds, both divine and human, near and far. He cognizes the minds of other persons, other beings, mentally penetrating them.—He recollects many a past existence, as unto one rebirth, two, three, four and five rebirths, one hundred, two hundred, three hundred, four hundred and five hundred rebirths, one thousand rebirths, one hundred thousand rebirths; he recollects many world-evolutions and world-devolutions: 'There I have been and had such a name, belonged to such a family, had such an appearance, ate such kinds of food, partook of such pleasures and sufferings, and such was my life span. Having departed from there, entered existence elsewhere; and there I had such a name . . . and such was my life span. Having departed from there I entered existence here.' Thus he recollects many a past existence with all its characteristic features and particulars.—With the Divine Eye, purified and superhuman, he sees how beings depart and reappear, beings base and noble, beautiful and ugly, happy and miserable; he sees how beings reappear according to their deeds. —After the eradication of the taints (*āsava*) he dwells, free of taints, in the liberation of the mind, in the liberation by wisdom, having understood and realized it by himself.

If Mindfulness of the Body has been cultivated and regularly practised, made a vehicle (of progress) and a firm possession of the mind; has been consolidated, strengthened and perfected, these ten blessings may be expected.'

Thus spoke the Exalted One. Glad in heart the monks rejoiced in the words of the Blessed One.

38. From the Verses of the Venerable Ānanda

The friend[33] has passed away, the Master, too, has gone.
There is no friendship now that equals unto this:
The Mindfulness directed bodywards.

39. The Discourse on Mindfulness of Breathing[34]

. . . Mindfulness of Breathing, monks, cultivated and regularly practised, is of great fruit and great benefit. Mindfulness of Breathing, cultivated and regularly practised, brings to perfection the four Foundations of Mindfulness; the four Foundations of Mindfulness, cultivated and regularly practised, bring the seven Factors of Enlightenment to perfection; the seven Factors of Enlightenment, cultivated and regularly practised, bring wisdom and deliverance to perfection.

And how cultivated and regularly practised, is Mindfulness of Breathing of great fruit and benefit?

Herein, monks, a monk having gone to the forest, to the foot of a tree, or to an empty place, sits down cross-legged, keeps his body erect and his mindfulness alert. Just mindful he breathes in, mindful he breathes out.

I. The First Tetrad (Contemplation of the Body)

1. Breathing in a long breath, he knows, 'I breathe in a long breath'; breathing out a long breath, he knows, 'I breathe out a long breath',

2. Breathing in a short breath, he knows, 'I breathe in a short breath'; breathing out a short breath, he knows, 'I breathe out a short breath,'

3. 'Experiencing the whole (breath-) body I shall breathe in,' thus he trains himself; 'Experiencing the whole (breath-) body I shall breathe out,' thus he trains himself,

4. 'Calming the bodily function (of breathing) I shall breathe in,' thus he trains himself; 'Calming the bodily function (of breathing) I shall breathe out,' thus he trains himself.

II. The Second Tetrad (Contemplation of Feelings)

5. 'Experiencing rapture I shall breathe in (I shall breathe out),' thus he trains himself,

6. 'Experiencing happiness I shall breathe in (I shall breathe out),' thus he trains himself,

7. 'Experiencing the mental functions[35] I shall breathe in (I shall breathe out),' thus he trains himself,

8. 'Calming the mental functions I shall breathe in (I shall breathe out),' thus he trains himself.

III. The Third Tetrad (Contemplation of the Mind)

9. 'Experiencing the mind I shall breathe in (I shall breathe out),' thus he trains himself,

10. 'Gladdening the mind I shall breathe in (I shall breathe out),' thus he trains himself,

11. 'Concentrating the mind I shall breathe in (I shall breathe out),' thus he trains himself,

12. 'Liberating the mind I shall breathe in (I shall breathe out),' thus he trains himself.

IV. The Fourth Tetrad (Contemplation of Mind-Objects)

13. 'Contemplating impermanence I shall breath in (I shall breathe out),' thus he trains himself,

14. 'Contemplating dispassion I shall breathe in (I shall breathe out),' thus he trains himself,

15. 'Contemplating cessation I shall breathe in (I shall breathe out),' thus he trains himself,

16. 'Contemplating relinquishment I shall breathe in (I shall breathe out),' thus he trains himself.[36]

In that way cultivated and regularly practised, monks, Mindfulness of Breathing brings great fruit and benefit.

Perfecting the Foundations of Mindfulness

And how cultivated, how regularly practised brings Mindfulness of Breathing the four Foundations of Mindfulness to perfection?

I. Whenever a monk mindfully breathes in and out a long breath, or a short breath; or when he trains himself to breathe in and out while experiencing the bodily function (of breathing); or while calming that function—at that time, monks, he dwells practising body-contemplation on the body, ardent, clearly comprehending and mindful; having overcome covetousness and grief concerning the world. For, breathing in and out, monks, I say is one of the bodily processes.

II. Whenever the monk trains himself to breathe in and out while experiencing rapture; or while experiencing happiness; or while experiencing the mental functions; or while calming the mental functions—at that time, monks, he dwells practising feeling-contemplation on feelings, ardent, clearly comprehending and mindful, having overcome covetousness and grief concerning the world. For, the full attention to breathing in and out, I say, is one of the feelings.

III. Whenever a monk trains himself to breathe in and out while experiencing the mind; or while gladdening the mind; or while concentrating the mind; or while liberating the mind—at that time he dwells practising mind-contemplation on the mind, ardent, clearly comprehending and mindful, having overcome covetousness and grief concerning the world. For one who lacks mindfulness and clear comprehension, I say, cannot develop Mindfulness of Breathing.

IV. Whenever a monk trains himself to breathe in and out while contemplating impermanence, dispassion, cessation or relinquishment—at that time he dwells practising mind-object contemplation on mind-objects, ardent, clearly comprehending and mindful, having overcome covetousness and grief concerning the world. Having wisely seen the abandoning of covetousness and grief,[37] he looks on with perfect equanimity.

Mindfulness of Breathing, monks, in that way cultivated and regularly practised, brings the four Foundations of Mindfulness to perfection.

And how do the four Foundations of Mindfulness, cultivated and regularly practised, bring the seven Factors of Enlightenment to perfection?

Whenever a monk dwells in the contemplation of body, feelings, mind and mind-objects, ardent . . . unclouded mindfulness becomes established in him. And when unclouded mindfulness is established in him, at that time the *enlightenment factor 'Mindfulness'* is initiated in the monk; at that time the monk develops the enlightenment factor 'Mindfulness'; at that time he gains perfection in the development of the enlightenment factor 'Mindfulness.'

Dwelling mindful in that manner, he wisely investigates, examines and scrutinizes the respective object; and while doing so, the *enlightenment factor 'Investigation of Reality'* is initiated in the monk; at that time the monk develops the enlightenment factor 'Investigation of Reality'; at that time he gains perfection in the development of the enlightenment factor 'Investigation of Reality'.

While he wisely investigates, examines and scrutinizes that object, unremitting energy is initiated in him. And when unremitting energy is initiated in the monk, at that time the *enlightenment factor 'Energy'* is initiated in him; at that time the monk develops the enlightenment factor 'Energy'; at that time he gains perfection in the development of the enlightenment factor 'Energy'.

In him possessed of energy unworldly rapture arises. And when in a monk possessed of energy unworldly rapture arises, at that time the *enlightenment factor 'Rapture'* is initiated in him; at that time the monk develops the enlightenment factor 'Rapture'; at that time he gains perfection in the development of the enlightenment factor 'Rapture'.

The body and mind of one who is filled with rapture, becomes tranquil. And when the body and mind of one who is filled with rapture, becomes tranquil, at that time the *enlightenment factor 'Tranquillity'* is initiated in him; at that time the monk develops the enlightenment factor 'Tranquillity'; at that time he gains perfection in the development of the enlightenment factor 'Tranquillity'.

The mind of one who is tranquil and happy, becomes concentrated. And when the mind of a monk who is tranquil and happy, becomes concentrated, at that time the *enlightenment factor 'Concentration'* is initiated in him; at that time the monk develops the enlightenment factor 'Concentration'; at that time he gains perfection in the development of the enlightenment factor 'Concentration'.

On the mind thus concentrated he looks with perfect equanimity. And when looking on his concentrated mind with perfect equanimity, at that time the *enlightenment factor*

'Equanimity' is initiated in him; at that time the monk develops the enlightenment factor 'Equanimity'; at that time he gains perfection in the development of the enlightenment factor 'Equanimity'.

The four Foundations of Mindfulness, in that way cultivated and regularly practised, bring the seven Factors of Enlightenment to perfection.

And how do the seven Factors of Enlightenment, cultivated and regularly practised, bring wisdom and deliverance to perfection?

Herein, monks, a monk develops the enlightenment factors Mindfulness, Investigation of Reality, Energy, Rapture, Tranquility, Concentration and Equanimity, based on detachment, based on dispassion, based on cessation, resulting in relinquishment.

The seven Factors of Enlightenment, in that way cultivated and regularly practised, bring wisdom and deliverance to perfection.

Thus spoke the Exalted One. Glad in heart the monks rejoiced in the words of the Blessed One.

40. Mindfulness of Breathing

This concentration of mind achieved through Mindfulness of Breathing, if cultivated and regularly practised, is peaceful and sublime, an unalloyed and happy state of mind that makes evil, unsalutary ideas immediately cease and vanish whenever they arise.

41. Mindful Dying

If, Rāhula, Mindfulness of Breathing has been cultivated and regularly practised, even the last in-breaths and out-breaths will pass consciously, not unconsciously.

Clear Comprehension
The Four Postures

42. Training for Enlightenment

While while going, standing, sitting or reclining when awake, a thought of sensuality, hatred or aggressiveness arises in a monk, and he tolerates it, does not reject, discard and eliminate it, does not bring it to an end, that monk who in such a manner is ever and again lacking in earnest endeavour and moral shame, is called indolent and void of energy.

If while going, standing, sitting or reclining when awake, a thought of sensuality, hatred or aggressiveness arises in a monk, and he does not tolerate it, but rejects, discards and eliminates it, brings it to an end, that monk who in such a manner ever and again shows earnest endeavour and moral shame, is called energetic and resolute.

When walking, standing, sitting or reclining,
Who cherishes thoughts of evil or of worldliness,
Beguiled by them, he goes the downward path;
Supreme Enlightenment can he never win.

But he who overcomes these evil thoughts,
While walking, standing, sitting or reclining;
Who finds delight in quieting thus the mind,
Supreme Enlightenment will he surely win.

43. Training in Determination and Insight

Devoted to virtue you should dwell, O monks, devoted to the discipline of the Order and restrained by that discipline! Perfect be your conduct and behaviour! Seeing danger even in the smallest transgression, you should train yourselves in the rules which you have accepted! But if a monk lives like that, what should he further do?

If a monk while walking, standing, sitting or reclining, is free from greed and hate,[37] from sloth and torpor, from restlessness and worry, and has discarded sceptical doubt, then his will has become strong and impregnable; his mindfulness is alert and unclouded; his body calm and unexcited; his mind concentrated and collected.

A monk who in such a manner ever and again shows earnest endeavour and moral shame, is called energetic and resolute.

Controlled when walking, standing, sitting and reclining,
Controlled in bending, stretching of his limbs,
Careful observer of the world around him :[38]
He knows how aggregates[39] arise and cease.
He who thus lives with ardent mind
And calm demeanour, free from restlessness,
Who trains himself in quietude of mind,
With constancy and perseverance—
As 'Ever-resolute' that monk is known.

44. The Bodhisatta's Training

Before the enlightenment, when I was not yet fully enlightened, a Bodhisatta still, I conceived this thought: 'How would it be if, in nights of special significance, on the fourteenth, fifteenth or the eighth of the half-month, I were to dwell in weird and frightful places, near sylvan shrines and tombs, in forests, under trees? Perhaps thus I may come to know that fear and terror? And after some time, if in nights of special significance, on the fourteenth, fifteenth or the eighth of the half-month, I dwelt near sylvan shrines and tombs, in forests and under trees. While I there dwelt, a deer would approach or a peacock would break a twig or the wind would rustle through a heap of leaves.' Then I thought: 'Might this be the fear and terror that now comes?' But then I considered: 'Why should I wait for that fear? Should I not better dispel that fear and terror in the very posture in which it meets me?' And fear and terror came when I walked up and down. Then I neither stood still nor sat nor did I lie down until I had dispelled that fear and terror even while walking up and down. Then fear and terror came while I stood. And I neither walked nor sat nor did I lie down until I had dispelled that fear and terror even while standing. Then fear and terror came while I sat. And I neither walked nor stood nor did I lie down until I had dispelled that fear and terror even while sitting. Then fear and terror came while I was lying down. And I neither walked nor stood nor did I sit up until I had dispelled that fear and terror even while I was lying down.

45. Clear Comprehension in Any Posture

If the mind of a monk inclines to walking up and down, he walks up and down with the thought: 'While I am walking up and down, covetousness and grief, and other evil, unsalutary thoughts shall not enter my mind!' Thus he has clear comprehension.

If the mind of a monk inclines to standing, sitting or reclining, he stands, sits or reclines with the thought: 'While I am standing (sitting or reclining), covetousness and grief, and other evil, unsalutary thoughts shall not enter my mind!' Thus he has clear comprehension.

46. Clear Comprehension in Talking

If the mind of a monk inclines to talking, he should think thus: 'I shall not engage in the low kind of talk that is vulgar, worldly and unprofitable; that does not lead to detachment, dispassionateness, cessation, tranquillity, direct knowledge, enlightenment, Nibbāna; namely talk about kings, thieves, ministers, armies, famine and war; about eating, drinking, clothing and lodgings; about garlands, perfumes, relatives, vehicles, villages, towns, cities and countries; about women and wine, the gossip of the street and the well, talk about ancestors, about various trifles, tales about the origin of the world and the sea, talk about things being so or otherwise, and similar matters.' Thus he has clear comprehension.

'But talk that is helpful for leading the austere life, useful for mental clarity, that leads to complete detachment, dispassionateness, cessation, tranquillity, direct knowledge, enlightenment and Nibbāna; that is talk on frugality, contentedness, solitude, seclusion, application of energy, virtue, concentration, wisdom, deliverance and on the knowledge and vision bestowed by deliverance—in such talk shall I engage.' Thus he has clear comprehension.

47. Clear Comprehension in Looking

Rightly, O monks, may Nanda be called noble, strong, lovable and filled with utmost zeal. If, monks, Nanda did not guard the doors of sense, were not moderate in eating, did not cultivate wakefulness and possess mindfulness and clear comprehension, he would be incapable of leading the perfect holy life that is entirely pure.

This now, monks, is how Nanda guards the sense doors: If Nanda has to look towards the eastern direction he does so only after having everything considered well in his mind: 'While I am so looking to the east, will not covetousness and grief, or other evil, unsalutary ideas enter my mind?' Thus he has clear comprehension.

If he has to look towards the western, southern or northern direction, he does so only after having everything considered well in his mind: 'While I am so looking to the west, south or north, will not covetousness and grief or other evil, unsalutary ideas enter my mind?' Thus he has clear comprehension.

This now, monks, is Nanda's mindfulness and clear comprehension: With full awareness arise feelings in Nanda, with full awareness they continue, with full awareness they cease. With full awareness arise perceptions in Nanda, with full awareness they continue, with full awareness they cease. With full awareness arise thoughts in Nanda, with full awareness they continue, with full awareness they cease. This, monks, is Nanda's mindfulness and clear comprehension.

The Contemplation of Feelings

48. How to Understand the Feelings

There are three kinds of feelings, O monks: pleasant feeling, unpleasant feeling and neutral feeling.

For the full understanding of these three kinds of feelings, O monks, the four Foundations of Mindfulness should be cultivated.

49. Giving Up

In pleasant feelings, monks, the inclination to greed should be given up; in unpleasant feelings the inclination to aversion should be given up; in neutral feelings the inclination to ignorance should be given up.

If a monk has given up in pleasant feelings the inclination to greed, in unpleasant feelings the inclination to aversion, and in neutral feelings the inclination to ignorance, then he is called one who is free of (unsalutary) inclinations, one who sees clearly. He has cut off craving, sundered the fetters, and, through the destruction of conceit,[40] has made an end of suffering.

If one feels joy, but knows not feeling's nature,
Bent towards greed,[41] he will not find deliverance.

If one feels pain, but knows not feeling's nature,
Bent towards hate,[42] he will not find deliverance.

And even neutral feeling which as peaceful

The Lord of Wisdom has proclaimed,
If, in attachment, he should cling to it,
Will not set free him from the round of ill.

But if a monk is ardent and does not neglect
To practise mindfulness and comprehension clear,
The nature of all feelings will he penetrate.

And having done so, in this very life
Will he be free from cankers, from all taints.

Mature in knowledge, firm in Dhamma's ways,
When once his life span ends, his body breaks,
All measure and concepts will be transcended.

50. Feelings, Internally and Externally . . .

Be it a pleasant feeling, be it painful, neutral,
One's own or others', feelings of all kind—
He knows as Ill, deceitful, evanescent.
Aware of their repeated impact and their disappearance,
Wins he detachment from the feelings, passion-free.

51. Mindful Examination of Feeling

Once the Exalted One dwelt at Vesāli, in the Great Forest, in the Gabled House. In the evening, after the Exalted One had risen from his seclusion, he betook himself to the sick room and sat down on a prepared seat. Being seated he addressed the monks as follows:

'Mindfully and clearly comprehending, monks, should a monk spend his time! This is my injunction for you!

'If a monk is thus mindful and clearly comprehending, ardent, earnest and resolute, and a pleasant feeling arises in him, he knows: "Now a pleasant feeling has arisen in me. It is conditioned, not unconditioned. Conditioned by what? Even by this body it is conditioned. And this body, indeed, is impermanent, compounded, dependently arisen. But if this pleasant feeling is conditioned by the body which (on its part) is impermanent, compounded, dependently arisen, how could such a pleasant feeling be permanent?"

'In regard to both the body and the pleasant feeling he dwells contemplating impermanence, dwells contemplating evanescence, dwells contemplating detachment, dwells contemplating cessation, dwells contemplating relinquishment. And in him who thus dwells, vanishes the inclination to greed in regard to body and pleasant feeling.

'If a painful feeling arises in him, he knows: "Now a painful feeling has arisen in me. It is conditioned, not unconditioned. Conditioned by what? Even by this body it is conditioned. And this body, indeed, is impermanent, compounded, dependently arisen. But if this painful feeling is conditioned by the body which (on its part) is impermanent, compounded, dependently arisen, how could such a painful feeling be permanent?"

'In regard to both the body and the painful feeling he dwells contemplating impermanence, dwells contemplating evanescence, dwells contemplating detachment, dwells contemplating cessation, dwells contemplating relinquishment. And in him who thus dwells, vanishes the inclination to aversion in regard to body and painful feeling.

'If a neutral feeling arises in him, he knows: "Now a neutral feeling has arisen in me. It is conditioned, not unconditioned. Conditioned by what? Even by this body it is conditioned. And this body, indeed, is impermanent, compounded, dependently arisen. But if this neutral feeling is conditioned by the body which (on its part) is impermanent, compounded, dependently arisen, how could such a neutral feeling be permanent?"

'In regard to both the body and the neutral feeling he dwells contemplating impermanence, dwells contemplating evanescence, dwells contemplating detachment, dwells contemplating cessation, dwells contemplating relinquishment. And in him who thus dwells, vanishes the inclination to ignorance in regard to body and neutral feeling.

'If he experiences a pleasant feeling, he knows it as impermanent; he knows, it is not clung to; he knows, it is not indulged. If he experiences an unpleasant feeling . . . a neutral feeling, he knows, it is impermanent; he knows, it is not clung to; he knows it is not indulged.

'If he experiences a pleasant feeling, he feels it as one unfettered by it. If he experiences an unpleasant feeling, he feels it as one unfettered by it. If he experiences a neutral feeling, he feels it as one unfettered by it.

'Having painful feelings endangering the body, he knows: "I have a painful feeling endangering the body". Having painful feelings endangering life, he knows: "I have painful feelings endangering life". And he knows: "After the dissolution of the body, when life ends, all these feelings which are unindulged, will have to come to rest, even here".

'It is like a lamp that burns by strength of oil and wick, and if oil and wick come to an end, it is extinguished through lack of nourishment. Similarly a monk knows: "After the dissolution of the body, when life ends, all these feelings which are unindulged, will have come to rest, even here".'

The Contemplation of the State of Mind

52. The Visible Teaching

Once the venerable Upavāna went to the Exalted One, saluted him respectfully and sat down at one side. Thus seated he addressed the Exalted One as follows:

'People speak of the "Visible Teaching". In how far, Lord, is the Teaching visible here and now, of immediate result, inviting "Come and see", onward-leading, directly experiencable by the wise?'

—'Herein, Upavāna, a monk having seen a form with his eyes, is aware of the form and aware of his desire for the form. Of the desire for forms present in him, he knows: "There is in me a desire for forms". If a monk having seen a form with his eyes, is aware of the form and aware of his desire for the form, knowing that desire for forms is present in him, in so far, Upavāna, is the Teaching visible here and now, is of immediate result, inviting "Come and see", onward-leading, directly experiencable by the wise.

'Further, Upavāna, a monk having heard a sound with his ears—having smelled an odour with his nose—having tasted a flavour with his tongue—having felt a tactile sensation with his body—having cognized a mental object (idea) with his mind, he is aware of the mental object and aware of his desire for the mental object. Of the desire for mental objects present in him, he knows: "There is in me a desire for mental objects". If a monk having cognized a mental object with his mind, is aware of the mental object and aware of his desire for the mental object, knowing that the desire for mental objects is present in him, also in so far, Upavāna, is the Teaching visible here and now, is of immediate result, inviting "Come and see", onward-leading, directly experiencable by the wise.

'There is here, Upavāna, a monk who, having seen a form with his eyes, is aware of the form and aware that there is no desire for the form. Of the absent desire for forms, he knows: "There is in me no desire for forms". If a monk having seen a form with his eyes, is aware of the form and aware that there is no desire for the form, knowing that no desire for forms is present in him, also in so far, Upavāna, is the Teaching visible here and now, is of immediate result, inviting "Come and see", onward-leading, directly experiencable by the wise.

'Further, Upavāna, a monk having heard a sound with his ears—having smelled an odour with his nose—having tasted a flavour with his tongue—having felt a tactile sensation with his body—having cognized a mental object with his mind, he is aware of the mental object, and aware that there is no desire for the mental object. Of the absent desire for mental objects he knows: "There is in me no desire for mental objects". If a monk having cognized a mental object with his mind, is aware of the mental object and aware that there is no desire for the mental object, knowing that no desire for mental objects is present in him, also in so far, Upavāna, is the Teaching visible here and now, is of immediate result, inviting "Come and see", onward- leading, directly experiencable by the wise.'

53. Beyond Faith

'Is there a way, monks, by which a monk without recourse to faith, to cherished opinions, to tradition, to specious reasoning, to the approval of views pondered upon, may declare the Final Knowledge (of Sainthood): "Rebirth has ceased, the Holy Life has been lived, completed is the task, and nothing more remains after this"?'

—'For us, O Lord, the teachings are rooted in the Exalted One. May the Exalted One speak! The monks will preserve his words.'

—'There is such a way, O monks. And which is it?

'Herein, monks, a monk has seen a form with his eyes, and if greed, hate or delusion are in him, he knows: "There is in me greed, hate, delusion"; and if greed, hate or delusion are not in him, he knows: "There is no greed, hate, delusion in me".

'Further, monks, a monk has heard a sound, smelled an odour, tasted a flavour, felt a tactile sensation, cognized a mental object (idea), and if greed hate or delusion are in him, he knows: "There is in me greed, hate, delusion"; and if greed, hate or delusion are not in him, he knows: "There is in me no greed, hate, delusion".

'And if he thus knows, O monks, are these ideas such as to be known by recourse to faith, to cherished opinions, to tradition, to specious reasoning, to the approval of views pondered upon?'

—'Certainly not, Lord.'

—'Are these not rather ideas to be known after wisely realizing them by experience?'

—'That is so, Lord.'

—'This, monks, is a way by which a monk, without recourse to faith, to cherished opinions, to tradition, to specious reasoning, to the approval of views pondered upon, may declare the Final Knowledge (of Sainthood): "Rebirth has ceased, the Holy Life has been lived, completed is the task, and nothing more remains after this".'[43]

Satipaṭṭhāna, Combined with Other Methods of Training

54. The Lawfulness in the Teaching

Sequence: Overcoming of the Five Hindrances—Satipaṭṭhāna—The Seven Factors of Enlightenment.

Once the Exalted One dwelt at Nālandā, in the Mango Grove of Pāvārika. And the venerable Sāriputta betook himself to the Exalted One, saluted him respectfully and sat down to one side. Thus seated he spoke to the Exalted One as follows:

'Thus, Lord, have I trust in the Exalted One: "There was not, there will not be and there is not now any ascetic or brahmana who has deeper knowledge than the Exalted One, that is in regard to Enlightenment".'

—'Lofty, bold and assured indeed are your words, Sāriputta, a veritable lion's roar—when you said: "Thus have I trust in the Exalted One: There was not, there will not be and there is not now any ascetic or brahmana who has deeper knowledge than the Exalted One, that is in regard to Enlightenment."

'Then, Sāriputta, you actually know those Holy Ones, Fully Enlightened, who lived in times past, having encompassed all these Exalted Ones in your mind: "Such and such was the virtue of these Exalted Ones; such and such their teachings; such and such was their wisdom; such and such was their abode (in meditation); such and such their deliverance"?'

—'Not so, Lord.'

—'Then, Sāriputta, you actually know those Holy Ones, Fully Enlightened, who will live in times to come, having encompassed all these Exalted Ones in your mind: "Such and such will be the virtue of these Exalted Ones; such and such their teachings, such and such their wisdom; such and such will be their abode (of Meditation) such and such will be their deliverance"?'

—'Not so, Lord.'

—'Then, Sāriputta, you actually know me who is now the Holy One, Fully Enlightened, having encompassed me in your mind: "Such and such is the virtue of the Exalted One; such and such are his teachings; such and such his wisdom; such and such is his abode (of meditation); such and such is his deliverance"?'

—'Not so, Lord.'

—'You have, then, Sāriputta, no encompassing knowledge of the Holy Ones, the Fully Enlightened Ones of the past, the future and the present. How, then, Sāriputta, could you now utter such a lofty, bold and assured word, a veritable lion's roar: "There was not, there will not be and there is not now any ascetic or brahmana who has deeper knowledge than the Exalted One, that is in regard to Enlightenment"?'

—'Though, Lord, I do not have such knowledge about the Holy Ones, the Fully Enlightened Ones, of the past, the future and the present, encompassing all these Exalted Ones in my mind, yet the lawfulness in the Teaching[44] is known to me.

'Suppose there is a king's border town with strong ramparts and turrets on strong foundations, and with a single gate; and there is a gate keeper, intelligent, experienced and prudent, who keeps out people unknown, and admits those who are known. That gate keeper walks along the path that girdles the town all round, and he does not notice in the ramparts any hole or crevice, not even enough to allow a cat to slip out. So he knows: "Any larger creatures that enter or leave this town, can enter or leave it only by that gate."

'Similarly, Lord, I know of the lawfulness in the Teaching: Those, Lord, who in times past have been Holy Ones, Fully Enlightened, all these Exalted Ones have awakened to incomparable, perfect Enlightenment after they had removed the five hindrances that defile the mind and weaken the understanding; and, with their minds firmly established in the four Foundations of Mindfulness, have developed the seven Factors of Enlightenment in their true nature.

'Also those, Lord, who in times to come, will be Holy Ones, Fully Enlightened, all these Exalted Ones will awaken to incomparable, perfect Enlightenment after they have removed the five hindrances that defile the mind and weaken the understanding; and, with their minds firmly established in the four Foundations of Mindfulness, will develop the seven Factors of Enlightenment in their true nature.

'And also the Exalted One, Lord, who is now the Holy One, Fully Enlightened, he awakened to incomparable, perfect Enlightenment after he had removed the five hindrances that defile the mind and weaken the understanding, and with his mind firmly established in the four Foundations of Mindfulness, had developed the seven Factors of Enlightenment in their true nature.'

—'Well said, Sāriputta, well said. Therefore, Sāriputta, you may often recite this exposition of the Teaching to monks and nuns, to male and female lay followers. And also in those foolish persons who have doubt and uncertainty concerning the Perfect One, after they have listened to this exposition of the Teaching, doubt and uncertainty about the Exalted One will vanish.'

55. Failure and Accomplishment

Sequence: Satipaṭṭhāna—'The Saint's Power'.

Once while the venerable Anuruddha was in solitude, in seclusion, he thought thus:

'Those who fail in the four Foundations of Mindfulness, fail also on the noble path that leads to the complete extinction of suffering.

'Those who accomplish the four Foundations of Mindfulness, also accomplish the noble path that leads to the complete extinction of suffering.'

Now the venerable Mahā-Moggallāna cognized in his mind the thoughts of the venerable Anuruddha, and just as a strong man may stretch his bent arm or bend his stretched arm, so quickly appeared he before the venerable Anuruddha, and spoke to him thus:

'In how far, brother Anuruddha, are the four Foundations of Mindfulness accomplished by a monk?'

—'Herein, brother, a monk dwells contemplating origination-factors in the body, internally; he dwells contemplating dissolution-factors in the body, internally; he dwells contemplating both origination- and dissolution-factors in the body, internally, ardent, clearly comprehending, having overcome covetousness and grief concerning the world.

'He dwells contemplating origination-factors—dissolution-factors—origination- and dissolution-factors in the body, externally, ardent....

'He dwells contemplating origination-factors—dissolution-factors—origination- and dissolution-factors in the body, both internally and externally, ardent....

'If he should wish: "May I dwell perceiving the unrepulsive in the repulsive," he dwells perceiving the unrepulsive.

'If he should wish: "May I dwell perceiving the repulsive in the unrepulsive," he dwells perceiving the repulsive.

'If he should wish: "May I dwell perceiving the repulsive in the unrepulsive as well as in the repulsive," he dwells perceiving the repulsive.

'If he should wish: "May I dwell perceiving the unrepulsive in the repulsive as well as in the unrepulsive," he dwells perceiving the unrepulsive.

'If he should wish: "Avoiding both (considerations), as unrepulsive and as repulsive, I shall dwell in equanimity, mindful and clearly comprehending," he dwells in equanimity towards that (object), mindful and clearly comprehending.[45]

In the same manner, he dwells contemplating origination-factors, etc., in the feelings—in the mind—in mind-objects, internally, etc.

56. Well-Developed Concentration

Sequence: The Four Sublime States—Jhāna—Satipaṭṭhāna—Jhāna.

'Thus, O monk, should you train yourself: "My mind shall be firmly grounded within, and evil, unsalutary ideas that arise, shall not take hold of the mind!"

'If, O monk, your mind becomes firmly grounded within, and the evil, unsalutary ideas that arise, do not take hold of your mind, then you should further train yourself thus:

"Loving-kindness, the liberation of the heart, should be cultivated in me and regularly practised, should become a vehicle (of progress) and a firm possession (of my mind), and should be consolidated, strengthened and perfected!" Thus, O monk, should you train yourself.

'If, O monk, this concentration of mind has been cultivated by you, well cultivated, then you may develop this concentration together with thought-conception and sustained thinking; or without (new) thought-conception, only with sustained thinking; or without thought-conception and without sustained thinking; or you may develop it with rapture; without rapture; with joy; or with equanimity.[46]

'If, O monk, this concentration of mind has been cultivated by you, well cultivated, then you should train yourself thus: "Compassion. . . . Sympathetic Joy. . . . Equanimity, the Liberation of the heart, should be cultivated in me and regularly practised, should become a vehicle (of progress) and a firm possession (of my mind), and should be consolidated, strengthened and perfected!"[47] Thus, O monk, should you train yourself.

'If, O monk, this concentration of mind has thus been cultivated by you, well cultivated, then you may develop it together with thought-conception and sustained thinking. . . . (*as above*).

'If, O monk, this concentration of mind has been cultivated by you, then you should train yourself thus: "I shall dwell practising body-contemplation on the body, ardent, clearly comprehending and mindful, having overcome covettousness and grief concerning the world."

'If monk, this concentration of mind has thus been cultivated by you, well cultivated, then you may develop it together with thought-conception and sustained thinking. . . . (*as above*).

"If O monk, this concentration of mind has been cultivated by you, well cultivated, then you should train yourself thus: "I shall dwell practising feeling-contemplation . . . mind-contemplation . . . mind-object contemplation. . . ."

'If, O monk, this concentration of mind has thus been cultivated by you, well cultivated, then, O monk, wherever you go, you will go being at ease; wherever you stand, you will stand being being at ease, wherever you sit, you will sit being at ease; wherever you lie down, you will lie down being at ease.'[48]

And that monk, having been admonished by the Exalted One with this exhortation, rose from his seat, saluted the Exalted One respectfully, and keeping him to his right, went away. And that monk then lived alone and secluded, earnest, ardent and resolute. And the goal for the sake of which noble sons go forth from home to homelessness, that highest perfection of the Holy Life he soon came to know directly, in that very life, realizing it for himself: 'Rebirth has ceased, the Holy Life has been lived, completed is the task, and nothing further remains after this,' thus he knew. And then this monk became one of the Arahats.

57. The Gradual Training

First in the sequence of the Gradual Training come 1. Virtue, 2. Sense-control, 3 Moderation in Eating, 4. Wakefulness (reduction of sleep). After dealing with these, our text proceeds with the next stages: 5. Mindfulness and Clear Comprehension, 6. Abandoning of the five Hindrances, 7. Satipaṭṭhāna, 8. Meditative Absorption (jhāna).

When the noble disciple has cultivated wakefulness, the Perfect one gives him further guidance: 'Come, O monk, equip yourself with mindfulness and clear comprehension! Be one who acts with clear comprehension when going forward and going back; In looking straight on and in looking elsewhere, in bending and stretching (your limbs), in wearing the robes and carrying the alms bowl, in eating, drinking, chewing and savouring; in obeying the calls of nature; in walking, standing, sitting, falling asleep, waking, speaking and in being silent, be one who acts with clear comprehension!'

When the noble disciple has equipped himself with mindfulness and clear comprehension, the Perfect One gives him further guidance: 'Come, O monk! Live in a secluded place; in a forest, under a tree, on a hill, in a rock cleft, a mountain cave, in a cemetery, a jungle thicket, an open space, a shelter of straw (in the fields)!' The monk then lives in such secluded places, and after the meal, having returned from the alms round, he sits down, cross-legged, keeping his body erect and his mindfulness alert. Having given up *covetousness* concerning the world, he dwells with a heart free from covetousness; he cleanses his mind from covetousness. Having given up the blemish of *hatred* concerning the world, he dwells with a heart free from hatred, friendly and compassionate toward all living beings; he cleanses his mind from the blemish of hatred. Having giving up *sloth and torpor,* he dwells with a heart free from sloth and torpor, in the contemplation of light, mindful and clearly comprehending; he cleanses his mind from sloth and torpor. Having given up *restlessness and worry,* he dwells with a heart that is unagitated, with a mind that is at peace; he cleanses his mind from restlessness and worry. Having given up *doubt,* he has left uncertainty behind, and is no longer uncertain about things salutary; he cleanses his mind from doubt.

Having given up these five hindrances that defile the mind and weaken the understanding, he practises body-contemplation on the body—feeling-contemplation on feelings—mind-contemplation on the mind—mind-object contemplation on mind-objects, ardent, clearly comprehending and mindful, having overcome covetousness and grief concerning the world.

Suppose an elephant trainer has driven a strong post into the ground, and to it he ties a forest elephant by his neck, for subduing in him the behaviour of the forest, for subduing in him the longings of the forest, for subduing in him the anxieties, fatigue and heat of the forest life, for making him amenable to village life, for training him in a behaviour agreeable to men.

Similarly are the four Foundations of Mindfulness for the noble disciple a fastening of his mind, for subduing in him his worldly behaviour, for subduing in him his worldly longings, for subduing in him his worldly anxieties, fatigue and heat; for reaching the right path: for realizing Nibbāna.

Then the Perfect One gives him further guidance: 'Come, O monk! Practise body-contemplation on the body, and do not think thoughts connected with sense desires! Practise feeling-contemplation of feelings, and do not think thoughts connected with sense desires! Practise mind-contemplation on the mind, and do not think thoughts connected with sense desires! Practise mind-object contemplation on mind-objects, and do not think thoughts connected with sense desires!'

Then, after the stilling of thought-conception and sustained thinking, he gains the inner tranquillity and harmony of the *second absorption* that is free of thought-conception and sustained thinking, born of concentration and filled with rapture and joy.[49]

Now follow, in the original text, the third and fourth absorption, the threefold Gnosis (te-vijjā), *culminating in Sainthood* (arahatta).

Similes

58. The Gate Keeper—I

Suppose there is a king's border town with strong ramparts and turrets on strong foundations, and with six gates. And there is a gate keeper, intelligent, experienced and prudent, who keeps out people unknown and admits those who are known. Now there arrived from the eastern direction a pair of messengers, and they ask the gate keeper: 'Where, friend, is the lord of this town?' And the gate keeper replies: 'He lives at the central square, dear sirs.' And that pair of messengers now quickly carry the true message to the lord of the town and return by the way they had come. (Similarly it is with messengers arriving from the western, northern and southern direction.)

This simile I have given to make the meaning clear. And its significance is this:

'The town' is a name for this body consisting of the four elements, begotten by father and mother, nurtured on rice and gruel, subject to (the law of) impermanence, to decaying, to wasting away, to dissolution, to disintegration.

'The six gates' is a name for the six internal sense bases.

'The gate keeper' is a name for mindfulness.

'The swift pair of messengers' is a name for Tranquillity and Insight.

'The lord of the town' is a name for consciousness.

'The central square' is a name for the four primary elements: the earth element, the water element, the heat element, the air element.

'The true message' is a name for Nibbāna.

'The way traversed' is a name for the Noble Eightfold Path, namely Right Understanding, Right Thought, Right Speech, Right Action, Right Livelihood, Right Effort, Right Mindfulness and Right Concentration.

59. The Gate Keeper—II

In a king's border town, O monks, there is a gate keeper, intelligent, experienced and prudent, who keeps out people unknown and admits those who are known, to protect the residents of the town and to ward off outsiders. Similar to that gate keeper is a noble disciple who is mindful, endowed with a high degree of mindfulness and circumspection. Even what has been done and spoken long ago, he will remember, he will recollect. A noble disciple who has mindfulness as his gate keeper, will reject what is unsalutary and cultivate what is salutary; he will reject what is blameworthy and cultivate what is blameless, and he will preserve his purity.

60. The Probe

Suppose a man has been wounded by an arrow thickly smeared with poison, and his friends and companions, relatives and kinsmen call a physician, a surgeon. And the physician, the surgeon, widens the wound with his knife and searches for the arrow point with the probe. Having found the arrow point, he extracts it and completely removes the poison until he thinks that nothing of it is left. . . .

This simile have I given to make the meaning clear. And its significance is this:

This simile have I given to make the meaning clear. And its significance is this:

'The wound' is a name for the six internal sense bases.

'The poison' is a name for ignorance.

'The arrow' is a name for craving.

'The probe' is a name for mindfulness.

'The knife' is a name for noble wisdom.

'The physician, the surgeon' is a name for the Perfect One, the Holy One, the Fully Enlightened

61. In a Crowd

Once the Exalted One lived in the Sumbha country, in a town of the Sumbha people called Sedaka. There the Exalted One addressed the monks:

'Suppose a large crowd of people has gathered on hearing the news that a beauty queen[50] has come. And if that beauty queen is also highly gifted in dancing and singing, on knowing that a still larger crowd would gather. Now a man comes who wishes to live and not die, who desires happiness and abhors suffering. The people say to him: "Here, friend, is a vessel filled to the brim with oil. That you must carry through the large crowd to the beauty queen. A man with drawn sword will follow behind your back, and if you spill even a little of the oil, he will cut off your head!" Now, what do you think, monks? Will that man carry the oil-vessel carelessly, without paying heed to his environment?'

— 'Certainly not, Lord.'

—'This simile have I given to make the meaning clear. And its significance is this:

'"The vessel filled to the brim with oil" is a name for mindfulness concerning the body.

'Hence, O monks, you should train yourselves thus: "We shall cultivate Mindfulness concerning the Body, we shall practise it regularly so that it may become a vehicle of progress and a firm possession of our minds; so that it may be consolidated, strengthened and perfected in us!" Thus, O monks, should you train yourselves!'

62. Ploughshare and Goad

Mindfulness is like the ploughshare and the goad.[51]

Commentary.—In the Exalted One's 'husbandry', the place of the farmer's ploughshare and goad is taken by mindfulness that is associated with Insight (*vipassanā*) and conjoined with the Path (that is, the stages of emancipation). Just as the ploughshare precedes and protects the plough-handle, similarly mindfulness protects the plough of wisdom by examining the development of the salutary processes of mind and keeping the respective objects present before the mind. Therefore, in scriptural passages like 'he dwells with a mind guarded by mindfulness', mindfulness is called a 'guard'. Also in the sense of 'absence of confusion', mindfulness precedes the 'plough of wisdom', because wisdom can penetrate only such ideas that have been carefully examined by mindfulness, and hence are free from confusion.

Further, just as the goad instils in the oxen the fear of being beaten and so prevents them from lying down and restrains them from taking a wrong path; similarly it is the function of mindfulness to stir the energy—which is, as it were, mind's drawing animal—and fill it with the fear of being reborn in lower worlds of misery, and thus does not allow energy to slacken. Mindfulness further keeps energy from turning to a wrong field, that is to the pursuit of sense pleasures; it harnesses energy to the subject of meditation and prevents it from straying to a wrong path. Hence it is said: 'Mindfulness is like the ploughshare and the goad'.

Post-canonical Pali Literature

***From the Questions of Milinda*[52]**

63. The Characteristic Quality of Mindfulness

King Milinda asked: 'What is the characteristic quality of mindfulness, Venerable Sir?'

The Venerable Nāgasena replied: 'It is the quality of keeping check and of retaining.'

—'In how far, Venerable Sir, is "keeping check" characteristic of mindfulness?'

—'If mindfulness has arisen, one keeps check of things salutary or unsalutary, blameless or blameworthy, excellent or inferior, and (other) contrasts of dark and bright; and one knows: "These are the four Foundations of Mindfulness, these the four Right Efforts, the four Roads of Spiritual Success, the five mental Faculties and Powers, the seven Factors of Enlightenment, this is the Noble Eightfold Path." Knowing this, one practises what ought to be practised, and does not practise what ought not to be practised; one adopts what ought to be adopted, and does not adopt what ought not to be adopted. In that way, great king, has mindfulness the quality of keeping check.'

—'Give a simile.'

—'It may be likened to the treasurer of a world-ruling monarch who reminds him early and late of his might, keeping count of the king's possessions thus: "Your Majesty has so many elephants, so many horses, chariots and soldiers; so much is your money, gold and other treasure. May Your Majesty remember it!" Similarly, great king, has mindfulness the characteristic of keeping check (of one's mental possessions).'

—'And in how far, Venerable Sir, is "retaining" characteristic of mindfulness?'

—'If mindfulness has arisen, great king, one can examine the outcome of things beneficial and those not beneficial; one will know: "These things are beneficial, and those are not; these things are helpful and those are not." Knowing this, one will discard things that are not beneficial and not helpful, and one will retain those which are beneficial and helpful. In that way, great king, is "retaining" a characteristic quality of mindfulness.'

—'Give a simile.'

—'Suppose there is a monarch's councellor who knows: "These people are well disposed towards the king, and those are ill-disposed; these are useful to him, and those are harmful." Knowing this, he wards off the ill-disposed and harmful, and retains those who are well-disposed and useful. Similarly, great king, is "retaining" a characteristic quality of mindfulness.

'Also the Exalted One has said that "Mindfulness is helpful everywhere".'

—'You are a capable man, Venerable Nāgasena.'

64. Attention and Wisdom

The king asked: 'What is the characteristic quality of attention (*manasikāra*) and what is the characteristic quality of wisdom (*paññā*)?'

—' "Gathering-in", great king, is the characteristic quality of attention, and "cutting off" is the characteristic quality of wisdom.'

—'In what way? Please give a simile.'

—'Do you know, great king, the way of the barley-reapers?'

—'Yes, I know it, Venerable Sir.'

—'How do they cut the barley?'

—'With the left hand they take hold of a sheaf of barley, and holding the sickle with the right hand, they cut it off.'

—'Similarly, great king, he who is devoted to meditation (*yogāvacara*), takes hold of the mind through attention and with wisdom he cuts off the defilements.

'In that way, great king, is "gathering-in" characteristic of attention, and "cutting off" characteristic of wisdom.'

—'You are a capable man, Venerable Nāgasena.'

65. From the Simile of the Cock

Just as the cock, even if chased away with stones, sticks, clubs, cudgels or switches, will nevertheless not abandon his home, similarly a monk devoted to meditation, whether he is busy with his robes,[53] doing repairs, attending to his monastic duties and observances, whether studying or teaching, should not abandon wise and thorough attention (*yoniso manasikāra*); because this is the meditator's own home, namely thorough attention. This is a quality of the cock that should be taken up by him.

Also by the Exalted One, divinest of the divine, it was said: 'What, monks, is the monk's domain, his very own paternal home? It is the four Foundations of Mindfulness.'

66. The Grain of Seed

'You have said, Venerable Nāgasena, that one should take up two qualities of the seed grain. What are these two?'

—'If there is, great king, good soil and proper rain, even a small quantity of seed will produce ample fruit. Similarly virtue should be so well observed by the meditating monk that it will produce the entire fruit of the ascetic life. This, great king, is the first quality of the seed that should be taken up.

'Further, great king, if seed is sown on a well cleared field, it will quickly grow. Similarly, if the meditator has well mastered his mind and has purified it in solitude, and if he throws (as it were, the seed grain of his mind) on the excellent field of Satipaṭṭhāna, then it will quickly grow.'

67. The Cat

Just as the cat goes out for prey only close by, similarly the meditating monk contemplates the arising and vanishing of these very five aggregates of his own which are the objects of clinging (*upādāna-kkhandha*): 'Thus is corporeality, thus it arises, thus it vanishes; thus is feeling, thus it arises, thus it vanishes; thus is perception, thus it arises, thus it vanishes; thus are the mental formations, thus they arise, thus they vanish; thus is consciousness, thus it arises, thus it vanishes.'

Also the Exalted One, divinest of the divine, has said:

'Not far from here you have to seek:
Sublimest heavens what will they avail?
Here in this present aggregation,
In your own body will you find it all.'

68. From the Spider Simile

It was said by the venerable Anuruddha Thera:

At the five sense doors spread the net
Of Mindfulness, so fine and subtle.
In it defilements will be caught,
And can be killed by insight clear.

From the Commentarial Literature

69. The Sole Way

Satipaṭṭhāna is the 'one and only way'[54] because it is a single (and straight) path, not one that branches off. It is a way that has to be taken by oneself alone: having given up association with the crowd, one should live secluded and detached. *A two-fold seclusion is meant here: bodily seclusion, that is living without a companion, away from the crowd; and inner seclusion, that is keeping free from craving which is called 'man's companion'.*[55]

Further, Satipaṭṭhāna is the 'one and only way' because it is the way of the One, in the sense of the best, the unique. This refers to the Exalted One, the Buddha, who is the best of all beings. Though others, too, walk on that Way, it is the Buddha's because he had discovered it, and it exists only in his Teaching and Discipline, not elsewhere.

Satipaṭṭhāna is the Only Way because there is no other road that leads to Nibbāna. Here one may object: Is it only Satipaṭṭhāna that is meant by the word 'way'? Are there not several other factors that comprise the (eightfold) way—such as right understanding, right thought, etc.?—That is true. But all these other factors are comprised in Satipaṭṭhāna and cannot exist without it.

70. Typology

Why did the Exalted One teach just *four* Foundations of Mindfulness, neither more nor less? He did so for the benefit of different types of character among those susceptible to instruction.

For a character bent on *Craving* (*taṇhā-carita*), if he is of slow intelligence, the suitable way of purification is the Satipaṭṭhāna concerned with the Contemplation of the Body, which is coarse and distinct; for a craving-type of keen intelligence, it is the subtle Contemplation of Feeling.

For a character bent on *Theorizing* (*diṭṭhi-carita*), if he is of slow intelligence, the suitable way of purification is the Satipaṭṭhāna concerned with the not too diversified Contemplation of the State of Mind; for a theorizing type of keen intelligence, it is the greatly diversified Contemplation of Mental Objects.

Body and Feelings are the chief inducements to enjoyment (which stands foremost for one of the craving type). For overcoming (his particular propensity) it is easier for the craving type of slow intelligence to see the impurity in the coarser of those two bases of craving, that is in the body. For the craving type of keen intelligence it is easier to see the suffering in the subtle object of feeling.

Similarly, the state of mind (citta) *and mind contents* (dhammā) *are the chief inducements to theorizing since they may become the basis for a tenacious belief in permanency and selfhood. For giving up the belief in permanency it is easier for the theorizing type of slow intelligence to see the impermanence of consciousness* (citta) *in its not too diversified classification as 'mind with lust', etc. For giving up the belief in selfhood it is easier for the theorizing type of keen intelligence to see the absence of selfhood* (anattā) *in the mental concomitants* (cetasika) *with their greatly detailed classification as perception, sense impression, etc.; or as the Five Hindrances, etc. (according to the Discourse).*

But mind and mind contents can as well be bases for craving (and not only for theorizing); while body and feelings may also be bases for theorizing (and not only for craving). But for indicating which of the four are the stronger conditions for craving and theorizing respectively, the above differentiation has been made and the word 'chief (inducement)' has been added to qualify these statements.

71. Having Overcome Covetousness and Grief . . .

'Having overcome covetousness and grief', that is either by overcoming a bad quality by its opposite good quality (*tadanga-ppahāna*) or by temporary suppression (*vikkhambhana-ppahāna*) during *jhāna*.

Because the term *covetousness* is meant to include sense-desire (*kāma-cchanda*), and the term *grief* comprises ill will (*byāpāda*), therefore this statement of the Discourse refers to the abandonment of the five Hindrances (*nīvaraṇa*), by naming the two strongest of them.

In particular, this passage intends to convey the following: *Overcoming of covetousness* means: giving up the satisfaction caused by bodily gratification; giving up delight in the body; ceasing to be carried away by the illusory beauty and the illusory bliss of the body. *Overcoming of grief* means: giving up the dissatisfaction caused by bodily misfortune; giving up the discontent with the (continued) contemplation on the body; ceasing to recoil from the actual impurity and misery of the body.

Hereby the yogi's yogic power and yogic skill are shown. For just this is yogic power: to become free of satisfactions and dissatisfactions;[56] to master one's likes and dislikes;[57] to cease alike from being carried away by the unreal and from recoiling from the real. And to accomplish all this is yogic skill.

72. Ardent, Clearly Comprehending and Mindful

Because for one who is not *ardent* (in his meditative effort), inner stagnation will become a hindrance; because one without *clear comprehension* will be confused as to the employment of the right means and the avoiding of the wrong means; because one of feeble *mindfulness* will be unable to avoid rejecting the right means and employing the wrong means—(because of these defects) such a one will not be successful in his meditation. For showing those qualities by virtue of which one can succeed, it is said in the Discourse: *he dwells ardent, clearly comprehending and mindful.*

73. Mindfulness as Harmonizing Quality

Mindfulness should be strong everywhere. It protects the mind against restlessness into which the mind may fall by the influence of those faculties (*indriya*) which incline to it, namely Faith, Energy and Wisdom. Mindfulness protects also against lassitude into which the mind may fall by the influence of the faculty that inclines to it, namely Concentration. Therefore, mindfulness—like salt in all dishes, like a minister versed in all affairs—is required everywhere. . . . Without mindfulness there is no spurring nor restraining of the mind.[58]

74. Gleanings from the Commentarial Literature Mindfulness and Clear Comprehension

Because these two qualities serve to remove hindrances and to foster meditative development, they are to be considered as helpers, and this at all times, for all types of meditators, and in the practice of all subjects of meditation.

- The functions of Mindfulness and Clear Comprehension are of equal importance.
- There is no mental process concerned with knowing and understanding, that is without mindfulness.
- Negligence is, in brief, absence of mindfulness.
- Mindfulness is that unremitting heedfulness that brings about perseverence in any activity.
- Developed sense-faculties[59] are called those which, under the impact of habitual work at mind-development,[60] have become impregnated

with the fragrance of mindfulness and clear comprehension.

From the Mahāyāna Literature

75. Nāgārjuna

The four Foundations of Mindfulness have unmistakably been shown as the Only Way trodden by the Buddhas. Guard them at all times! Negligence in them makes all efforts useless, and it is the persevering practice of them that is called 'concentration of mind' (*samādhi*).

76. Aśvaghoṣa

Keep to mindfulness and clear comprehension in all activities, as in sitting, standing, walking, looking around and talking.

He who has established mindfulness as a guard at the doors of his mind, cannot be overpowered by the passions, as a well-guarded city cannot be conquered by the enemy.

No passion will arise in him who possesses mindfulness concerning the body; he will protect his mind under all circumstances as a wet-nurse protects the infant.

He who lacks the protective armour of mindfulness, is truly like a target board for the passions; just as a warrior in battle, who has no coat of mail, is exposed to the arrows of the enemy.

The heart if not protected by mindfulness, must truly be regarded as utterly helpless. It resembles a blind man walking on uneven ground without a guide.

Attracted by evil are men, and upon their own true weal they turn their back; regarding the perils that are so close to them, they feel no apprehension. All that is due to lack of mindfulness.

Moral conduct and all the other good qualities remain each in its own domain (as if isolated); but mindfulness follows them as a cow herd goes after his straying cattle (and collects them).

He who loses mindfulness, loses the Deathless (Nibbāna). But he who possesses Mindfulness concerning the Body, holds the Deathless in his hands.

He who is without mindfulness, how can he acquire the Noble Method (of Deliverance)? And he who lacks that Noble Method, has missed the Right Path.

He who has missed the Right Path, also misses the Deathless. He whohaslostsightoftheDeathless,cannotwinfreedomfro msuffering.

Therefore it is meet that, while going, you know 'I am going'; while standing 'I am standing', and that you thus preserve mindfulness at all times.

Therefore it is meet that, while going, you know 'I am going'; while standing 'I am standing', and that you thus preserve mindfulness at all times.

Śāntideva

'The Compendium of Spiritual Training' (Śikṣa-Samuccaya)

77. From Chapter VI: On Self-Protection

How does one guard oneself?
By shunning what is base.
And how is this achieved?
By shunning fruitless waste.
And how can this be done?
By constant mindfulness,
Which gains in keenness by devoted zeal.
And zeal arises if one comes to know
The greatness that in inner stillness lies.

Kārika 7–8

There are twelve applications of mindfulness that lead to the avoidance of fruitless waste (or useless effort):

1. One should have reverential mindfulness of the result of observing and not transgressing the Tathāgata's injunctions.

2. One should be mindful of keeping the body in a motionless state (if no activity is required).

3. But if there is occasion for activity, one should not react at once, but should first remain motionless because of the need for still stronger mindfulness (to be applied to the activity ahead). Keeping one's wishes under control, mindfulness should then be directed to fully circumspect[61] action.

4. One should be mindful of keeping the body under control if there is any disturbance like festivities or danger.

5. One should be mindful in contemplation of the four postures.

6. One should be mindful of watching from time to time the adroitness of the posture for guarding against distortions in the posture.

7. While talking one should be mindful that there are no excessive and unseemly movements of hands, feet and head, or changes of facial expression, due to excessive pleasure, arrogance, excitement, partiality, etc.

8. One should be mindful to talk only in such a voice that the hearer can understand it, and not too loudly; otherwise there will be the fault of rudeness.

9. If one comes into the difficult situation of meeting uneducated people, one should be mindful that one's own thoughts remain acceptable and intelligible to the minds of others.

10. One should be mindful that the mind that resembles an elephant in rut, is always tied to the post of inner calm.

11. One should be mindful to examine from moment to moment the condition of one's mind.

12. In a large gathering of people one should remember the above rules for the preservation of mindfulness, even if it means giving up other activity.

By such employment of mindfulness one will be successful in avoiding fruitless waste (or useless effort). And this 'mindfulness gains in keenness by devoted zeal'. 'Devoted zeal' means turning to one's task wholeheartedly; it is the opposite of a casual way (of attending to one's work).

And this devoted zeal 'arises if one comes to know the greatness that in inner stillness lies'. What is that 'stillness' (*śama*)? It is that tranquillity (*śamatha*) described in the *Ārya Akṣayamati Sūtra:*

'What is imperturbable tranquillity? It is peacefulness of mind, peacefulness of body, the control of sense faculties that are undistracted; it is freedom from agitation, from unrestraint, restlessness and fickleness; the possession of gentleness, self-control, amenability, cultured manners, a collected mind; shunning company and delighting in solitude; bodily seclusion and undistractedness of mind; a mind bent towards the forest life; frugality, control of postures; knowing the right time, the right opportunity, the right measure, and keeping deliverance in mind; being easy to support, easy to satisfy, and so forth.'

And what is 'the greatness that in inner stillness lies'? It is the capacity to produce understanding of things as they really are. Therefore, the Great Sage (the Buddha) has said: 'He who is concentrated, understands things as they really are'.[62]

One should further know that through 'the greatness that in inner stillness lies', one may secure, for oneself and for others, escape from immeasurable misery, for instance that of rebirth in the worlds of misery; that one may bring about, for oneself and others, immeasurable bliss, mundane and supramundane; and that, finally, one may attain to the Other Shore (Nibbāna). Knowing this, one should cultivate an ardent spirit of longing for that inner stillness. As one who is inside a burning house, will long for cool water, imbued with a longing as strong should be one's keen and devoted zeal for the training (in virtue, meditation and wisdom). Through that zeal, mindfulness will be firmly established; and firm mindfulness will avoid what is fruitless. In him who avoids what is fruitless, base and unprofitable things will not arise.

Therefore, he who wishes to protect himself, should go down to the root which is mindfulness, and should ever keep that mindfulness alive.

78. From the Ārya-Ratnamegha Sūtra

'All things have mind as their forerunner.[63] If mind is known, all things will be known.

'Mind whirls around like a swung fire-brand; mind vacillates like a wave; mind burns like a forest fire; mind swells like a mighty flood. If one considers this well, one will live with mindfulness well directed on the mind. One will not succumb to the mind's mastery, but will exercise mastery over the mind. If the mind is mastered, all things are mastered.'

79. Avoidance of Diversion

Through the loss of clear comprehension and the lack of mindfulness, the mind becomes unsteady, because it allows itself to be diverted from the goal. But if an excessive preoccupation with external activities has been avoided with the help of mindfulness and clear comprehension, then, thanks to them, the mind can steadily keep to a single object as long as it wishes.

80. Self-Protection

Ārya-Sāgaramati Sūtra. 'There is yet another rule that can serve as the epitome of Mahāyāna: "By taking care to avoid stumbling oneself, one will protect all beings".'[64]

Bodhisattva-Prātimokṣa. 'If, O Sāriputra, one wishes to protect others, one should protect oneself.'(See text No. 15)

From Chapter XIII:

'The Foundations of Mindfulness' (*smṛtyupasthāna*): With a mind that has become pliant (by the preparatory practices described in the earlier chapters of the *Śikṣasamuccaya*), one should enter upon the practise of the Foundations of Mindfulness. Herein the

81. Foundation of Mindfulness Concerned with the Body

has been stated by way of contemplating the body's impurity. This has been said in the *Dharma-sangīti Sūtra:*

'And further, O noble son, the Bodhisattva directs his mindfulness to the body thus: "This body is nothing but a collection of feet, toes, legs, chest, hips, abdomen, navel, spine, heart, ribs, hands, arms, shoulders, neck, jaws, forehead, head and skull. It has been built up by the builder of the Karmic life-process (*karma-bhava-kāraka;* i.e. Craving), and it has become the abode of a hundred thousand of various defilements, desires and fancies....

'This body did not come from the past and will not go over into the future. It has no existence in the past or future, except in unreal and false conceptions. It is void of an (inherent) active or percipient entity;[65] neither its beginning nor its middle nor its end have firm roots anywhere; it is not a master, it is not my own and is itself propertyless. By adventitious conventional names it is called: body, bodily frame, "treasure", "receptacle", "carcass", etc. Without a core is this body, procreated by the mother's blood and the father's semen; it is of an unclean, putrefying and evil-smelling nature; it is upset by the intrusion of such thieves as greed, hatred, delusion, fear and despair; it is constantly exposed to collapse and fall, decrepitude, dissolution and destruction; and it is the breeding-place of a hundred thousand different diseases.'

82. The Foundation of Mindfulness Concerned with Feeling

It is said in the *Ārya-Ratnacūḍa Sūtra:*

'When the Bodhisattva practises feeling-contemplation on feelings, he conceives a great compassion for those beings who cling to the happiness of feelings. And he thoroughly learns to understand: "Happiness is where there is no feeling".[66] He practises feeling-contemplation on feelings, for the sake (of helping) all beings to give up (attachment to) feelings. For (effecting) the cessation of feelings in beings, he dons his armour; but for himself he does not strive after the cessation of feelings.[67]

'Any feeling felt by him is pervaded by deep compassion. When experiencing a pleasant feeling, he conceives deep compassion for beings whose character is strongly inclined to lust, and he himself gives up the propensity to lust.[68] When experiencing an unpleasant feeling, he conceives deep compassion for beings whose character is strongly inclined to hatred, and he himself gives up the propensity to hatred. When experiencing a neutral feeling, he conceives deep compassion for beings whose character is strongly inclined to delusion, and he himself gives up the propensity to delusion.

'He is not attracted by a pleasant feeling, but strives after the eradication of attraction. He is not repelled by an unpleasant feeling, but strives after the eradication of repulsion. He is not left in ignorance by a neutral feeling, but strives after the eradication of ignorance.

'Whatever feeling he experiences, all feeling he knows as transient; all feeling he knows as painful; all feeling he knows as not-self. He feels the pleasant feeling as transient; the unpleasant feeling as a thorn; the neutral feeling as peaceful.[69] Thus, indeed, what is pleasant, is transient; the unpleasant is (transient) just as the pleasant, and the neutral is without an ego.'

83. The Foundation of Mindfulness Concerned with the Mind

It is said in the *Ārya-Ratnacūḍa Sūtra:*

'He examines his mind thus: "Is it a mind that lusts or hates or is deluded?[70] Is it a mind of the past, the future or the present? What is past, has ceased; the future has not yet come, and in the present mind, there is no stability. The mind, Kāśyapa cannot be found within, nor outside, nor between. Mind, O Kāśyapa, is formless, invisible, intangible, unconceivable, without support, without abode. . . .

'Mind, O Kāśyapa , is like a magician's illusion; it takes on various forms of arising (or rebirth; *upapatti*), through thinking that is not according to reality. Mind, O Kāśyapa , is like a river's current, never at a standstill: arising, breaking, vanishing. Mind is like the light of a lamp, kept burning by causes and conditions. Mind is like a flash of lightning that, in a moment, comes to an end, and does not abide. Mind is like space; defiled by adventitious impurities.[71] . . . Mind is like a bad friend because it brings about all kinds of misery.

'Mind, O Kāśyapa , is like a bait for fishes: with a pleasant appearance, but pain-causing; it is like bluebottle flies, taking for pure what is impure. Mind is like an enemy who causes much vexation. Mind is like a vampire that sucks one's vigour and ever seeks for access. Mind is like a thief: it steals one's good dispositions.'

84. The Foundation of Mindfulness Concerned with the Factors of Existence[72]

It is said in the *Ārya-Ratnacūḍa Sūtra:*

'A Bodhisattva contemplating the Factors of Existence in the Factors of Existence, thinks thus: "Only factors of existence arise in a process of arising; only factors of existence cease in a process of ceasing.[73] But there is not in them any selfhood, any abiding being, soul, creature, a man, a man's eternal principle (*puruṣa*), a personality, a human being[74] that (as an identical entity) arises, grows old, departs and is reborn. It is the very nature of these Factors of Existence that they appear if produced (by appropriate causes and conditions); but if they are not thus produced, they will not appear. In whatever way they are produced, in that way they will appear: be they salutary, unsalutary or imperturbable (mind processes).[75] There is, however, no "producer" (or creator), but there is also not any production of factors of existence, without (appropriate) causes.'

In the same Sūtra it is said: 'Even if a Bodhisattva contemplates Factors of Existence that have little profundity in them, he does not abandon the remembrance of the thought of omniscient enlightenment.'

85. Śāntideva

'The Entrance into the Life of Enlightenment' (Bodhicaryāvatāra)

He who wishes to follow the Training,[76] should carefully guard his mind; he cannot follow the Training if the fickle mind is unguarded. (V, 1)

Untamed elephants in rut do not cause as much harm as that caused by an unrestrained mind (and experienced) in the Avīci hell and other worlds of woe. (V, 2)

But if that unruly elephant, the mind, has been completely bound by the rope of mindfulness, then all danger has ended and everything good has come. (V, 3)

The Truthfinder (the Buddha) has proclaimed that all dangers and fears, and the immeasurable sufferings (of existence) arise only from the mind. (V, 6)

Whereto could I remove the fishes and other creatures, to save them from being killed? But if the thought of abstention (from killing and other evil deeds) has been conceived, it is deemed to constitute the Perfection of Virtue (Śīla-Pāramitā). (V, 11)

How many evil men could I kill? Their number is as boundless as the sky. But if the thought of anger is killed, all enemies are killed. (V, 12)

Where could I find enough leather to cover the whole earth?[77] But by the leather of one pair of sandals the earth will be covered. (V, 13)

External circumstances cannot be guarded against like that.[78] But if I guard my own mind, what other protection do I then need? (V, 14)

In vain do those wander about in the worlds[79] who wish to destroy suffering and win happiness, without having developed this hidden mind, the essence of the Dharma.[80] (V, 17)

Hence I must see to it that my mind becomes firm and is well guarded. If I neglect this observance, the guarding of the mind, what use have for me all the other many observances? (V, 18)

As one injured will carefully protect his wound in the midst of an excited crowd, so, amidst evil folk, one should always guard the mind which is like a (sensitive) wound. (V, 19)

With folded hands I pay reverence to those who are willing to guard the mind. May you, with all your might, preserve mindfulness and clear comprehension! (V, 23)

As a man weakened by illness, is unfit for any work, so also is a mind inefficient in any activity if those two qualities are weak. (V, 24)

A mind devoid of clear comprehension is like a pot with holes; it cannot retain in memory what has been learned, thought over or meditated. (V, 25)

Many who are learned, and also possess faith and energy, become tainted by the blemish of transgression due to the fault of thoughtlessness. (V, 26)

Those who are robbed of their mindfulness by the thief 'Thoughtlessness', go to an unhappy destiny, even if they have accumulated meritorious deeds. (V, 27)

Therefore, mindfulness should never be allowed to leave the door of the mind; and if it has left, it should again be reinstated there, remembering the miseries in the worlds of woe. (V, 29)

If mindfulnes stands guard at the door of the mind, clear comprehension will likewise join and, having come, will never-leave. (V, 33)

'So-and-so must be my bodily posture'; having thus decided on a course of action, one should from time to time verify the body's position.[81] (V, 39)

What, after consideration, one has started to do, should first be accomplished with singleness of mind, and without thinking of anything else (until it is completed). (V, 43)

In that way, everything will be done well; but in the other case, both (activities)[82] will come to naught, and the defilement consisting in the lack of clear comprehension, will increase. (V, 44)

Wishing to move or to speak, one should first consider it in one's mind, and then act with skill and energy. (V, 47)

But when noticing that the mind is swayed by attraction or repulsion one should neither act nor speak but be like a piece of wood. (V, 48)

Similarly if the mind is conceited, derisive, arrogant, sarcastic, insincere, deceitful, inclined to self-praise, to blaming, despising or insulting others, or to quarrelsomeness—then one should be like a piece of wood. (V, 49–50)

One should think: 'My mind ever craves for gain, honour and fame, for a large following paying obeisance—therefore I shall be like a piece of wood.' (V, 51)

If one notices that the mind is defiled by passions or intent on vain pursuits, one should, as a valiant man, curb it vigorously by suitable countermeasures—and this at all times. (V, 54)

By my body's (observance) I shall study (the Teaching): what use is the (mere) study of words? Can a sick man cure himself by reading prescriptions? (V, 109)

Having first examined all the circumstances and one's own capacity, one may start on some work, or not; for it is better not to start than, having started, to give up.

Also in another existence that habit might continue; and through that fault suffering will increase. Besides, the work remains unfinished, whilst the time spent in starting on it, is lost. (VII, 47–48)

Beware of the blows aimed at you by the passions, and return the blows vigorously as if engaged in a sword fight with a skilful foe.

If, in such a fight, one has dropped the sword, one will, full of fear, quickly pick it up again. Similarly, if the sword of mindfulness has been dropped, one should take it up, remembering the worlds of woe. (VII, 67-68)

As one carrying a vessel full of oil and followed by sword bearers, will, in fear of death, beware of stumbling, so one should act in following the observances.[83] (VII, 70)

One should seek company or attend to one's work with this in view: 'How will the habit of mindfulness fare in these situations?' (VII, 73)

Remembering the (Buddha's last) word on Heedfulness, make yourself so quick of response that you are always ready before a situation arises. (VII, 74)

Therefore, enough of the ways of the world! Remembering (the Master's last) words on Heedfulness, I shall follow after the wise and ward off all sloth and torpor.

Hence, for defeating all hindrances, I shall engage in concentration, pulling the mind back from wrong paths and binding it to its own object constantly. (VIII, 185–186)

If one like me, still not free from the defilements, should propose to set free from the defilements the beings extending throughout the ten directions (of space), I should speak like a madman, ignorant of my own limitations. Hence, without turning back, I shall always fight the defilements. (IV, 41-42)

Thus resolving I shall put forth effort to follow the Training as it was proclaimed. How can anyone recover health through an effective medicine, if he ignores the physician's advice? (IV, 48)

Notes

1. *paṭisaraṇaṁ*; lit.: recourse, refuge.

2. *Those in Higher Training* is a paraphrase of the Pali term *sekha,* 'trainee'. It refers to disciples who, in the threefold Training (*sikkhā;* i.e. in virtue, concentration and wisdom), have advanced to such an extent that they have reached those stages of sanctitude where final deliverance is assured; namely, the Paths and Fruitions of Stream-entry, Once-return and Non-return, and the Path of Holiness (*arahatta- magga*).

3. The term 'full understanding' (*pariññā*) refers to a high stage of methodical Insight-meditation (*vipassanā-bhāvanā*) where the true nature of all phenomena is comprehended by direct and penetrative experience, as being impermanent, unsatisfactory, void of a self and any abiding substance, and as conditioned.

4. *Asekha;* one who has attained to final deliverance, the Fruition of Holiness (*arahatta-phala*); see Note 2.

5. *Āsava*; often rendered by 'cankers' or 'biases'. The Pali term implies a 'flow'; but what is meant are not 'influences' from outside, but tainted inner thought currents, the motive powers or 'drives' for wandering in the Round of Existences. Other texts mention a fourth *āsava,* the Taint of Wrong Views.

6. We would say to-day: 'he will not accept other philosophical theories.'

7. Literally: 'by repeated practice (*āsevanāya*), by mental development (or meditation; *bhāvanāya*) and frequent work on it (*bahulīkammena*).'—

Commentary: 'There is a monk who, after having giving up Sensuality and the other Hindrances, and devoting himself, day and night, to his principal subjects of meditation, has attained to Holiness (*arahatta*). Another person sees him and thinks: "Admirable, indeed, is that monk who lives such a perfect life!". Inspired by that thought, his heart feels joyful confidence (in the Buddha and his Teaching), and after his death he appears in a heavenly world. In that way one protects and helps others by protecting and helping oneself (by meditation).'

8. *Commentary:* 'There is a monk who, through meditating on one of the first three of the Sublime States (*brahma-vihāra*; i.e. loving-kindness, compassion, and sympathetic joy), has produced the first three meditative Absorptions (*jhāna*). Taking this as his basis, he contemplates the bodily and mental formations, strengthens his Insight and attains Holiness. In that way he protects and helps himself by protecting others (through his cultivation of loving-kindness, etc.).'

9. This text succinctly sets forth the principles of Buddhist ethics which, as the Buddha's own Enlightenment, are based on the 'twin virtues' of Compassion (*karuṇā*) and Wisdom (*paññā*). In the two terse maxims of our text, self-protection and protection of others are closely interrelated, and each of these maxims is the postulate of Compassion as well as of Wisdom. But both, Compassion and Wisdom, require true self-protection as their indispensable condition of sound development. Therefore, in our text, it is the apprentice's view that the Buddha approves. See also Text 77.

The introduction of Satipaṭṭhāna in this context, confirms the Buddha's statement that 'Mindfulness is useful everywhere'. Self-protection and protection of others require mindfulness which receives its requisite training through that triple chord of the practice: its application to the internal (self), the external (others) and the combination of both. Possibly the last paragraph of our text is an allusion to that triple practice: the sentences 'I shall protect myself', 'I shall protect others' refer to the internal and the external; while the last two statements of the text correspond to the combination of the internal and external.

10. The five lower Fetters (*saṁyojana*) are: 1. Personality-belief, 2. Sceptical Doubt, 3.Attachment to rites and rituals, 4. Sensual Lust, 5. Ill-will.

11. The Non-returner (*anāgāmī*) who has entered the third of the four stages to consummate Holiness (*arahatta*), is no longer reborn in the Sense Sphere, but reaches Nibbāna in one of the heavenly worlds of the Fine-corporeal Sphere.

12. The Pali term is *vipassati*, alluding to *vipassanā*, the meditative development of liberating insight.

13. This refers to Nibbāna.

14. *Vijjā-vimutti-phala.*

15. In thoughts, words and deeds.

16. According to this instruction, the mind should be trained to stop at the initial observation of the bare perceptual object, without any interference by likes and dislikes, or by any other emotional or intellectual judgements. The purpose and value of this practice is manifold: it will act as a brake to any rashness in thoughts, words and deeds; it makes it possible to distinguish the single phases of a seemingly compact perceptual process which is very often identified with its subsequent evaluation; it offers direct insight into the evanescent, conditioned and unsubstantial character of reality. See Texts 53, 54, and p. xiv.

17. *Commentary:* 'If there is bodily agitation caused by defiling passions, or if there is lassitude or distraction, one should not be influenced by these defilements. One should rather lay down (temporarily) the subject of meditation, and should direct the mind towards any object that inspires confidence, such as the Recollection of the Buddha.'

18. He reverts to his original subject of meditation.

19. *Commentary.* He no longer reflects upon, and considers, thoughts of defilement.

20. *Commentary: paṇidhāya bhāvanā;* that is an interrupted meditation where the original subject is temporarily laid off (*ṭhapetvā*).

21. *Commentary: apanidhāya bhāvāna,* without laying off (*afhapetvā*), i.e. uninterrupted.

22. That is, away from the original subject.

23. The Pali term is here again *apaṇihitaṁ,* 'undirected' (see *apaṇidhāya* in Note 21); that is, without directing the mind to another subject.

24. Sense impression, or Contact (*phassa*), is sixfold: as produced by the five physical sense faculties or by the mind. See the 5th link of the formula of Dependent Origination (*paṭicca-samuppāda*).

25. *Citta.* In the translation of the Discourse rendered by (state of) mind.

26. *Commentary:* Through the origination of wise attention (*yoniso manasikāra*) the mental objects of the Factors of Enlightenment originate; through unwise attention (*ayoniso manasikāra*) the mental objects of the Hindrances originate.

27. *Upaṭṭhāna*: corresponds to *paṭṭhāna* in the term *satipaṭṭhāna;* see p. xiv.

28. That is, the knowledge connected with the Seven Contemplations.

29. Or 'consciousness'.

30. What remains are the Aggregates of Perception (*saññā-kkhandha*) and of Mental Formations (*sankhāra-kkhandha*).

31. *Rati*, 'lust'.

32. *Arati*, listlessness, boredom.

33. Sāriputta, one of the two chief disciples of the Buddha who died before the Master.

34. The first section of this Discourse, not dealing with Mindfulness of Breathing, has been omitted.

35. *Citta-sankhāra*; this refers to feelings, perceptions and other mental concomitants arising in connection with breathing.

36. According to the Commentary, the first tetrad may apply to the development of Tranquillity (*samatha*) or of Insight (*vipassanā*). See Ch. 5.

The second and third tetrad refer to one who has reached the meditative Absorptions (*jhāna*), while the fourth tetrad concerns only the development of Insight.

37. These are synonyms for the first two of the five Hindrances which, on their part, form the first section in the Contemplation of Mind-objects. The 'abandoning' is effected by the contemplations of impermanence, etc., by which notions of permanency, etc., are abolished.

38. Literally: 'Above, below, and in-between, as far as the earth's reach goes.'

39. These are the five Aggregates or Categories (*khandha*) which constitute personal existence: corporeality, feeling, perception, mental formations and consciousness.

40. 'Conceit' (*māna*) refers in particular to 'self-conceit' (*asmi-māna*), i.e. personality-belief, and other wrong conceptions.

41. 'Greed' includes all degrees of attraction.

42. 'Hate' includes all degrees of aversion.

43. The Texts 52 and 53 are, in the first place, illustrations of the Contemplation of Mind, as given in the Discourse, i.e. knowing mind as being with lust or without, etc. In addition, these two texts may serve as an illuminating example of the 'Instruction to Bāhiya' (Text 29), that is, for 'stopping at bare perception': 'In what is seen there must be only the seen . . .'

Text 52 enjoins the meditator to distinguish clearly the perception proper from the reaction to it (for instance, by greed), which is a separate and subsequent mind process: 'He is aware of the form and aware of his desire for it (or, that there is no desire).' This application of mindfulness is said to be one of the instances in which the Buddha's Teaching reveals those chacteristics which are expressed in the ancient formula of homage to the 'Jewel of the Dhamma': 'Visible here and now is the Teaching . . . It is noteworthy that this applies also to the case when desire has been found to be present but was identified as a separate process. In the kindred Text 53, this way of practice is said to be independent of belief, tradition, opinions, etc., and to offer a direct access to the goal of deliverance, through one's own indubitable experience.

44. *Dhammanvayo*; the inner consistency of the Teaching.

45. These five modes of perceiving things as repulsive, etc., and the mastery of these modes, are called in Pali *ariya-iddhi*, 'noble magic' or 'the power of the noble ones (the Saints)'. They are a kind of subtle 'magic of transformation' by which habitual emotional attitudes can be changed at will, or replaced by complete equanimity. An equanimity that has gone through this training has, indeed, stood the severest test. By that training full control of emotive reactions

to one's environment can be achieved, and complete independence from the influence of habits and passions. As indicated by the name of that training, 'The Saints' Power', perfection in it can be attained only by the Accomplished Ones, the Arahats. But earnest attempts in practising it, will be of great benefit to anyone who can muster the required determination. Previous experience in mind-control will, however, be indispensable, and therefore, our text mentions first the practice of Satipaṭṭhāna. It is, in particular, the Contemplation of Feeling and the distinction between a perception and one's reaction to it (see Texts 52, 53), which are important in this context. See *Dīgha-Nikāya* No. 28; *Majjhima-Nikāya* No. 152; *The Path of Purification,* transl. by Ñāṇamoli (Colombo 1956), p. 417.

46. This paragraph refers to the mental factors which are present or absent in the different stages of meditative Absorption (*jhāna*).

47. Loving-kindness, Compassion, Sympathetic Joy and Equanimity are called the four 'Sublime States' or 'Divine Abidings' (*brahma-vihāra*). About their meditative development see *The Path of Purification*, Ch. XI; *The Four Sublime States*, by Nyanaponika Thera (Buddhist Publication Society, Kandy, Ceylon).

48. This refers to Sainthood (*arahatta*); because the Saint (*arahat*) is in a state of well-being (or ease; *phāsu*) in any of the four bodily postures, that is in all his activities. The method given in this text, is that of Insight preceded by Tranquillity (*samatha-pubbaṅgama-vipassanā*), according to a division of meditative practice given in the *Aṅguttara-Nikāya* (*The Gradual Sayings*, The Fours, No. 170). 'Tranquillity' is Absorption, while the practice of Satipaṭṭhāna stands here for Insight.

49. The method given here, is that of Tranquillity (Absorption) preceded by the practice of Insight (*vipassanā-pubbaṅgama-samatha*). After a practice of Satipaṭṭhāna, with a temporary suppression of the five Hindrances, stress is laid that during that practice no thoughts of sense desires are entertained. Now follows the entry into the Second

Absorption, without any reference to a prior attainment of the First Absorption. There is no comment on that omission in the exegetical literature. The following remarks may be offered as a tentative explanation.

The temporary abandonment of the five Hindrances indicates that during the practice of Satipaṭṭhāna a high stage of Insight-development has been reached that is characterized by a strength of concentration approaching that of full Absorption, and therefore called Neighbourhood- or Access Concentration (*upacāra-samādhi*); in the latter, as in Jhāna itself, the five Hindrances are temporarily subdued. The Second Absorption is described as being 'free of Thought-conception and Discursive Thinking'. The direct entry onto it, as mentioned in our text, is facilitated by the fact that in the bare observation of physical and mental processes as cultivated in Satipaṭṭhāna, ratiocination is greatly reduced. This fact makes it also easier to follow the specific injunction of our text, to avoid thoughts of sense desire, which is the starting point for the First Absorption, 'Detached from sense objects . . .'

50. *Janapada-kalyānī;* 'the lovely one of the country (or province).'

51. A farmer of the Brahmin caste blames the Buddha for not sowing and ploughing, and yet, as a mendicant ascetic, expecting to be fed. The Buddha replies that he cultivates the field of the mind, and he gives a sequence of similes from which these two are taken.

52. The *Questions of Milinda* are an outstanding work of later Pali literature. The original, however, is believed to have been written in a vernacular (Prakrit) of North West India; the oldest parts have been dated to the 1st Century B.C. In Burma, the work is included in the canonical scriptures (*Tipiṭaka*), but also in other Theravāda countries it enjoys a high esteem. King Milinda has been identified with the Greco-Indian king Menandros who reigned 160–140 B.C.

53. That is, in stitching, mending, washing or dying.

54. *Ekāyano maggo:* the opening words of the Discourse.

55. The passages printed in *italics* are taken from the Sub-commentary to the Satipaṭṭhāna-Sutta.

56. These terms (in Pali: *anurodha, virodha*) also imply: partisanship and opposition, approval and condemnation.

57. *Rati, arati:* overeagerness and boredom: lust and distaste.

58. Mindfulness is one of the five Spiritual Faculties (*indriya*); the other four are: Faith and Wisdom, Energy and Concentration. Each of these two pairs of faculties should be well balanced, for achieving full potency; that is, there should be neither excess and one-sided development, nor neglect and underdevelopment, in either of these faculties. It is mindfulness that watches over them and acts as the harmonizing factor.

59. *Indriyāni bhāvitāni;*, including the sixth, the mind faculty.

60. *Vāsanā-bhāvanā,* 'habitual meditation'.

61. *Sarva-dhīra,* alternative rendering: 'fully determined' or 'wholeheartedly energetic'.

62. In the Pali Canon, this saying occurs at *Saṁyutta-Nikāya* XXII, 5.

63. *Cittapurvangamaśca sarva dharmaḥ;* see *Dhammapada* v. 1: *manopubbaṇgamā dhammā.*

64. *Aparo eko dharmo mahāyāna-samgrahāya saṁvartate; svaskhalita-pratyavekṣaṇatāya sarvasattvānurakṣe'ti.*

65. *Kāraka-vedaka-rahito.* This identical phrase occurs very often in the commentarial Pali literature, e.g. in the Commentary to the Satipaṭṭhāna Sutta, and the *Visuddhi-Magga.* By this phrase those

speculative views are rejected which ascribe to an assumed self (*ātma*) either an active or passive (receptive) part in the life process.

66. This is probably an allusion to passages in the Pali Canon as *Anguttara Nikāya* (PTS), vol. IV, pp. 414 ff (*Gradual Sayings*, the Tens, Discourse 34), where Sāriputta says that 'Nibbāna is happiness', and when questioned about this statement, replies 'Just that is happiness where there is no feeling.'

67. Here we find a deviation from Theravāda doctrine.

68. *Rāga-cariteṣu*; see in Text 70, the 'character bent on Craving' (*taṇhā-carita*).

69. Cf. the following stanza from the *Saṁyutta-Nikāya* (XXXVI, 5) of the Pali Canon:

> 'Who sees pleasure as pain, and pain as a thorn;
> And as transient the peaceful neutral state—
> Such clear-eyed monk has seen through feeling . . .
> And, having seen it, in this very life
> Will he be free from cankers, from all taints.'

See also the stanzas in Text 50.

70. See the Mind-Contemplation in the Discourse.

71. *Āgantukaiḥ kleśair upakliśyate.* Cf. in Pali: *Pabhassaram idam bhikkhave cittaṁ, tañca kho āgantukehi upakkilesehi upakkiliṭṭhaṁ,* 'Mind is radiant, O monks, but defiled by adventitious impurities' (*Anguttara-Nikāya,* I).

72. *Dharma-smṛtyupasthāna.* Here, as the context shows, the term *dharma* (Pali: *dhamma*) is not conceived as 'mental objects' (as rendered in the Pali texts of this anthology), but in the sense of the

factors, or constituents, of all existence, which are conditioned, and void of a self or of any other form of an abiding substance.

73. *Dharmā ev'olpadyamānā utpadyante: dharmā eva nirudhyamānā nirudhyanti.* This again has a parallel in the Pali where the same phraseology is applied to the term *dukkha,* 'suffering': *Dukkham eva uppajjamānaṁ uppajjati: dukkham eva nirujjhamānaṁ nirujjhanti'* (Samy. XII, 15).

74. The identical sequence of terms occurs frequently in the commentarial Pali literature.

75. *Kuśalā vā akuśalā vā āniñjyā vā;* the latter term refers to the meditative consciousness. In Pali literature, a similar threefold division is applied to the term *saṅkhāra* (karma formations, or karmic volitions), in the formula of Dependent Origination (*paṭicca-samupādda*).

76. *Śikṣāni* (plural); the threefold training (Pali: *sikkhā*) in virtue, concentration and wisdom.

77. As a protection against thorns, etc.

78. That is, by attempting external measures like killing all enemies, or covering the earth with a protective carpet.

79. Literally: 'are whirled about in the sky' (like a piece of cotton wool—a frequent simile in Indian literature).

80. Or: totality of things; *dharma-sarvasvaṁ.*

81. See in Text 77 the sixth of the twelve applications of mindfulness.

82. That is, the activity originally started, and that which interrupted the former.

83. See Texts 62, 80.

Source References

List of Abbreviations for the Books of the Pali Canon:

A.: Anguttara-Nikāya.—D.: *Dīgha-Nikāya.*—It.: Itivuttaka.—M.: *Majjhima-Nikāya.*—S.: *Saṁyutta-Nikāya.*—Snp.: *Sutta-Nipāta.*—Ud.: *Udāna.*

Text No. (1): S,47,11 (2): D.16 (3): S.47,22–23 (4): S.47,11 (5): M.123 (6): S.48,42 (7): S.47,4 (8): 8.47,26–27 (9): S.52,9 (10): S.52,8 (11): S.47,37 (12): S.47,50 (13): D.29 (14): A.4,17 (15): S.47,19 (16): S.47,29 (17): S.52,10 (18): Thag.30 (19): S.2,7 (20): Thag.100 (21): M.13 (22): S.47,5 (23): S.47,48 (24): S.46,53 (25): A.6,118 (26): S.46,6 (27): S.47,15 (28): S.47,21 (29): Ud.1,10 (30): S.47,10 (31): S.47,42 (32): D.18 (33): *Satipaṭṭhāna-Vibhanga* (*Abhidhamma-Piṭaka*) (34): *Paṭisambhida-Magga, Satipaṭṭhāna-Kathā* (35): M.36 (36): A.1,21 (37): M.119 (38): Thag.1035 (39): M.118 (40): S.44,9 (41): M.62 (42): It.110 (43): It.111 (44): M.4 (45): M.122 (46): M.122 (47): A.8,9 (48): S.47,49 (49): S.36,3 (50): S.36,2 (51): S.36,7 (52): S.35,70 (53): S.35,152 (54): S.47,12 (55): S.52,1 (56): A.8,63 (57): M.125 (58): S.35,204 (59): A.7,63 (60): M.105 (61): S.47,20 (62): Snp.77; Comy: *Paramatthajotikā* (Hewavitarne Ed.), 100f (63)–(68) *Milinda-pañhā,* Ed. of the 6th Synod (*Chaṭṭha Sangāyana*), in Burmese script (69)–(73): *Papañca-Sūdanī,* the Commentary to the *Majjhima-Nikāya, ad* No. 10: *Satipaṭṭhāna-Sutta* (*Aluvihāre* Ed. in Sinhalese script) (74) From the *Mūla-tīkā;* Comy. to the *Sutta*

Nipāta, etc. (75); Nāgārjuna, *Suhṛdllekhā* (76) Aśvaghoṣa, *Saundarānanda-Kavya,* Sanskrit text with Hindi transl., ed. by Suryanarayana Caudari (Bihar 1947) (77)–(84): Śāntideva, *Śikṣa-Samuccaya,* Sanskrit text, ed. by C. Bendall (Bibliotheca Buddhica, St. Petersburg 1902) (85): Śāntideva, *Bodhicaryāvatāra,* Sanskrit text, ed. by Louis de la Vallée Poussin (Bibliotheca Indica, Calcutta 1901).

Glossary of Pali and Sanskrit Terms

P—Pali; S—Sanskrit

Abhidhamma (P), *Abhidharma* (S). The Buddhist philosophy and psychology laid down in the third part of the Buddhist Canon, the *Abhidhamma Piṭaka,* and in later literature.

Anāgāmī (P). 'The Non-returner'; the third of the four stages of emancipation, leading to Sainthood (*arahatta*).

Ānāpāna-sati (P), 'Mindfulness of In- and out-breathing'.

Anatta (P), *Anatma* (S), adj., 'not-self'; egoless, impersonal, devoid of an abiding entity of any description.

Anicca (P), 'impermanent'; together with *dukkha* (suffering) and *anattā* (not-self), one of the three characteristics of all conditioned existence.

Anupassanā (P), 'Contemplation'.

Arahat, Arahant (P), 'Saint'; *arahatta* (P), 'Sainthood'.

Ariya-iddhi (P), 'the Power of the Noble Ones (i.e. the Saints)'; the power to see both the repulsive and non-repulsive aspects of phenomena, and remain equanimous.

Āsava (P), lit.: 'fluxes'; 'taints' of mind; cankers, corruptions, biases. There are four 'taints': the taint of sense-desire (*kāmāsava*), of desire for continued existence (*bhavāsava*), of wrong views (*diṭṭhāsava*) and of ignorance (*avijjāsava*). A saint is frequently called 'one who has eradicated the taints' (*khīṇāsavo*).

Asekha (P), a disciple 'beyond training'; a Saint (*arahant*): see *sikkhā, sekha*.

Aṭṭhaṅga-sīla (P), 'the eight precepts'; observed by Buddhist devotees in Theravāda countries on full-moon days, and during periods of strict meditation.

Āyatana, 'sense bases'. The six 'internal (or personal) sense bases' are the five sense organs and mind; the six 'external sense bases' are the five sense-objects and mind objects (ideas).

Bhikkhu (P), *Bhikṣu* (S), lit.: mendicant; a Buddhist monk.

Bodhisatta (P), *Bodhisattva* (S), a Buddha-to-be.

Bojjhaṅga (P), 'Factors of Enlightenment'.

Brahma-vihāra (P), 'Sublime States' or Divine Abodes, being the meditations on loving-kindness, compassion, sympathetic joy and equanimity.

Cittānupassanā (P), 'the Contemplation of (the state of) Mind'.

Dhamma (P), *dharma* (S). Among the numerous connotations of this term, those occurring in this book are:

The Buddha's Teaching
Mind-objects (mental contents)
Phenomena (bodily and mental processes).

Dhammānupassanā (P), 'the Contemplation of Mind-objects (mental contents)'.

Dhamma-vicaya-sambojjhaṅga (P), 'Investigation of Phenomena' as a Factor of Enlightenment.

Dhātu (P, S), 'elements'; here in the sense of the 'primary qualities of matter'.

Dhātu-vavatthāna (P), 'Analysis (of the body) into its elements'.

Diṭṭhi-carita (P), a type of character bent on theorizing.

Dukkha (P), suffering, ill; the unsatisfactoriness of all conditioned phenomena.

Ekāyano maggo (P), the sole or only way; the direct or straight path. A designation of Satipaṭṭhāna.

Gocara (P), here in the sense of 'domain', 'field of activity'.

Indriya (P), 'faculty'; here applied to the five Faculties of Faith, Energy, Mindfulness, Concentration and Wisdom.

Iriyāpatha-manasikāra (P), 'attention directed to the postures'; one of the exercises in Satipaṭṭhāna practice.

Jhāna (P), 'meditative absorption of the mind'.

Kamma (P), *karma* (S), 'action' (in Buddhism, never the '*result* of action'); rebirth-producing good or evil volition; the moral law.

Karuṇā (P, S), 'compassion'.

Kāyānupassanā (P), 'the Contemplation of the Body'.

Kāya-sankhāra (P), 'bodily functions'.

Kusala (P), good, skilful, right; karmically wholesome.

Mahāyāna (P, S), 'the Great Vehicle (or Career)'. Collective name for those later schools of Buddhism which advocate the Bodhisattva ideal.

Manasikāra (P), 'attention'.

Mettā (P), *maitri* (S), 'loving-kindness'.

Nāma, lit.: 'name'; in Buddhism, a collective term for all mental processes.

Nāma-rūpa-pariccheda (P), 'discernment of physical and mental phenomena'; a stage of Insight-meditation.

Nimitta (P), lit.: 'sign'; here in the sense of a 'mental image' appearing in meditation, and indicating a high degree of mental concentration.

Nīvaraṇa (P), 'mental hindrances'.

Paññā (P), 'wisdom'.

Papañca (P), the multiplicity, or diffuseness, of inner and outer phenomena.

Pāramī (P, S), 'perfections'; virtues and faculties required for the attainment of Buddhahood.

Pariññā (P), 'full understanding'.

Paṭicca-samuppāda (P), 'dependent origination'.

Phassa (P), lit.: 'contact'; sense-impression.

Prāṇayāma (S), breathing exercises in Hindu Yoga.

Rūpa (P, S), here in the sense of 'body', 'corporeal processes'.

Sacca (P), 'truth'; here, the four Noble Truths.

Samādhi (P, S), 'concentration of mind'.

Samatha (P), *śamatha* (S), 'tranquillity'
samatha-bhāvanā, 'tranquillity-meditation'; aiming at the attainment of the meditative Absorptions.

Sampajañña (P), 'clear comprehension'.

Saṁyojana (P), 'fetters' of mind binding to repeated existence.

Saṅgha (P, S), 'the community' of monks; the third of the three 'Jewels' (or ideals) and of the three Refuges.

Sati (P), *smṛti* (S), 'mindfulness'
-sambojjhaṅga (P), 'mindfulness as a Factor of Enlightenment'
-indriya (P), 'mindfulness as a Spiritual Faculty'
sammā-sati (P), 'right mindfulness' as a factor of the Noble Eightfold Path.

Satipaṭṭhāna (P), *smṛtyupasthāna* (S), 'the Foundations of Mindfulness.

Sekha (P), 'disciple in Higher Training'.

Sikkhā (P), *śikṣā* (S), 'training'; in virtue, concentration and wisdom.

Śīla-pāramitā (S), 'Perfection of Virtue'.

Sotāpatti (P), 'Stream-entry'; the first of the four stages of emancipation, culminating in Sainthood (*arahatta*).

Sukkha-vipassanā (P), 'Bare Insight' meditation.

Theravāda (P), lit.: 'the Teaching of the Elders', i.e. the monk-elders and Saints (*arahants*) who recited the texts of the Teaching at the First Council, soon after the Buddha's passing away. They thus consolidated the tradition which is maintained to the present day in Ceylon, Burma, Thailand, Cambodia, Chittagong and Laos.

Upacāra-samādhi (P), Access- or Neighbourhood-concentration.

Upādāna-kkhandha (P), the five 'categories (or aggregates) of clinging'; comprising both the physical and mental parts of what, conventionally, is called the personality.

Upaṭṭhāna (P), *upasthāna* (S), lit.: 'keeping near'; keeping present, establishing.

Vāyo-dhātu (P), 'wind-element'.

Vedanā (P, S), 'feeling'; sensation.

Vinaya (P, S), 'monastic discipline' and the code embodying and explaining the rules regulating the monk's behaviour.

Vipassanā (*-bhāvanā*, P), 'Insight(-meditation)'.

About the Author

Nyanaponika Thera (1901–1994) was a German-born, Sri Lanka-ordained Theravada monk, co-founder of the Buddhist Publication Society, author of numerous books, and teacher of contemporary Western Buddhist leaders such as Bhikkhu Bodhi.

To Our Readers

Weiser Books, an imprint of Red Wheel/Weiser, publishes books across the entire spectrum of occult, esoteric, speculative, and New Age subjects. Our mission is to publish quality books that will make a difference in people's lives without advocating any one particular path or field of study. We value the integrity, originality, and depth of knowledge of our authors.

Our readers are our most important resource, and we appreciate your input, suggestions, and ideas about what you would like to see published.

Visit our website at *www.redwheelweiser.com* to learn about our upcoming books and free downloads, and be sure to go to *www.redwheelweiser.com/newsletter* to sign up for newsletters and exclusive offers.

You can also contact us at *info@rwwbooks.com* or at

Red Wheel/Weiser, llc
665 Third Street, Suite 400
San Francisco, CA 94107

To Our Readers